CW01500348

Preface

This book is the based on the work of many people, and while I discuss many of them in the general context of this book in Chapter 1, I would like to emphasize here the contribution of all those people involved. My apologies in advance to any I have omitted to mention. The backbone of the book is based on a project, 'Farm Lives' conducted between 1999 and 2002, funded exclusively by the McDonald Institute for Archaeological Research at the University of Cambridge; without their essential financial support, this would not have been possible.

The project involved three components: archaeological fieldwork, archive research and oral history interviews. For the fieldwork, special thanks goes to Marcus Abbott, Jenny Bredenberg, Glenda Cox, Olivia Cyster, Andy Hall, Odile Peterson, and Sarah Winter; for post-excavation analysis of materials, I thank Duncan Miller (University of Cape Town), Peter Nilsson (South African Museum) and Jane Klose (University of Cape Town). For the archive research, I would like to thank J. Malherbe (Huguenot Museum) and Harriet Clift (South African Heritage Resources Agency), but most of all, Jaline de Villiers (Paarl Museum). For the oral history, my thanks go to Sarah Winter, Rowena Peterson and Jaline de Villiers for conducting interviews, and to the informants, Johanna Dressler, Louisa Adams, Geoffrey Leslie Hendricks, William Davids, Absolom David Lackay, John Cyster November and Lillian Aubrey Idas.

While I visited the Cape on the numerous occasions during this project, many others provided more general support or information: Gabeba Abrahams (South African Cultural History Museum), James Barker (Anglo-American Farms), Judy Dyer (Anglo-American Farms), Gabriel and Gwen Fagan, Tim Hart (Archaeology Contracts Office), Roger Jones, Ramola Naidoo, Wendy Pickstone, Gill Sutton, Don Tooth (Anglo-American Farms), Hennie Vos (Stellenbosch Museum) and Arthur Wilding. Special thanks, however, goes to a number of people who gave so much more, including their friendship and hospitality: Eleanor Damon, Quinton and Chrissie Fortuin, Marianne Gertenbach, David Hart and Johan van Rooyan, Antonia Malan, and Frank and Ronel Williams.

All the illustrations were created by the author, except for the porcelain in figure 2.5, which was drawn by Andy Hall. Many of the figures have been adapted from other sources and these are acknowledged in the captions. Photographs are either by the author or others, and these are likewise acknowledged; I would, however, like to thank the Cape Archives for permission to use several of the historic photographs in its collection.

Several people read over a draft of this book and for their comments and support, I am extremely grateful: Robert Ross (University of Leiden), Antonia Malan, (University of Cape Town), Marianne Gertenbach, Chuck Orser and an anonymous referee. I would like to thank the Cambridge Archaeological Unit, especially Chris Evans, for giving me (and others) leave of absence to conduct the fieldwork for this project and also Fornleifastofnun Íslands for the time in which to write it. Finally, I must thank Chuck Orser as series editor and Teresa Krauss of Kluwer for their positive and dynamic role in bringing this book to publication.

An Archaeology
of Colonial Identity

CONTRIBUTIONS TO GLOBAL HISTORICAL ARCHAEOLOGY
Series Editor:
Charles E. Orser, Jr., *Illinois State University, Normal, Illinois*

A Continuation Order Plan is available for this series. A continuation order will bring
delivery of each new volume immediately upon publication. Volumes are billed only upon
actual shipment. For further information please contact the publisher.

An Archaeology of Colonial Identity

Power and Material Culture in the Dwars Valley, South Africa

Gavin Lucas

Fornleifastofnun Íslands
Reykjavik, Iceland

 Springer

Library of Congress Control Number: 2005937177

ISBN-10: 0-306-48538-9
ISBN-13: 978-0306-48538-1

Printed on acid-free paper.

Printed in the United States of America.   (TB/IBT)

9 8 7 6 5 4 3 2 1

springer.com

For Dottie, Albert and Chrissie and David and Johan

Contents

Working Contexts | 1

INTRODUCTION: GLOBAL NETWORKS

Skálholt lies on top of a windswept hillside in the southwest of Iceland, a country lying on the edge of the arctic circle. Today, a large white, concrete cathedral dominates the landscape and in earlier centuries, an equally impressive but wooden cathedral stood on the same spot. Skálholt was the most important Episcopal see in the country during the medieval period, and until the 18th century, was the largest settlement on the island, its turf buildings home to a bishop, teachers and students and the labourers who kept the settlement running from day to day. In 2002, major excavations began on the site and uncovered some of the rooms and material culture belonging to the people living there in the mid 18th century. Among the finds were many sherds of Chinese porcelain—tea bowls and saucers, decorated with blue motifs and sometimes with brown exteriors. On the other side of the world, at the tip of Africa lies a farm called Good Hope, nestled amid vineyards and under a warmer sun. A whitewashed homestead with a thatched roof built in the early 19th century is the latest and grandest of several earlier homes on the site originally belonging to Huguenot families and their descendants who first settled here in 1688. In 2001, excavation behind the present homestead exposed the foundations of an earlier building, and associated with it, various broken objects including Chinese porcelain, in the same forms and decorated in a similar manner to those found at Skálholt.

By the 18th century, European capitalists had journeyed almost all over the globe and established colonies and trade networks, and one of the many commodities involved in this trade was Chinese porcelain. Its popularity as a tableware, especially among the more elite members of European society, meant that it can be found on archaeological sites all around the world—from South Africa to Iceland. The Netherlands held a particularly prominent position in this global network, especially in the 17th century. Much of their international trade was conducted explicitly to feed the north European trade. Good Hope at the Cape and Skálholt in Iceland are connected more than simply

1

by sharing a preference for Chinese porcelain; the very presence of porcelain at both places signifies the interconnection of trade networks under European capitalism. Indeed, in 1623 an Icelander Jón Ólafsson visited the Cape on board a Danish East India Company ship, though his comments were brief and indicated a dislike for a place he thought inhabited by cannibals (Raven-Hart 1967: 110–112). The Cape was tied into the Asian trade as a refreshment station for ships en route or homeward bound and consequently acquired many of the commodities being shipped from spices to porcelain dishes. Iceland was tied into the Baltic trade, and through Denmark, had access to many of the goods which Dutch traders were dealing in, from local clay pipes and earthenwares to imported Chinese porcelain. In the 18th century, Skálholt and Good Hope were enmeshed within a global network of European capitalism and though the people living in these two places at opposite ends of the earth, may have dimly if at all, been aware of the other's existence, they were nonetheless silently bound together, as both supped from porcelain bowls.

Such global networks are not just a thing of the past though; the modern phenomenon of globalism today is directly related to these earlier networks and the two are bound together as closely as my two sites on either ends of the earth. My presence in South Africa in 2001 and Iceland in 2002 is no accident; although the two projects are not intentionally related, a tie binds them nevertheless. The social context of academic knowledge, its production and reproduction through institutions, journals and books is as much a global network as the porcelain trade. And it is one that is directly descendant from the expansion of European culture around the globe since the 17th century, forming a hegemony of knowledge as well as technology. Archaeologists working in South Africa and Iceland speak the same language—they may have different interests and largely work on different materials (though not always as the example above attests), but they are part of the same broad scientific community that is held together in a global network.

This book, about a project I conducted in South Africa between 1999 and 2001, was written in Iceland, where I now live and work. On the whole, most of what I will write about will have little direct connection to Iceland, yet the two countries, and many others, remain bound together through this history of global networks. This issue of global capitalism—past and present—forms a key theme of this book, but it is intertwined with many others, such as colonialism and consumption. What unites all of these in this book, is a focus on the construction and articulation of identity. This book tells the stories of various people who have made one valley in the western Cape of South Africa their home since the late 17th century, and through them, the larger contexts that have framed their lives. Each chapter deals with a separate theme: Chapter 2 with the Dutch East India Company and how it negotiated its presence at the Cape; Chapter 3 with the free settlers who set up farms in the new colony and how they established themselves and created their own identity; and Chapter 4 with the slaves and their descendants who laboured for the Company or farmers, unwillingly giving their lives and freedom to create a new world at the tip of Africa. In the final chapter, I try and examine broader themes in the question of colonial identity, linking the specific stories at the Cape with larger issues in post-colonial theory. Each chapter begins with an overview of the themes to be discussed, and then goes into successively more detail, focusing on this one valley to illustrate the key themes, producing a history which I hope, is firmly grounded in the materiality of individual lives. This is a book about real people and real lives caught up in larger processes and how they articulated their lives in this larger context.

The writing here is by no means a solitary endeavour. Since it is partly intended for the reader who has very little familiarity with South African history and archaeology, I draw heavily on previous scholarship, especially in giving the broader background. I am very indebted to this work, which has not only been a foundation for my own work, but an inspiration too. Modern historical writing forms a particularly strong influence, much of it stemming from a major volume on South African History first published in 1979 and then substantially revised in 1989: *The Shaping of South African Society 1652–1840* (Elphick and Giliomee 1989). This book epitomized the new wave in South African historical writing, looking at issues of indigenous peoples, slavery and colonialism in a broader African and global context. Many of its contributors have subsequently written challenging books and articles on these issues such as Robert Ross, Nigel Worden, and Robert Shell (e.g. Ross 1983b; 1993; 1999b; Shell 1994; Worden 1985; Worden & Crais 1994). Similarly, archaeological writing in South Africa has also been incredibly inspiring; historical archaeology only properly emerged in the 1980s, but it has developed into a major research area, focused at the South African Cultural History Museum, the Stellenbosch Museum, but most of all, at the University of Cape Town and the Historical Archaeology Research Group (HARG) there (Abrahams 1984a; Hall 1988; Hall 1993; Hall & Markel 1993). Historical archaeology in South Africa has been heavily influenced by North American studies, and during the 1980s and early 1990s, much of it drew heavily on the structuralist analysis of Jim Deetz and others, and later, Mark Leone and critical archaeologies of power. Indeed, the links between North America and South Africa were forged when James Deetz visited the Cape several times over the mid to late 1980s, and many of his students set up research projects such as Margot Winer. Another link was through Carmel Schrire, who splits her time between UCT and Rutgers University in the States. However, South African historical archaeology has developed a more distinct identity over the decades, largely due to the fact that much of its material and history is very different to North America—especially with regard to issues such as slavery. In particular, the work of Martin Hall, Antonia Malan and Carmel Schrire have pioneered this field and provided a rich literature without which this book could hardly have been written (e.g. Hall 2000; Malan 1990; 1997; Schrire 1995).

But more than this, the research of my own project has been very much a collaborative effort, involving several people without whom the stories presented here would not have materialised. The working context of this book includes not only the wider academic discourse as just discussed, but also the specific context of its production. It is only right that I declare my own interests here, for as much as the stories in this book will be about other people who have lived or passed through the Cape, I should not omit my own story. Why was I there, unearthing these stories and what are my interests in writing this book? To begin at the beginning . . .

FROM CAMBRIDGE TO CAPETOWN: THE POLITICS AND PRODUCTION OF KNOWLEDGE

My first visit to South Africa was in 1996, where I spent several months after just completing my PhD at Cambridge. My doctoral research had been on the prehistoric archaeology in the north of England, but even before I had finished it, I was becoming more interested in the archaeology of the more recent past. In particular, I was interested in the processes of European imperialism and colonisation and its affect on the modern world. A close friend and colleague, David Hart, spent a large part of his childhood in South Africa and now works for the South African Heritage Resources Agency (SAHRA), and was my immediate reason for visiting the country in 1996. While I was there I discovered the expanding field of historical archaeology being practised at the Archaeology Department at the University of Cape Town, and worked part time as a research assistant for Martin Hall, who was head of the department at the time (Hall 1996a; Hall 1996b). Moreover, my friend's brother was an archaeologist who co-ran the Archaeology Contracts Office of the University, and at the time, he was excavating one of the levelled house plots in District Six for the Historical Archaeology Research Group of UCT on which I was invited to help out (Halkett and Hart 1996). Through them, I met many of the other archaeologists working there, in particular Antonia Malan who was to become an invaluable friend and supporter of the project discussed in this book. When I finally left South Africa to return to England, I was keen to continue the interest I had built up in the historical archaeology of the Cape, and when the opportunity finally came to initiate a project there, I jumped at the chance.

The project that forms the basis of this book began in 1998. A colleague of David Hart's, Sarah Winter, had just produced a heritage plan for a locality an hour's drive from Cape Town in the winelands (Winter 1999). At the heart of the Dwars valley was a community settlement called Pniel, with a strong sense of history as most of the population were descendants of ex-slaves, who had settled there after emancipation in the mid-nineteenth century. Originally established as a mission station for emancipated slaves, it grew to become an independent community but one that still retains strong ties to its church and missionary background. Apart from Pniel, the valley hosted several farmsteads originally settled in the late 17th century and a mid 18th century silver mine, high up on the slopes of the Simonsberg, the impressive mountain that forms the backdrop to the valley. As a context to explore processes of colonisation, it seemed ideal and so a proposal was drafted and funding applied to the McDonald Institute for Archaeological Research at the University of Cambridge. At the time, I was working for the University Field Unit of the University and spent most of my time in contract archaeology in Cambridgeshire. They funded the project, called 'Farm Lives', throughout its three seasons of fieldwork and one year of post-excavation, and without that funding, this project would have remained unrealised.

The project has, at all times, been a collaborative enterprise. Throughout the three seasons of fieldwork, the friendship and support of three local people living in the valley now has been invaluable: Quinton Fortuin, Marianne Gertenbach and Eleanor Damon are all driving forces in promoting the heritage of the area. Quinton Fortuin, formerly of the Pniel local council and now of Stellenbsoch municipal council (the district capital) was indefatigable in his help and sustains a vision of the valley as an important tourist attraction. Quinton's wife, Chrissy, works with Marianne Gertenbach who is curator of the impressive manor house and museum of Boschendal, once one of the most wealthiest farms in the valley and now owned by the multi-national Anglo-American corporation. Eleanor Damon is a local

school teacher at Kylemore, a smaller settlement close to Pniel, and re-
searching the genealogy of her family, the Cysters, one of the most important families of the emancipated slaves. These three people formed
my bridge with the local community, among whom I made many more
friends and acquaintances who helped the project in too many ways
to recount. It is the passion of the community in the Dwars valley
for their past which has been an inspiration to this project, but this
book is in no way meant to be a reflection of their views; indeed, our
agenda's are largely different, but nevertheless we share much common ground and our work and interests do intersect. For example, one
the most important elements of the local community's interest in history is a concern for genealogy, and although I was initially resistant
to its value, I have found it to be an increasingly critical part of my
work.

There have been three components to this project: archaeology,
archival research and oral history. All have brought very different
strengths to the research, but I have strived to make them work
together here in this book. Often there is little in which one seems to
intersect with the others, but all three have been crucial to writing the
stories in this book. The archaeology involved small scale excavations
at three sites. The first is a farm, called Goede Hoop which was
established in the late 17th century and is intimately connected to the
history of post-slavery settlements in the valley. The second is a silver
mine settlement dating to the mid 18th century and the third, a house
lot in Pniel, the main settlement in the valley which was established
in the mid 19th century for emancipated slaves. The excavations
were done with the assitance of a number of people: Marcus Abbott
(Cambridge), Jenny Bredenberg (London), Glenda Cox (Somerset
West), Olivia Cyster (Pniel), Andy Hall (Cambridge), Odile Petersen
(Pniel) and Sarah Winter (Cape Town). Archaeology, perhaps more
than most disciplines, is very much a team effort, especially when
it comes to fieldwork, but much of the post-excavation analysis
was also aided by various people. Specialist work on some of the
archaeological finds was done through institutions at Cape Town, in
particular Jane Klose's unrivalled expertise on ceramics has been
invaluable, while Duncan Miller conducted crucial scientific analysis
on metallurgical waste from the mining settlement. Peter Nilsson
from the South African Museum studied the assemblage of faunal
remains.

The archival research in many ways has been the backbone to this
project. Jaline de Villiers, now at Paarl Museum, conducted most of
the documentary work on archives in a language I could not read. She

went through title deeds, transfer histories, inventories, slaves registers, census returns and many other documents which have been essential part of the material used in this project. In particular, she managed to unearth the treasure of correspondence regarding the silver mine discussed in Chapter 2, which I was unable to locate. Her research is inscribed in almost every other page of this book, and reveals the vital dynamic between archives and material culture in the discipline of historical archaeology. Jaline also conducted one of the interveiws with a former resident of Goede Hoop farm, acquiring useful information on key themes of daily life. It was however Sarah Winter who conducted most of the oral history research, taking key interviews with six elderly residents of Pniel with the invaluable assistance of Rowena Peterson of Pniel; her work on these interviews as well as architectural investigations of the houses in the town formed a crucial bridge between archives and archaeology.

The task of writing this book has thus been heavily dependent on the texts produced by these people—whether written or spoken. However, much of these texts refer to other texts themselves, indeed the archive out of which this book was woven, is multi-layered in its referentiality. I see writing as an act of re-telling or re-writing as much as an originary event; if post-structuralism has taught us anything, it is that authors and texts are to some extent, dislocated and texts are produced by other texts as much as by the traditional 'author'. Inter-textuality is nowhere better expressed than through those silent, almost invisible marginalia which intersect any academic work: references. In this first chapter, I want to try and expose these references, to lay them bare for inspection so that some thing of this inter-textual nature of the book comes out. But more than that, I want to show how these 'references' are inflected by other narratives, not written and not even necessarily spoken, but inscribed in the material context in which they are produced. I therefore want to devote the rest of this first chapter to discussing the other working context on which this book is based: the social context of the archives I work with.

NARRATIVE GENRES: THE TEXTUAL AND VISUAL ARCHIVE

Eighteenth, nineteenth and twentieth century journals and letters, administrative documents, photographs, sketches, maps—all these texts were produced in a particular social context, and it is important to appreciate the nature of this context to be able to critically use them or interpret them. In this section I want to discuss the nature of these primary sources used throughout this book—though I admit to feeling some unease over using the term 'primary' here given the emphasis on inter-textuality which would seem to deny any hierarchy. Nevertheless, there is a sense in which the distinction is valid. I have already discussed in general, the background to the 'secondary' literature in which this book is situated—the exciting work in history and archaeology which has been produced since the late 1970s and early 1980s. Such work forms part of a wider academic discipline and style of writing and the intentions and nature of this literature are retrospective and historical and thus secondary insofar as they refer to a certain group of other texts which by default, become primary. The relationship however between primary and seconday is not so much a referential one—for a secondary text can quote a secondary text without the latter becoming primary—as a conceptual one. The difference lies in the genre to which the text belongs, in one case to academic discipline, in the other, to genres of administration, letters, art and so on. It is these genres which I want to explore in the following sections of this chapter.

White Writing

The South African novelist J. M. Coetzee was one of the first to critically examine the context in which European writing about South Africa occurred. His book *White Writing* (1988) raises the interesting issue of why European writers on the Cape never really considered it to be a New World like the Americas; in the moral geography of the European renaissance, Africa was always the Old(est) World and this cultural preconception coloured the views of the first settlers in both places: America was, and still is the land of opportunity, the land of the future: Africa was/is the land of stagnation, the land of the past (Coetzee 1988: 2). The constant fear of European colonials in Africa, Coetzee argues, was degeneration through living there, 'going native'—a theme which runs through the literature and is perhaps most famously epitomized by Kurtz in Conrad's *Heart of Darkness*. If America was the great utopia, Africa was its antithesis, a dystopia. South African literature coped with this by adopting the genre of a 'white pastoral'—writing about the landscape and countryside as if it were part of the European past, its gaze turned to a nostalgic past of white settlement where indigenous people and slaves are marginalized or completely forgotten.

The documents and texts that I draw on in this book are not novels, but mostly census returns, inventories and other colonial administrative documents. Nevertheless, Coetzee's points are as pertinent to these and other colonial transcripts as they are to fiction. The development of a farmer-settler society from the late 17th century—building itself up from a wild plot of land, founding family dynasties, and in places erecting spectacular houses in what has been called the 'Cape Dutch' style—can all be seen as material embodiments of this 'white pastoral' narrative. The infrastructure of European-style administration in deeds and transfers, census' and probates, birth, death and marriage registers, all helped to sustain this narrative with their textual inscription of property and descent. Such forms of documentation moreover carried within them, the seeds of social classification; census' do far more than simply reflect social categories, they actually help to construct them (Kertzer and Ariel 2002: 2). Indeed, in the context of British colonial India, the early 19th century census played a key role in objectifying and classifying Indian society for the Indian population, not merely the colonial administrators, and even influenced the caste system (Cohn 1987). Documents such as census are very much linked to the development of European nationalism and colonialism and its concern to map identity—census' were used to construct a particular vision of society which in the colonial context, was closely bound up with race (Kertzer and Ariel 2002: 10).

The other major type of textual archive apart from the administrative documents discussed above is more literary. Many Europeans who spent some time at the Cape wrote about their experiences in the form of letters, journals or travelogues and I variously draw on these too (Forbes 1965). They are very different in form but still inflected by similar beliefs and conceptions as the official documents; certainly in many of these texts, one can read the themes Coetzee raises, especially about the backwardness or parochial nature of Cape society, whether referring to its settlers, slaves or indigenous inhabitants—though of course, articulated in different ways for each group. For some of these writers, their visit to the Cape was short, often passing through. This is especially true of many of the Swedish travellers such as Sparrman and Thunberg who were both students of Carl Linne (Linnaeus), the great 18th century taxonomist who created a universal scheme for classifying all plants in his *Systema Naturae* (1735). As Pratt has discussed, this taxonomy epitomized the ideals of Enlightenment knowledge, and to render this abstract system more concrete, he sent his students all around the world to collect and classify new species. Two of these, Sparrman and Thunberg, came to the Cape in the 1770s, one as a naturalist on one of Cook's expeditions, the other as a surgeon for the Dutch East India Company. Both wrote up accounts of their travels, but their writings are heavily influenced by their interest in natural history (Sparrman

1975; Thunberg 1986). Pratt argues that their writings exemplify the European project of global hegemony through knowledge—their domestication and conquest of the Cape was through classifying its flora, rather than subjugating its people, although even its people did not escape their classificatory gaze (Pratt 1992: 33–34).

Sweden was a major political force in northern Europe in the 17th century, when, like the Dutch, it ostensibly had its 'golden age', called the Age of Greatness; by the mid 17th century, it was an imperial power in the Baltic controlling numerous cities and lands around its coastline, a position it maintained until the early 18th century. Overseas it even managed to acquire small, but short-lived colonies in North America and West Africa, and its vision of the world is nowhere better encapsulated that the late 17th century castle of Skokloster on the edge of lake Mälaren (Losman 1988). Here, travel books and ethnographic objects were entwined with a capitalist trade in tobacco and cocoa through the enterprise of its owner, Carl Wrangel. But it was not until the mid-18th century that such exotic material culture became more widely consumed—as Skokloster became an open attraction to visitors—and Sweden's overseas trade developed on a more substantial basis. In 1731 it started its own East India Company—a modest institution compared with the two giants, the English and Dutch Companies, but one which nevertheless managed to trade throughout the 18th century up to 1806 and was of vital importance to the economic growth of Sweden (Weibull 1991). Initially its trade goods were mostly re-exported into the north European market but very quickly a domestic demand also developed for these products from the east. Among them of course, was Chinese porcelain; Sweden had one of the first porcelain factories in Europe, Rörstrand, and its desire for this new, almost magical pottery was no less than any other European country (Fredlund 1997; Gleeson 1998). In 1745, two of the Swedish East India Company ships sunk close to home after a round trip to Canton; one of these wrecks, the *Götheborg*, has been salvaged and it included an impressive cargo of mid 18th century porcelain which provide direct parallels to vessels found at one of the Cape sites discussed in this book (Wästfelt et al. 1991).

Sweden is important in the context of the Cape colony not simply because it had a few students of Linnaeus writing about it, but because large numbers of its settlers came from Sweden. Although the Swedish East India Company ships stopped off via Cape Town, most of these settlers originally worked for the Dutch East India Company—indeed, between 1700 and 1779, the proportion of foreign employees in the Dutch company rose from 57 to 80% (Schutte 1989: 293). This is a staggering proportion, and among the largest numbers of these foreigners were Swedes and Germans. Indeed, German commentators form another major group of writers on the Cape, and include Peter Kolb and Otto Mentzel. Kolb went to the Cape in the early 18th century, originally to undertake astronomical and meterological research but ended up working for the Dutch East India Company as an administrator. Mentzel on the other hand arrived at the Cape as a soldier for the Company, and when released from service, worked as a tutor to various families; it has been suggested that he is one of the few 18th century commentators to have integrated fully into Cape society. Certainly his texts are among the more detailed and useful to the modern historian—despite being written decades after his experiences and in part, prompted by a reaction to the numerous other publications which came out such as Kolb's whose writing he disliked (Hall 2000: 12).

All these writers and others such as François Valentyn and Jan Stavorinus (also both servants of the Dutch East India Company), were living and working in a specific context and were present at the Cape for specific reasons—as scientist/explorer, administrator or settler, and their texts reflect this. Indeed, in some cases, the author's status changed with time. Alongside the position of the author however, was also the narrative genre in which they chose to write. Often this status of the author reflected the genre they chose, but in many cases the texts often reveal different genres entwined. I have already mentioned Pratt's analysis of the scientific genre of Linnaeus' students, but at the same time as this scientific, classificatory writing was being employed, a quite different style was emerging—the Romantic narrative of the picturesque. Orvar Löfgren has discussed how these two styles were exemplified by two journeys to the north of Sweden in the 18th century, one by Linnaeus and other by Linnerhielm (Löfgren 1999: 16–21). While Linnaeus described the soils, rocks, vegetation and fauna, Linnerhielm described the landscape; while in Linnaeus' saddlebag was a microscope, in Linnerhielm's was the 18th century equivalent of the camera—the Claude-glass, a small convex mirror used to render the landscape in miniature. As Löfgren so eloquently puts it, if Linnaeus set out to collect minerals and plants, Linnerhielm collected views and moods.

Linnerhielm's journey and text was written half a century after Linnaeus, but both narrative genres existed side by side, continuing into the 19th century; and just as one developed into the scientific discourse of today, the other continues as the narrative of modern travel and tourism (Gilroy 2000; Löfgren 1999). This narrative genre of landscapes and the picturesque is particularly prominent as the Cape fell from Dutch to British control in the late 18th/early 19th century. Lady Anne

Barnard, who lived at the Cape in the last years of the 18th century and whose husband worked for the British colonial administration, wrote a series of letters and a lengthy journal of her stay at the Cape. Many of her descriptions of places evoke the concept of the picturesque, the 'pastoral', and can be seen as part of a very different genre of writing to those from the earlier 18th century. Margot Winer has discussed this genre in terms of the settlement of the Eastern Cape in the early 19th century and shown, despite the harsh reality often conflicting with preconceptions of the picturesque, that pastoral narratives of the Cape landscape win out (Winer 1995). It is, presumably, the translation of this genre into fiction, which Coetzee charts and describes as a 'white pastoral'.

Compare Kolb's description of the valley which is the subject of this book: "And, indeed, 'tis a Road full of dangers. 'Tis frequently infested with Lions, Tigers &c, is very steep, narrow and stony; and leads you on the Edges of precipices and Pits of Water." (Kolb 1967: 50), with Lady Anne Barnard's written half a century later: "The road from Stellenbosch leads thro' a pass formed between the above mountain and Simon's Berg, called Bange Kloof, or the tremendous passage. This last Parnassian Mountain with its high forked top has also its Helicon but no Apollo nor the Muses." (Barnard, in Fairbridge 1924: 39). While Kolb's eyes see wild, untamed nature and danger, Lady Anne Barnard sees a classical landscape; for Kolb, it was Africa as the wild, for Anne Barnard, Africa as Europe. While the actual landscape may have altered somewhat in the time between Kolb and Barnard, farms had been in the valley since the late 1680s. The ultimate vision of a pastoral however comes from a visitor of the early twentieth century, Madeline Alston: "When your eyes have taken in the beauty of those glorious blue mountains which guard the valley in horseshoe formation, you turn your gaze downwards and see, first, great clumps of restful trees—oaks, pines and poplars—sheltering orchards and vineyards and orange-groves, which break though and also climb up the mountain-sides. Everywhere you see mathematically-straight rows of well-kept fruit trees sunning themselves in the undisturbed glory of a South African summer day." (Alston 1929: 4–5).

The Cape Camera

Many of the same themes discussed above can be repeated with the visual archive—of maps, sketches, paintings and photographs. The idea that visual images also conform to genres and share a wider context with literature has been a common theme in current theory. Images of the southern hemisphere helped to promote certain European perceptions of this region which inter-connected with the textual narratives (e.g. Eisler 1995). In the South African context, Martin Hall has explored the relation between art and archaeology (Hall 1991b), but Margot Winer's work here again is of vital importance. She discusses not only narratives but also paintings, sketches and maps, and shows how the same genre of the picturesque is present in images of the Eastern Cape (Winer 1995). The images attempted to render the South African landscape in the same pictorial genre as European scenes, employing the same perspectives and motifs; even though the exotic was often incorporated into such scenes—indigenous flora, fauna and people—the composition was explicitly that of the European landscape genre. Not only did this translate current visual ideologies into the colony, it also helped to tame or domesticate this potentially alien world, especially for an audience back home or for the new immigrants (Winer 1995: 84).

Winer also discusses maps of the Eastern Cape, which reveal a different genre—that of the colonial administration. Through various strategies, maps are just as partial a means of representing the landscape as paintings or narratives; issues of accuracy, which are in themselves ideological signs of control and authority, especially in the colonial context, are of less relevance here that cartographic conventions. The selection or omission of details on a map, the naming, size and emphasis given to these details, and the design of marginalia all given silent witness to the ideology present in the imagery of maps (Harley 1988; Wood 1992). In the context of colonial mapping in particular, Ryan has raised the critical significance of the 'blank spaces' (Ryan 1994; 1996). Ryan discusses the colonial mapping of Australia, as a *tabula rasa*, a blank slate; crucially, he argues that the blank areas on colonial maps are not simply reflections of *terra incognita*, the unknown but an active erasure of existing perceptions and occupation. The blank areas do not so much signify the limits of European knowledge as the deliberate attempt to represent the land as a blank slate on which to impose a new order (Ryan 1994: 116). This clearly suited the project of colonialism and territorial acquisition; the fact that European maps are not conceptually able to represent nomadic inhabitation is no coincidence either.

Ryan's arguments for Australian cartography apply just as well to South Africa, where there are plenty of blank areas, especially on the edges of settlement. A map from *c.* 1700 of the study area for this book illustrates this (Figure 1.1). The fact that the nomadic Khoikhoi are depicted on this map is interesting precisely because they are represented in the same way as the European settlers, as fixed settlements, despite

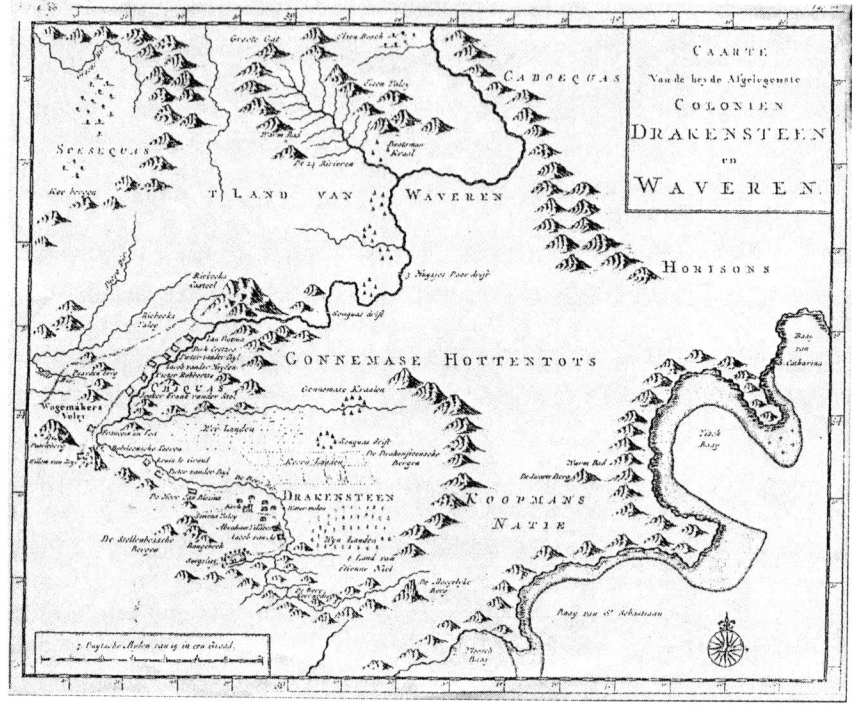

Figure 1.1. Map of the Cape, dated 1690. (*Source*: Cape Archives 1/1159)

the fact that all the narrative accounts are quite cognizant of their mobile lifestyle. However, these 'settlements' always exist on the edges of the colonial settlement, never within it, and they are named generically after their tribal or regional ascription, while the European settlers are given personal and individual names. The large open areas that take up more than half the space on the map are only sparsely occupied by these Khoikhoi, inviting the settler to claim new lands, which have already even been named. I examine this map in more detail in Chapter 3, but its conventions differ quite markedly from later maps, and it is not simply a question of accuracy. Indeed, the latitude and longitude scales that frame the 1700 map are clearly meant to be read as part of the scientific genre of mapping.

The maps of the 17th and 18th centuries at the Cape were largely produced through the Dutch East India Company. In 1617, the Company appointed an exclusive map maker who oversaw the acquisition and production of all charts and maps for the merchant ships, to create some consistency and order; template maps were created from which copies could be easily made and annotated, any changes or corrections being then fed back to the mapmaker who could modify the template if necessary. A number of mapbooks or atlases were compiled by the various mapmakers over time and these provided the information in a single, usable form for the Board of Directors as well as the map-maker (Zandvliet 1998). In general, most of the maps commissioned by the Dutch East India Company of the Cape were not about territorial expansion or geographical knowledge—rather the iconography is more complex as they were primarily aimed at giving information to the Board of Directors to enable them to make decisions about locating forts, settlements, ship routes and agricultural or mineral exploitation. They are maps of a commercial rather than imperial organization (Zandvliet 1998). Apart from the navigation charts, there were essentially two kinds of maps produced by the Company: cadastral maps of agricultural plots and fort or town plans. These maps enabled the Board of Directors to plan and manage their stations and posts throughout the Indian Ocean—although often the reality fell short of the ideal (Hall et al. 1990a). Cadastral maps more generally were an established part of European State control which had emerged in the 16th century, and a critical tool in articulating the relationship between private property and State control (Jowett et al. 1992).

Finally there are the photographs. Like paintings, sketches and maps, photographs contain a hidden voice—an ideology which guides the selection of the subject, its framing and the use of light and so on (e.g. Tagg 1988). In the context of colonialism, Ryan has addressed the role of photographs in presenting the imperial vision, especially to an audience 'back home' (Ryan 1998; also see Maxwell 1999). At the Cape, photography began in the mid-19th century and as in Europe, was predominantly a portrait medium and especially as a commercial profession, this is how it continued into the early twentieth century (Schoeman 1996). Formal portrait photographs at the Cape from the 1870s increasingly included material goods that underlined the class and status of the sitter, in contrast to the austerity of the earlier images that concentrated on the sitter alone (Schoeman 1996). Photography in this period was—inevitably—practised almost entirely by whites, with the role of blacks being that of 'subject'. Photographs of blacks were primarily taken either for scientific and ethnographic reasons or in their working roles as servants and labourers (also see Bull & Denfield 1970; Bensusan 1966).

However there was always a more artistic genre alongside portraiture—photographs of wildlife or landscape, but perhaps the most

Figure 1.2. Photograph of the farm Goede Hoop taken by Arthur Elliot in the early 20th century. (*Source*: Cape Archives E754)

famous genre to emerge at the turn of the century was that of old Cape buildings. Architecture became a focus for articulating a 'photographic pastoral' of what was considered a disappearing past, epitomized by Cape Dutch farmsteads and its leading exponent was Arthur Elliot (Lighton 1956). Many of the photographs in the Cape Archives are in this genre, and a large part from the Arthur Elliot collection. Elliot was an American who came to the Cape in about 1900, and sustained himself as a portrait photographer, but taking more 'artistic' photographs which he exhibited in Cape Town; his 1920's exhibitions in particular of Cape Dutch houses sparked a new interest in these buildings. Elliot's photographs and those of others, more than anything, perhaps helped to create and sustain the mythological tradition of European settlement and a 'white pastoral' through the focus on architecture (Figure 1.2).

Out of the Shadows

While maps, paintings and photographs inscribe a certain vision of the Cape, employing tropes and articulating genres as in textual narrative, it needs to be remembered that such inscriptions are usually authored by an elite—whether the administrative officials governing the colony or a leisured class consuming the picturesque. Running counter to these perceptions, or representations of the landscape as *tabula rasa* or African arcadia, are the experiences of those inhabiting the landscape who leave no written or depicted inscription. In an extremely provocative paper on travel in the Cape, Jessica Dubow discusses how colonial subjectivity was defined by a very different spatial modality to that presented in such inscriptions (Dubow 2002). In contrast to the imperial gaze of the map or the Romantic prospect afforded by painting, is the experience of travel, of motion, either on foot or by ox-wagon—the principal means of transport at the Cape in the 18th and 19th century. Dubow argues that such journeys defined a colonial form of spatial inhabitation of the landscape, a spatiality which even some authorities were aware of, stood in tension with the abstract representation of landscape given in maps (Dubow 2002: 251–3). However, it is not simply that the one spatiality stands opposed to the other, but that intrinsically, the two are related. Maps do not just represent the landscape, but perform it. The (imaginary) journeys implicit in the map shown in Figure 1.1 are, to borrow a term from Dubow, 'serpentine'—they follow the topography and rivers, where the journey itself is not distinct from its destination and embody a specific mode of transport (ox-wagon). In contrast, later and modern maps imply a separation of journey from destination; the straight roads, laid down by the British imperial road builders re-inscribed the landscape and ushered in a new colonial spatiality. It is a different landscape, not only being represented, but being performed.

Such materiality embodied in these archives ultimately brings us to the non-textual—the material world of architecture, porcelain cups, glass bottles or food remains. It is this material culture in the form of buildings and broken objects, that provides an alternative perspective from the textual and visual sources at our disposal. Indeed, archaeology and more generally the study of material culture offers quite unique advantages in these terms because it is directly implicated in the very nature of inscription. Texts and images are, for the most part, explicit representations produced by the elite, by those in power, while architecture and artefacts are the implicit articulations of everyone in society—although equally inflected by networks of power. The perspective I take in this book is that shared by many in archaeology and material culture studies, namely that material culture is very actively implicated in the articulation of social life and identity. People express who they are, who they want to be and who they want others to be, through material culture as much as, if not more so, than through writing or depiction. Moreover, material culture is not simply a surface veneer to such identities but is deeply and fundamentally constitutive of them. In a profound sense, we are the houses, clothes, furniture and objects we use and inhabit. This belief underlies everything written in this book, and it is developed in further specific ways, particularly insofar as identity is inextricably linked with power.

I employ material culture as a means of articulating a politics of identity; this politics of identity is about the power for someone to be what they want to be, and is in potential, constant tension with the power another person exerts over what they want that first person to be. Inequality is fundamentally an inequality in ability to articulate identity, and material culture plays a key role here. This is not solely about the 'have' and 'have-nots', or even a linear gradation of wealth, but how the particular consumption of goods is distributed and articulated between members of the population. In the colonial—and post-colonial context of the Cape, such consumption is inflected along the familiar lines of ethnicity, gender and class as elsewhere, but which will be given more specific designation in this book, through the politico-legal constructs of Cape society. I will talk of male and female slaves, free blacks, Khoikhoi, burghers, officials, coloureds and whites among many others, and how material culture was used to articulate these various identities that were variously fluid. As a means of exploring those who have no voice in representational discourse—the subaltern, the study of material culture is particularly suitable. It enables an exploration of the more subtle and yet perhaps more intractable ways, in which identity and power are articulated. The very ambiguity often inherent in material culture makes it an ideal form of both domination and resistance; avoiding the more explicit discourse of language, its ambiguity can often more easily sustain the contradictions of both an oppressive yet benign authority, and an obedient yet rebellious populace.

My aim in this book is to examine the question of how identity has been articulated through material culture at the Cape from the late 17th to the late 20th century. There are multiple levels at which this occurs, from the global processes of capitalism, colonialism and imperialism, to the local processes of settlement, farming, mining and household creation and maintenance. I try and keep these different levels inter-locked, so that the global and local remain part of the same story. My narrative crosses back and forth between general historical process and the local events in the study area and thus the book is simultaneously about the Dwars valley and the Cape of South Africa—and beyond.

The Archaeology of Dutch Capitalism and the Colonial Trade

In late summer of 1748, the Dutch East Indiaman, the *Geldermalsen* started on its maiden voyage from the Netherlands to the East Indies, a journey that took nearly eight months before it docked at Batavia in Java, the headquarters of the Company in the East. It spent the next year and a half traveling between Japan, China, India and Indonesia buying, selling and trading goods in order to fill up for its return voyage. In late December 1751, it left Canton laden with its cargo and bound for Batavia before starting its long journey back home. However, early in the new year it hit a reef; of 112 on board, there were only 32 survivors who made it back to Batavia (Jörg 1986: 44). From the records we know what the full cargo list was supposed to be—the primary commodity was tea (60% by value), followed by textiles (chiefly silks—32%) and then to a lesser extent, porcelain, medicinal roots and lacquer ware (Table 2.1). Most of this had been acquired at Canton, which took about five months of negotiation and waiting. If the cargo had made it back to Europe, it would have been sold at public auction for a huge profit. Instead, it sunk to the bottom of the sea.

In the 1980s, the wreck of the *Geldermalsen* was found; divers, on encountering the remains, found a soup of congealed, decaying organic matter over the top, several metres thick: tea (ibid.: 51). Beneath it was the only part of the cargo to survive, and yet exactly what the divers were after: porcelain. They retrieved over 150,000 pieces of Chinese export ware, all from Jingdezhen in Xiangsi province, which included dinner plates, soup plates, serving dishes, tea, coffee and chocolate cups, saucers and jugs and various other vessels. According to the records, there were 203 chests of porcelain stowed on board—they would have been placed in a middle layer of the ship's storage, above the ballast of wood and beneath the tea and textiles. Apart from the porcelain cargo, there was also found gold bars, intended for Batavia and coarse Provincial porcelain, to be loaded off at the Cape. The story of the *Geldermalsen* more or less sums up the nature of European presence in the Indian

Table 2.1. Cargo of the *Geldermalsen*.
(*Source*: Jörg 1986: 115)

Tea	686, 997 pounds
Textiles	
Woven Silks	5,240 pieces
Raw Silks	9,935 pounds
*Nankeens**	3,060 pieces
Porcelain	c. 239,200 pieces
Lacquerware	625 pieces
Medicinal Roots	4,936
Wood (ballast)	60,000 pounds

* Shiny linen

Ocean in the 17th and 18th centuries: trade in exotic goods that fetched very high prices back in Europe. Colonial settlement in places like Batavia and the Cape were all initially and primarily serving this one commercial interest.

Europeans had been stopping off at the Cape of Good Hope since the late 15th century as part of the eastward expansion of mercantile capitalism under the lead of the Portuguese (Raven-Hart 1967). As the center of mercantile power shifted from Portugal, then Spain to the Netherlands, so the Cape increasingly became a stopover for Dutch trading ships. The Dutch settlement at the Cape in the mid 17th century needs to be seen in the context of the Dutch overseas trade and its significance to the new Republic's position in the north European economy and as well as its own domestic culture. In this chapter, I want to examine the nature of Dutch colonialism in the Cape in the wider context of Dutch capitalism and the role material culture played in this process. The key case study of this chapter will be the archaeological investigations of a failed silver mine venture of the mid 18th century, but it will be linked into other archaeological sites and stories, and ultimately, the discussion will revolve around the nature of trade and commodities in a nascent global capitalist system.

THE NEW REPUBLIC AND THE DUTCH EAST INDIA COMPANY

The cultural and economic prosperity of the Netherlands in the 17th century, epitomized as the 'Dutch Golden Age', has been the subject of many books, most particularly, Huizinga's *Dutch Civilization in the 17th Century*, Peter Geyl's *The Netherlands in the Seventeenth Century* and more recently Simon Schama's *The Embarrasment of Riches* (Geyl 1961; Huizinga 1968; Schama 1991). The mutually sustaining relationship between 'culture' and 'economy' seems to be only too well expressed in this case, with Dutch paintings frequently depicting the very material culture that participated in the Republic's economic success—tobacco, porcelain, silks, spices, and other exotic foodstuffs. This new material culture was transforming European society, and in this transformation, the Netherlands was at the vanguard. The 1590s was a period of major economic transformation for the newly formed Dutch Republic or United Provinces, and a large part of this transformation came through the redistribution of colonial goods in the north European market. The development of Dutch hegemony in this trade was to some extent prefigured and enabled by the establishment of a fairly modern agricultural system where land had become commodified and alienable and the social system democratic rather than feudal (Aymard 1982). Through unique agricultural and then industrial production, it became first a trade and then a financial leader in the north European market (Wallerstein 1982).

Although Spain controlled the direct trade with the east, in 1590 it lifted a trade embargo and allowed Dutch (but not English) traders into Lisbon, giving them access to the luxury or 'rich trade' items which they could then re-export into north Europe (Israel 1995: 311–313; Israel 1989). With its edge in high value commodities such as spices, sugar, silk and wine as well as American silver, Dutch traders managed to rapidly contest the English and German (Hanseatic) primacy of trade in the Baltic. Although Spain was short-lived in its generosity and in 1598, reimposed the embargo, by this time the Republic had already initiated its own long distance trade through a private company (*Compagnie van Verre*) in 1594. The new embargo of 1598 only stimulated greater investment in direct traffic with the East Indies, and the formation of new trading companies, especially as in 1604, Spain lifted its trade embargo with England (Israel 1995: 320). The overseas trade however was not without its problems. The economic insecurity of having several independent companies—eight by 1599—was jeopardizing the success of this trade, so in 1601 it was decided to amalgamate them into a single, chartered joint stock company backed by the State. The United East India Company (*Vereenigde Oostindische Compagnie*, hereafter abbreviated to its acronym, VOC or simply the Company) was granted its charter the following year, which licensed them to maintain a military force, conduct treaties and alliances with other peoples and also establish governors in foreign lands (Boxer 1965). The company consisted of six chambers, reflecting the independent origins of the partners, but with differential division of power according to the different investment strengths of these partners. Power lay with the Board of Directors known as the *Heren XVII*, and Amsterdam, being the strongest, had eight seats on this board, Zeeland four and two each to the North Quarter and South Holland. The seventeenth director was nominated by the three smaller chambers by rotation (Israel 1995: 321).

The first half of the 17th century saw the VOC establish itself in the East Indies, specifically through the capture of the 'Spice Islands' or Moluccas (Malaku, Indonesia) from the Portuguese. It also set up an overseas headquarters in Bantam, Java, which it later transferred to Jakarta, which was named Batavia by the VOC. The name is interesting insofar as it was an emphatic attempt to invoke the mythic origins of the Dutch nation and perhaps suggest that this center to their eastern colonies which was an offspring of its mother country, was destined for equal greatness. The 'Batavii' was the name of the tribe occupying the Netherlands region in the 1st century AD as recounted by Tacitus, and there were many histories in the 17th century which attempted to trace Dutch culture back to these ancestors as part of the new nationalist spirit (Schama 1991: 72–81). As well as being used for their chief eastern colony, the name was also employed in place of United Provinces for the new Batavian Republic in the early 19th century in the wake of the French Revolution—and probably with similar connotations. The success of the VOC fluctuated as conditions in northern Europe changed however. In 1609, Spain lifted its trade embargo, which saw a slight loss of momentum in overseas trade, but then it was re-imposed again in 1621 until 1647. It was however, only during the second half of the 17th century that the overseas trade really flourished and brought economic prosperity to the Republic through its 'rich trade'. It was in its context of safeguarding its trade routes to the East Indies that a trading post was established at the Cape of Good Hope in 1652, its primary function to supply outward and homeward bound VOC ships with supplies.

The Dutch direct trade with the East Indies was intimately linked with their power in the north European trade, not simply about their own consumption of these luxury commodities. Indeed, its trading expeditions needed to be conducted on such a scale as to supply the north European market, not just its domestic quota. This north European market consisted not only of the re-distribution of colonial goods but also domestic products, and the more success Dutch traders had with colonial goods, the more it stimulated domestic production. The growth of domestic industries such as textiles, clay pipes, tin-glazed earthenware among others was directly linked into the success of the trade in colonial goods (Israel 1995: 611–12). This domestic trade within the north European market is well known archaeologically, especially in terms of ceramics, where products from China and South-east Asia, Italy, Spain, Portugal, France, Netherlands and Germany are among the more widely distributed goods (Hurst et al. 1986). However, work on specific consumption patterns among different communities in northern Europe is less well known but is increasingly a focus of research, particularly in the Netherlands.

Urban excavations in major towns throughout the Netherlands since the 1950s has been producing a wealth of archaeological material on domestic material culture, which can inform us of the dynamics of Dutch consumption between the 17th and 19th centuries (Baart 1987; 1990). In particular, a number of recent publications are providing pioneering data on a whole range of goods, especially ceramics, glass and clay pipes using a new and standardized system of classification (Baart et al. 1986; Bartels et al. 1993; Bartels 1999; Bitter et al. 1997; Bult 1992; Clevis et al. 1990; Ostkamp et al. 2001). It was during the later 17th century that major structural changes occur in domestic industries in the Netherlands, including the mass production of tin-glazed earthenware at Delft and clay pipes at Gouda. At the same time, exotic imports such as Chinese porcelain become a major component of ceramic assemblages, especially after 1680. These changes in material assemblages are also coincident with architectural transformations, specifically the development of passageway houses with gabled fronts from an earlier open hall type plan (Figure 2.1). These changes are clearly illustrated in the excavations at 115/117 Langestraat in the town of Alkmaar which had buildings from the early 15th century onwards, and a sequence of rich assemblages of artifacts associated with privies in the back of the lots (Bitter et al. 1997). To date, the most substantial study of archaeological assemblages however is the Rubbish Pit and Cesspit project (part of the Delft Heritage Conservation Plan), which has analysed the chronological changes in 172 assemblages from four towns—Deventer, Dordrecht, Nijmegen and Tiel—between 1250 and 1900 (Bartels et al. 1999). This reveals in close detail, across a range of households, transformations in material culture for urban populations in the Netherlands. Taking an amalgamated selection of sites for three broad periods covering the 17th and 18th centuries, the basic shift in the ceramic repertoire can be shown (Table 2.2). From the late 17th century, tin-glazed earthenwares form a substantial proportion of assemblages, basic lead-gazed earthenwares making up the majority however. Both oriental porcelain and stonewares show a major increase in the early 18th century, with a corresponding decline in the role of lead-glazed earthenwares. However, both, along with tin-glazed earthenwares,

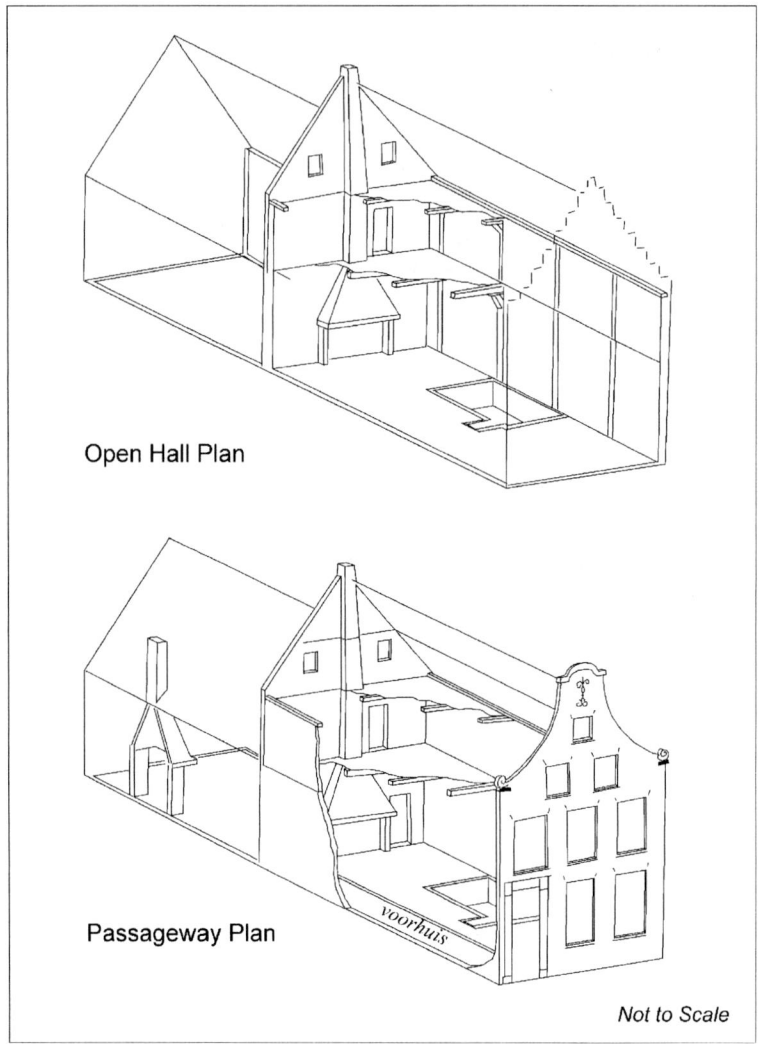

Figure 2.1. Dutch town house development, 115/117 Langestraat, Alkmaar. (*Source*: Adapted from Bitter et al. 1997)

decline in the latter half of the century as English industrial ceramics swamp the market. It was only in the mid-19th century that Dutch factories, centred in Maastricht, started to compete and outstrip the British imports. This pattern will be very useful later when comparing it to assemblages from the Cape, for there are some major differences.

Table 2.2. Summary of selected Dutch ceramic assemblages. (*Source*: Bartels 1999)

Date (N = no. of assemblages)	1650–1700 (4)		1700–1750 (9)		1750–1800 (6)	
	MNV	%	MNV	%	MNV	%
Stonewares	19	4.95	111	12.35	18	6.45
Lead-glazed earthenwares	238	61.98	334	37.15	110	39.43
Tin-glazed earthenwares	123	32.03	330	36.71	37	13.26
Oriental porcelain	4	1.04	118	13.13	15	5.38
European porcelain	0	0.00	2	0.22	22	7.89
Industrial earthenwares and stonewares	0	0.00	4	0.44	77	27.60
Total	*384*	*100*	*899*	*100*	*279*	*100*

Although some ceramics were exported from the Netherlands to its eastern colonies such as the Cape (e.g. tin-glazed earthenwares, coarse lead-glazed earthenwares, stonewares), local ceramics were generally cheaper and better—particularly Chinese and Japanese porcelain. Indeed, ceramics in the form of oriental porcelain was more likely to travel the other way, being imported into Europe (see below). A more common element of Dutch material culture in its colonies was tobacco pipes and glassware. Clay tobacco pipes were manufactured in various places in the Netherlands, but the major center was in Gouda which formed a guild with registered makers, who often stamped their pipes with their mark (Duco 1981; 1982; van der Meulen 2003). They were exported to the Cape and other places in large numbers—at the Cape, they were a major item of barter with the indigenous Khoisan, along with copper, but also of course used by the VOC employees. A study of excavated and stamped clay pipe fragments from the two VOC Forts in Table Bay showed three peaks in frequency: the 1670s, the 1730s and the 1760s, corresponding to peak shipping at the Cape (Abrahams 1984b). After 1790 there is a sharp decline in Dutch pipes, concurrent with the transition of the Cape colony from Dutch to British hands. According to the shipping registers and pipe frequencies, the 1730s was the height of trade during the VOC occupation of the Cape.

Apart from clay pipes, glassware—particularly wine bottles, were also exported to the Cape colony; glass was not made at the Cape until the late 19th century, but successful production only began in the 20th century, and so all glassware was imported, chiefly from Europe. This included some tablewares such as beakers and goblets, but the main find on archaeological sites is bottle glass, either globular wine bottles or square case gin bottles. Wine and beer were common drinks at the Cape, both made locally, wine as early as 1659 and beer in 1658 (Abrahams 1987: 11; Penn 1999). While these drinks were generally stored and sold in casks, it was more common to decant them into glass bottles or ceramic flagons in taverns and households. Cape wine was primarily made for domestic consumption, but some was exported, chiefly the famous Constantia wine, produced first by the Governor of the Cape colony Simon van der Stel in the 1680s. It became an exclusive and expensive wine in northern Europe into the 18th century, its label kept through changes of ownership and was initially exported in casks. However, towards the mid 18th century, bottled Constantia wine started to be exported, and was marked with its own seal (Abrahams 1987: 11–13). Examples of such bottles, made in the Netherlands, shipped to the Cape and then re-imported back to the Netherlands with contents, have been found on archaeological sites in Holland (Henkes 1994: 293).

The archaeological assemblages in Netherlands and the Cape attest to the global networks of European capitalism as articulated through the VOC: a global material culture was emerging in Europe and its colonies through items such as porcelain, clay pipes, and wine, and while such items helped to maintain a broad sense of Dutch or European identity, particularly in the colonies among the VOC servicemen, ultimately different identities emerged. This book is largely about the forging of colonial identities in just one of these colonies at the tip of Africa, but at the same time, identity was slowly being transformed in the mother country by the same processes and in which material culture played a key part. There is a recognizable tension between global and local processes, especially in relation to material culture in the modern world, and while global capitalism may have facilitated a global culture which was already emergent in the late 17th century, local articulations of this global culture always pull in a divergent direction. If wine was the 18th century Coca-Cola, its meaning in places such as the Cape colony increasingly varied not only from that in the Netherlands, but also among different sections of the Cape population. My concern in this chapter, is primarily with how the official organization at the Cape Colony—the VOC—tried to regulate such meanings and therefore, identities.

While the Board of Directors was composed mostly of Dutch nobility and some elite merchants, the men in service were generally from modest or humble backgrounds (Israel 1995: 948–9). At the Cape, many of the higher ranks of the VOC had worked their way up from being common soldiers and though some may have come from European nobility, on the whole most did not. This social mobility within the VOC—not that dissimilar to Dutch society as a whole at the time—was complemented by the power structures of the Company. The VOC worked by consultation and favoured dispersal of power rather than concentration; at the head of its overseas government in Indonesia was a Governor-General working as the head of a council (*raad*), and in most of the major colonies, this system was duplicated with a Governor and Political Council. The governor could never act on his own but only with his council, and key decisions had to go through the Board of Directors, via the Indonesian headquarters. Consequently, some decisions took a long time to be resolved. However, there is also a peculiarly modern feeling to this kind of power structure—a sense of detachment, of power at a distance. Despite the fact that the Company servants working in posts in the Indian Ocean were several months travel away from the Board of Directors, their ultimate power was still highly affective. This is not to deny the abuses of privilege or contravention of Company rules—most notably, private trading by individuals, which was widespread; but such breaches only contested the authority of the Board in a minor way, for ultimately all the Company servants depended on the VOC for their employment and position.

These two factors in the VOC organisation—the dispersed nature of its power and the lack of inherited social differentiation within the ranks of the Company servants—created quite unique conditions in their colonies, the Cape included. Indeed, in many ways the VOC can be seen as an institutional innovation in the context of European mercantilism (Steensgaard 1982). It was unique in that it integrated the functions of a sovereign power with a business partnership, with political decisions being made by the same people making economic decisions, both motivated by one thing: profit. Moreover, it used its monopoly status in the Netherlands to control the longer-term stability of the market against short-term fluctuations, through the accumulation of stock reserves. Finally, it distributed the Asian imports to wherever in Europe it could get the best price, not preferentially to the Netherlands. Fundamentally, its greatest strength lay in its creation of a permanent capital, although this was by no means intentional. Most contemporary companies would return their profits to their shareholders at the highest rate: the higher the profits, the higher the dividends. However, because the shareholders of the VOC were not involved in executive or management decisions—this was the role of the Board of Directors—a large part of the profits were invested back into the infrastructure of the Asian network. Ultimately, this led to the accumulation of an anonymous capital stock, over and above what was paid as dividends to the shareholders. This was something very new, even if it was not planned (Steensgaard 1982: 250).

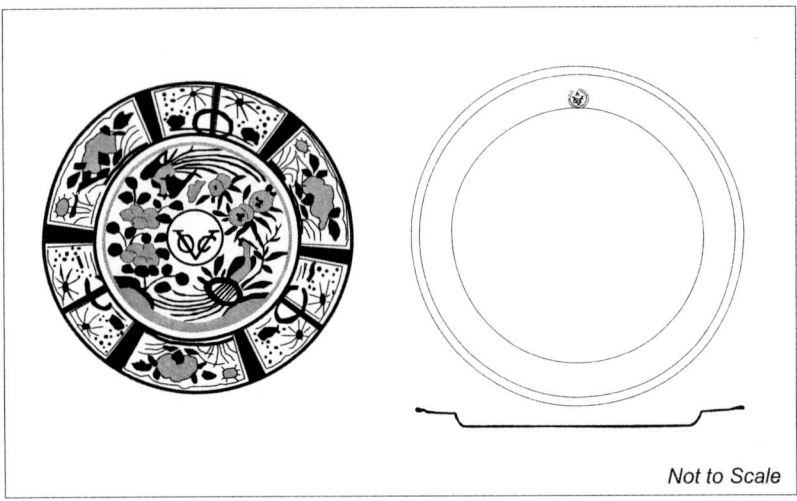

Not to Scale

Figure 2.2. VOC monogrammed porcelain (left) and pewter (right) plate—not to scale. (*Source*: Adapted from Woodward 1974 and Cowan et al. 1975)

The VOC was very much a corporate enterprise, and while I would not want to overplay the similarities to modern multi-nationals, there are certainly a number of interesting similarities. In terms of creating a corporate identity for example, the VOC had its own logo, which it placed on all kinds of objects—official documents bore the VOC monogram seal, its packaged crates of goods were branded with the same, its property—from cannons to pewter to porcelain, all were variously monogrammed (Figure 2.2). Of course this is not to say everything was thus marked, but the presence of the VOC monogram on such a diversity of objects attests to a power of corporate identity which could be mobilized in certain important contexts. VOC monogrammed porcelain for example, specially commissioned, might have been brought out only on certain state or official occasions, but even so, during such events it helped to sustain and forge a sense of corporate identity, both for those in the Company and those outside.

One of the key themes I want to address in this chapter is how this organization of the VOC affected the development of Cape society in the late 17th and 18th centuries, and it is perhaps the first factor that will be discussed most in this chapter. Indeed, the intentional dispersal of power can be said to have articulated itself in other ways, especially in the degree to which the VOC wanted to tie itself down to its colonial enterprises. As will be seen, all too frequently, much of the infrastructure development at the Cape occurred through private enterprise endorsed and backed by the VOC. Rather than take on direct responsibility, they preferred to delegate much of it into private hands, yet without losing ultimate control. This is part of the wider recognition that the VOC were generally very reluctant to establish colonial settlements and certainly invest too heavily in them. Their chief priority was the trade and any settlements they made were intended to safeguard this trade, not develop into extensive colonies of the homeland. Yet throughout, there was a continual tension and ambiguity in the degree of investment required, and as I hope to demonstrate in the case of the Cape colony, this very ambiguity allowed the space for the development of the outpost at Table Bay into a major colonial settlement. It is in the interstices of VOC equivocation that Cape society developed during the late 17th and 18th century.

THE CAPE COLONY, 1652–1795

The VOC colony at Table Bay was established in 1652 as a refreshment station for ships passing outward and homebound on the East Indies trade route. It remained a Dutch colony until 1795 when it was annexed by the British, and apart from a brief period between 1802 and 1806 when it fell back into Dutch hands (as part of the Batavian Republic), it was part of the British Empire until 1910 when it became part of the union of South Africa. As elsewhere on the East Indies trade route, the post at Table Bay at the southwestern tip of Africa was fortified. The VOC established fortified posts throughout the Indian Ocean in southern Africa, southern India, Sri Lanka, and Indonesia, and all were of fairly similar form. Their role was defensive, primarily against other European colonial powers, chiefly Portugal, Spain and England, but also local populations. A recent project from Amsterdam Archaeological Centre at the University of Amsterdam (http://www.frw.uva.nl/eura/ipp_expans.html) in collaboration with other institutions has started to investigate the archaeology of VOC forts in the Indian Ocean, including Fort Frederik Henrdrik in Mauritius and Katuwana Fort in Sri Lanka (Lakdusinghe 2001).

In South Africa, the archaeology of VOC forts is much better known, thanks to excavations at the Fort and Castle of Good Hope (Abrahams 1993; Hall et al. 1990a) and a smaller outpost at Oudepost (Schrire 1995; Schrire and Cruz-Uribe 1993). The fort *de Goede Hoop* in Table Bay was built in 1652 when the VOC decided to keep a permanent post there. Outside the fort which garrisoned the contingent of VOC soldiers, sailors and others, there was also a small cultivated area known as the 'garden', which still exists today as a public park. The Company Gardens were intended to grow vegetables and fruits to help supply the ships, while meat was primarily gained by trade with the local Khiokhoi—although this proved insufficient for their needs and they were soon forced to start keeping their own herds of livestock, traded or raided from the Khoikhoi. Indeed, the initial role of the post at Table Bay as a refreshment station for VOC trade ships was ironically reversed during much of Van Riebeeck's time there as the fort was often dependent on these very ships for supplies rather than vice versa (Worden et al. 1998: 19). Although colonization was not the policy of the VOC, if the Cape post was to properly serve its function, it was soon realized that it needed to become more self-sufficient and to do this, required a greater emphasis on local production by colonists over local trade with the Khoikhoi. Since the VOC were commonly reluctant to take a direct role in this, in 1657 they approved the granting of freehold lands to ex-employees who would farm land in the nearby Liesbeeck valley. These first free citizens or burghers (*vrijburgers*) were loaned tools and seeds and in return, their produce had to be sold exclusively to the VOC at fixed prices.

This attempt at initial colonisation was of limited success, and exacerbated by the Khoikhoi's refusal to respect the VOC's increasing presence at Table Bay, which led to open conflict in the late 1650s. Slowly, the Dutch started to demarcate their possession with palisades, watchtowers and thorny hedges in an attempt to cut their outpost off from the rest of southern Africa. Despite the settlement by free burghers, the VOC still had no wish to turn this outpost into a proper settlement. Yet whatever their intentions, private and company development around the fort and gardens began an unstoppable process of urbanization. By the early 1660s, the victualling station was on its way to becoming a town as taverns and tradesmen became established in the shadow of the fort (Worden et al. 1998: 28). During the latter decades of the 17th century and first decades of the 18th, the VOC remained ambiguous about encouraging settlement—though they had assisted with some European emigration, especially French Huguenot refugees in the 1680s (see Chapter 3), they were not sure how far this should be pushed. While recognizing the need for the Cape colony to be producing supplies for its ships, the VOC was indecisive whether this should be developed through free burgher farmers or slaves; it was not until 1717 that they decided to stop assisting all further emigration and promote the slave base (Elphick and Giliomee 1989: 533). But by this time, it was almost too late as the colony had expanded, both in terms of farm land which now stretched deep into the interior and population of burghers.

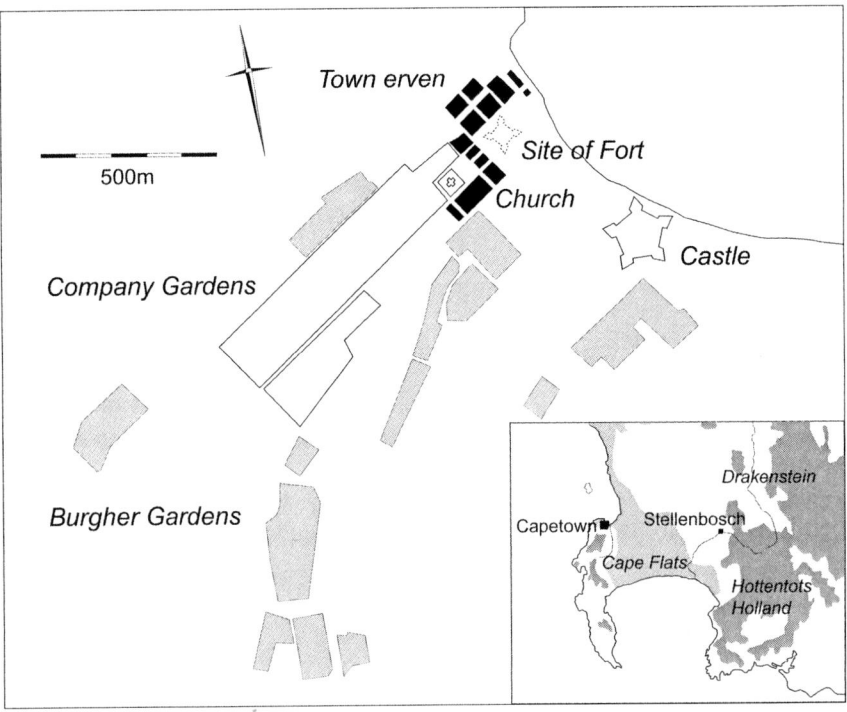

Figure 2.3. Cape Town c.1700. (*Source*: Adapted from Algemeen Rijksarchief map VEL 828)

Throughout the later 17th and early 18th century, the town developed, but at some distance from the castle and gardens, separated by an open area of land called the *plein*, under part of which lay the site of the leveled remains of the first fort (Figure 2.3). This seems to have been a regular and intentional pattern for VOC settlements elsewhere and where there were already towns in existence, VOC forts were usually placed with an empty space between them and the town (Zandvliet 1998: 260). This town at the Cape was laid out on a regular grid of streets and plots, another feature of VOC planning, and although occupied by an ever expanding burgher population, it included many key public buildings owned by the VOC such as the Dutch Reformed Church, a hospital, and a slave lodge. Moreover, the town was under the political control of the fort, and through various administrative structures, it governed the growing colony. The main power at the colony itself resided with the Governor and Council of Policy, but there were various other bodies with specific roles, and while there was some burgher representation in this machinery, it was dominated by VOC officials

(Schutte 1989). The Governor was a post only established in 1679, up-grading the former post of Commander of the Fort, which had been held by Van Riebeeck and then Wagenaer; the first Governor was Simon van der Stel, the son of the Governor or Mauritius.

In governing the new colony, the VOC distinguished very early on between the different groups of people, according them different legal status; there were four main groups defined: Company servants (i.e. VOC employees), free burghers, slaves and the Khoikhoi (called 'Hottentots'). Although not explicitly racial, these categories had very clear racial assumptions and associations with the first two groups be-ing largely white Europeans and the second, non-white, non-Europeans. There were however, some exceptions—a few Asians in the employ of the VOC and a few manumitted slaves or Asian immigrants who essentially became free burghers, though they were distinguished as 'free blacks'. While not denying that racism was ingrained in the Cape colony from the start, it was certainly not as rigid as it later became, though there are different viewpoints on how South African racism de-veloped (see Elphick and Giliomee 1989). Certainly it seems there was no *systematic* expression of racial attitudes in the early Cape colony, a fact supported by the practice of miscegenation. Mixed sexual relations were frequent, but chiefly between European men and slaves; mixed marriages however were rarer, yet still occurred. The first governor, Simon van der Stel was himself the grandchild of a Dutch sea cap-tain and a local from Coromandel. The VOC categorizations were then, primarily legal rather than racial, in the first instance; but the racial assumptions associated with them—systematic or not—nevertheless helped to sustain racial divisions, especially through the official ma-chinery that differentiated these groups through various proscriptions such as marriage, domicile, taxation, movement and land ownership (Elphick and Giliomee 1989: 529).

From a total population of less than 400 in the late 1650s, the Cape colony by the 1730s had reached over 3000; nearly a third were VOC employees, well over a third, slaves and the remainder, burghers and 'free blacks'—i.e. mostly freed slaves or more rarely, free non-European immigrants (ibid.: 50). Such figures do not however, reveal the proper extent of cultural diversity at the colony; within the VOC and free burgher classes, there were many nationalities apart from Dutch, pri-marily German and Scandinavian, many of whom came to the Cape as VOC employees. Indeed, in 1700, over half the VOC personnel was com-posed of people of non-Dutch origin (Schutte 1989: 293). Of the slaves and free blacks, the population was even more diverse with people from all around the Indian Ocean basin such as Madagascar, Mozambique,

Sri Lanka, Bengal and Indonesia, as well as Cape-born slaves of mixed descent (Elphick and Shell 1989: Shell 1994). Moreover, although the Dutch Reformed Church was the official church at the colony and many of the slaves were baptized, much of the slave and ex-slave population came from Islamic societies, and produced a distinctive and alternative culture at Cape Town to the official VOC one.

Given that when the Dutch first established their post in 1652, the relations at the Cape were primarily between the VOC and the Khoikhoi, in less than a century, a community with diverse origins and classified into four separate groups, must have opened up many new problems for the VOC. Not that it did not face similar situations elsewhere; at its main headquarters in Java, the town of Batavia was developing in similar ways to the Cape colony though on a larger scale— between 1624 and 1700, its total population increased from c. 8000 to 70,000 people (Israel 1995: 324). But both the population composition and context were very different. The question I want to address is how the VOC at the Cape attempted to shape this emerging society and how it, in turn, shaped itself, through material culture. I will focus on two elements—architecture and ceramics.

Jan van Riebeeck, a surgeon of the Dutch East India Trading Company (VOC) landed at Table Bay with a small party and set about constructing the fort according to instructions—a square fort with four corner bastions, made from local clay and timber. It took eighteen months to complete. Within a year, part of it collapsed, and over the next two decades, the fort was continually repaired due to the effect of rain on the clay walls, until finally, in 1674 it was abandoned and leveled, as the post re-located to a new, stone-built castle started in 1665 by Van Riebeeck's replacement, Zacharias Wagenaer (see Hall et al. 1990a). The site of the fort currently lies under a major open area in central Cape Town, Grand Parade, which is used for market stalls and a car park; between 1983 and 1991, sections of the fort were investigated in archaeological trenches (Abrahams 1993). Excavated evidence conforms to the historical descriptions, with structural foundations made from various clays and showing signs of repair (Figure 2.4). The finds were numerous, however none were directly associated with the fort, most being from disturbed layers post-dating its abandonment (see Abrahams 1984b; 1987; 1994 for studies of the clay pipes, ceramics and glass). The site is famous in modern times for where Nelson Mandela gave his first speech after his release from prison, as president-elect, in 1994.

Better preserved and thus more informative in many ways, is the excavation of a smaller fort around 120 km up the western coast from

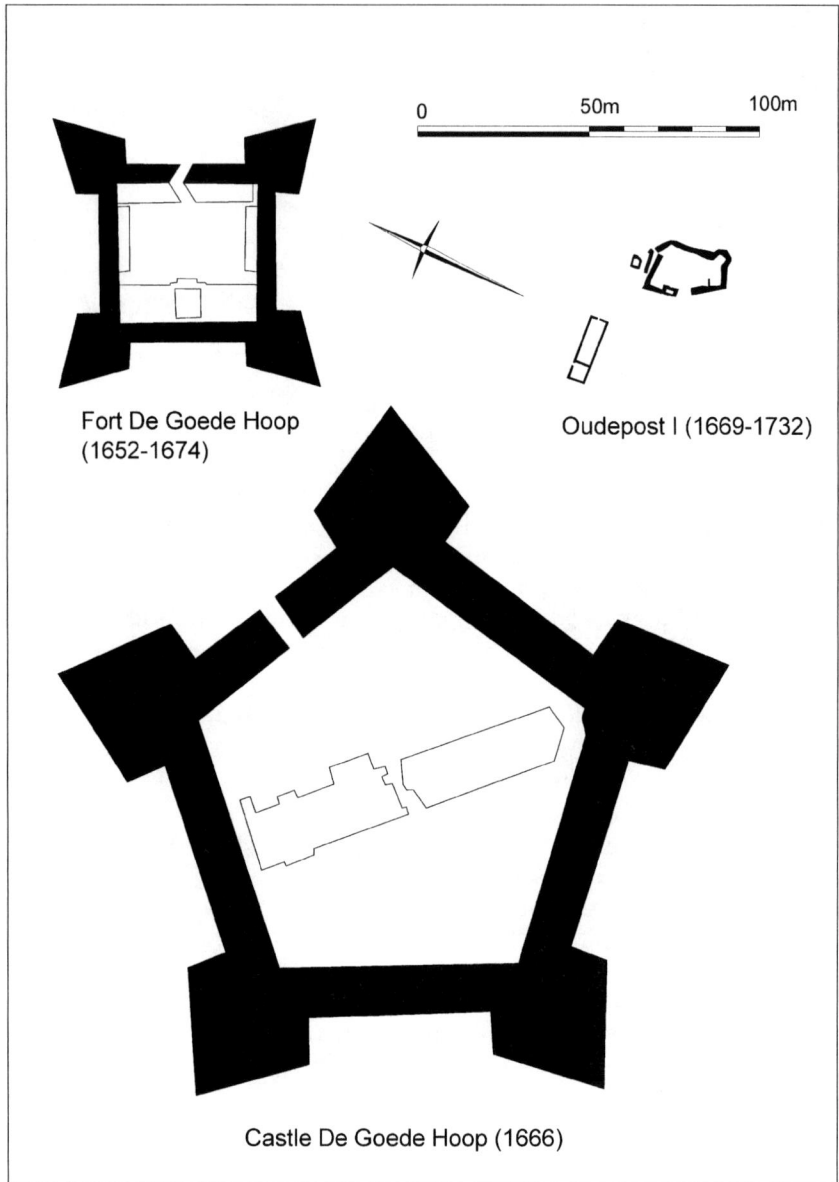

0   50m   100m

Fort De Goede Hoop
(1652-1674)

Oudepost I (1669-1732)

Castle De Goede Hoop (1666)

Figure 2.4. Plans of Fort, Castle and Oudepost. (*Source*: Adapted from Abrahams 1993, Hall et al. 1990 and Schrire 1995)

Good Hope in Saldanha Bay. In 1669, the VOC decided to establish a small outpost here to prevent the French from claiming the area, and serve as a provisioning station for ships on the East Indies trade route. Indeed, at the start, the VOC were half considering this as a better location than Table Bay for their main station given the bad weather at the Cape. In the end however, Good Hope retained its position and Oudepost was only occupied until 1732, with a short hiatus between 1673 and 1684/6 after a massacre of the garrison by Khoikhoi. After 1732, the post was re-located a few kilometers away (Oudepost II). Archaeological excavations focused on the early fort (Oudepost I) and between 1984 and 1987, uncovered a rich story in the material remains of this small outpost (see Schrire 1995 for the most engaging narrative of the site). The remains of a small, stone built fort or redoubt were investigated (with detached cell) along with a rectangular lodge, which served as the main residence of the garrison. The most interesting aspect to the site has been the interpretative potential it offers for studying Dutch-Khoikhoi interactions, especially through its material culture assemblage (Schrire 1987; 1988; 1990; Schrire and Merwick 1991).

The redoubt at Oudepost was very irregular in plan and clearly contrasting with the formal layout of the fort at Good Hope (Figure 2.4). The difference is not surprising—Oudepost was small and run by no more than 10 men while the fort at Good Hope was larger and housed around 90 men and as many slaves at the start, but whose number grew. Nevertheless, irregular though Oudepost was, it can still be seen to some extent to embody the principles of the polygon which were more regularly laid out for the fort and later the castle. Both these latter followed actual plans sent from the *Heren XVII* in the Netherlands, which drew on conventional models of military fortification from northern Europe (Abrahams 1993; Hall et al. 1990a). Translating the Company's design for the new fort (i.e. the Castle) at Good Hope to the local context of Table Bay proved as difficult as the old fort, and it suffered similar problems of collapsing walls. Indeed, the disparity between the intended or ideal plan and the actual plan reveals the symbolic aspirations of the forts at Good Hope as much as, if not more than its functional utility. Indeed, like the earlier fort, the castle was never tested in conflict. As Hall has argued, the castle served as a symbol of Dutch colonial power and presence in the landscape as much as anything and in practice, this symbol was constantly being compromised by its inability to live up to its ideal (Hall et al. 1990a).

Hall has also studied the town plans and architecture of Dutch colonial settlements to reveal the tensions between privilege and poverty or high and low in such contexts (Hall 1991a; 1992b; 2000: 57–60). He has shown how the layout of Cape Town is similar to other Dutch colonies such as at New Amsterdam (Manhatten Island), Willemstad (Curaçao) in the Caribbean or Mauritsstad in Brazil, in their deployment of geometric forms as an expression of 'converting the "wild" landscape to a "civilized" townscape' (Hall 1991a: 44). The basis of central Cape Town today was laid out in 1660 by the Company surveyor on a regular grid, which mimicked on a larger scale, the layout of the Company Gardens. Similar geometries of order, expressed in the design of the forts are thus also present in the town layout, and both can be seen to reflect very specific 'regimes of order' to quote Hall (2000). Yet just as the fort 'ideal' often fell short of reality, so with the townscape; though regular streets and plots could be laid out, the houses occupying the plots and the condition of the streets often presented a very different picture at street level than on the map. Moroever, Cape Town, along with all the other places also had an underbelly, a part of the town where the streets were more chaotic, where housing was more simple—and where the poorer classes lived.

Apart from the architecture, other aspects of material culture are equally vocal on the tensions between VOC ideals and actuality. One of the commodities in which the VOC traded was porcelain. It never formed a major part of their trade, yet was nonetheless, highly desirable in Europe and of course, forms a major element of archaeological assemblages, especially at the Cape (Jörg 1982; Volker 1971; Woodward 1974). The VOC traded predominantly in the basic blue and white wares from China and Japan, with lesser amounts of enamelled wares, and millions of pieces were shipped all over the world. There were two basic types of porcelain being carried in this trade—the fine porcelain from the Jingdezhen factories and a 'coarse' provincial ware from southern China and other neighbouring countries in the Malaysian peninsula (Figure 2.5). Almost all the porcelain destined for Europe was the former type, while in the VOC's posts in the Indian Ocean, provincial porcelain formed a substantial part of the pottery alongside the finer wares. Porcelain was relatively cheap at source—the VOC could acquire large quantities and it was an easy substitute for imported European utilitarian ceramics such as German stonewares or Dutch earthenwares. The price in Europe in no way reflected its purchase value for there was a typical mark-up of between 200 and 300% in the mid 18th century (Jörg 1982). Given its cheapness at colonies such as the Cape, it forms the major part of archaeological ceramic assemblages until the 19th century (Klose 1993; Klose & Malan 1993; Vos 1985).

However, the predominance of porcelain as a utilitarian ware at the Cape must not simply be seen as an economy or practical necessity; it also links in to competing perceptions of its value among the

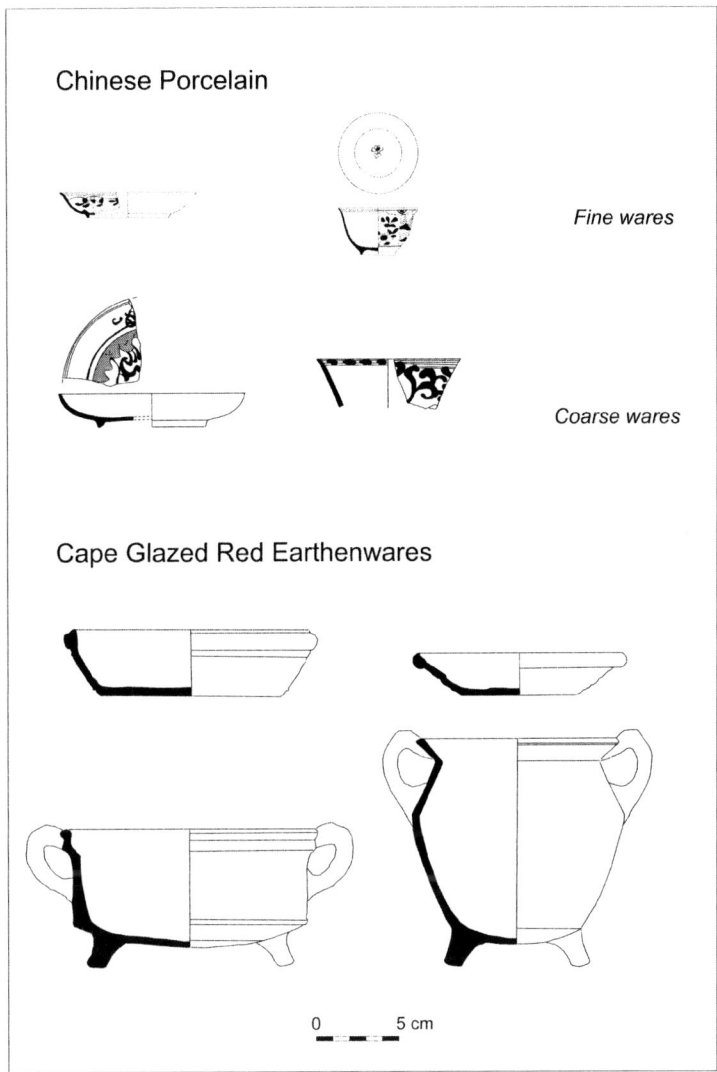

Figure 2.5. Examples of main pottery types at the Cape.

population. The fact that a large part of the population at the Cape—
i.e. the slaves—were more familiar with these vessel forms as everyday
ceramics than the European colonists to whom they represented an
expensive item is not to be overlooked. Indeed, the porcelain at the
Cape perhaps not only reflected the ethnic origins of the slaves but the

cultural world to which many in the colony looked—Asia, not Africa or Europe. Although porcelain was the most common ceramic in use at the Cape, the use of European style earthenwares and stonewares was not absent at the Cape, indeed within years of the colony's establishment, a local pottery was set up to produce European style glazed earthenwares (Abrahams 1994; Jordan 2000). The second commander of the garrison, Zacharias Wagenaer who oversaw the construction of the new Castle, also requested potters to be sent out to provide a supply of basic utilitarian vessels for his men. The VOC pottery works was established in 1665 and operated throughout the 18th century, and its output has been found on numerous archaeological sites. Vessels produced were essentially similar to contemporary north European types—lead-glazed red-bodied earthenwares in the form of basic kitchen wares such as tripod cooking pots, pipkins or skillets, all with lids and table wares such as plates, dishes and bowls (Figure 2.5).

Despite local production however, there was only a small market for these products; people at the Cape, both VOC and burghers preferred porcelain or metal, as archaeological assemblages and inventories attest. Indeed, as Jordan has suggested, the establishment of a local pottery earthenware industry in the Cape colony might be seen as an attempt to preserve European styles of cuisine and foodways in opposition to the developing multicultural nature of Cape society (Jordan 2000: 138). Not only that, it might also have been initiated to maintain social distinctions within the colony as a result of the availability of porcelain which in Europe, carried status distinction. In other words, while the VOC high officials made earthenwares available for its servants and the burghers in order to maintain their distinction through use of porcelain, the cheapness and greater availability of porcelain undermined this attempt at every stage. But more than that perhaps, the very people who they were marketing the earthenwares for, were in fact increasingly re-defining themselves because of the multi-cultural nature of the society, and in this context, porcelains were preferable not simply because of cheapness but through cultural choice. The dynamics of social differentiation as articulated through material culture in the homeland was being steadily eroded and contested in the new context of the Cape colony.

These tensions between VOC intentions and day to day processes, between the Company elite and the common soldiers, slaves and settlers, has revealed itself in very interesting ways in the material culture. Moreover, perhaps the various sides increasingly saw things very differently, a perception that may have only fragmented further over time. This is something I address further in the next chapter, but for now I want to explore the themes I have been discussing here in more detail, using a case study of a VOC backed industrial operation in the mid-18th century. In particular, I want to explore the VOC ambiguity over the process of colonization and power in terms of how it was articulated through the social relations between the VOC elite, its servants, slaves and burghers. More generally though, the case study illustrates some of the broader workings of the VOC in the Asian sphere and how an industrial settlement in the rural western Cape was enmeshed within the broader global processes of Dutch capitalism.

GOEDE VERWACHTING: THE SILVER MINE ON THE SIMONSBERG

A silver mine which was operated for several years in the 1740s lies on the eastern slopes of the Simonsberg, the landmark mountain range in the study area of the Dwars valley. The Dwars is a tributary of the Berg river which runs through the Drakenstein, a mountainous area c. 55 km to the northwest of Cape Town (Figure 2.6). By the time the silver mine operations had started, much of the valley was claimed by numerous farms that spread out along the valley bottom (see Chapter 3). As it happened, the mines were devoid of any silver, and the whole operation was a total failure—the story to have passed down is that it was a confidence trick by a German ex-VOC serviceman, Frans Diedrick Muller, and is most popularly related by Burman (1969: 66–73). This story probably originated soon after the events of the 1740s, as this is how it was referred to by a British visitor to the Cape in the 1790s, Lady Anne Barnard (Fairbridge 1924: 39; Robinson 1994: 255). The story I believe is more complicated than that, but however one views the personal motivation of Muller, the fact is the VOC invested heavily in the project and it persisted for many years before it was closed down. Indeed, the operation provides significant insights into the role of silver in the global economy and the VOC's desire for increasing its stock of silver.

The possible potential of the Simonsberg was first identified in the late 17th century under the Governorship of Simon van der Stel. The first traveler to mention the mines was Peter Kolb, who was at the Cape in the early 18th century; he writes in 1731: "A silver- and a copper mine were some time ago discover'd near it. Samples of Ore, very promising ones, were immediately sent to the Directors in Holland. But the Directors, for reasons I shall give hereafter, have not hitherto thought fit to order these mines to be further open'd." (Kolb 1968: 51).

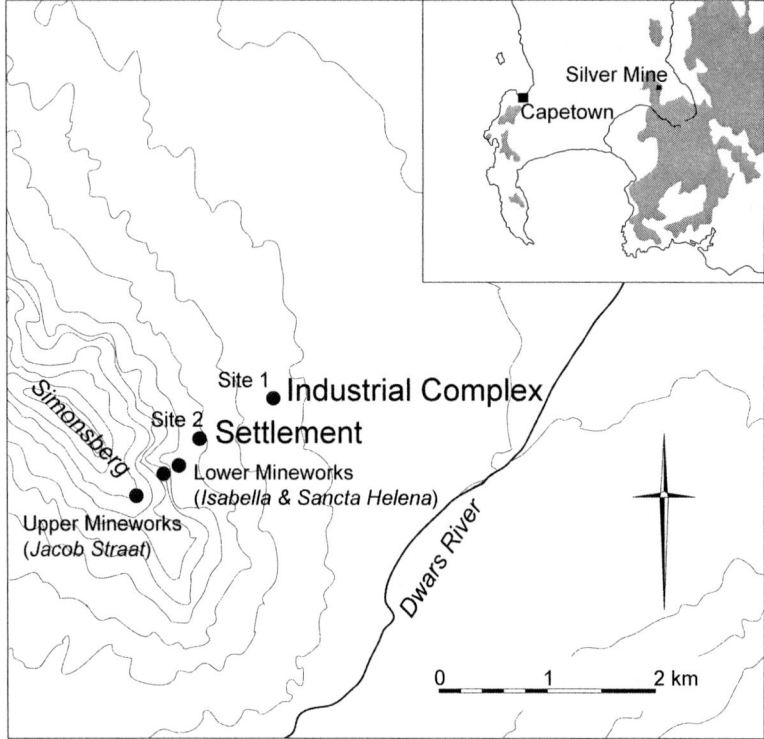

Figure 2.6. Location of the silver mine and Simonsberg at the Cape.

The reasons, according to Kolb, were a lack of labour and lack of fuel (Kolb 1967: 310). A minister working for the VOC, Francois Valentyn, who visited the area in 1705, also mentions that a "...silver-mine was also opened here, but has not been further exploited owing to the great cost (Valentyn 1971: 161). Neither Kolb nor Valentyn say anything about a confidence trick, rather the mine was closed because it was too expensive to work. The story of the confidence trick appears much later and indeed refers to a different and more concerted attempt to mine the mountain; this story can be seen in two further travelers accounts. The first is Lady Anne Barnard, writing in a journal and letters in the closing years of the 18th century. The first is from her journal:

> But let me not forget to mention that to Stillinbosch we passed thro' the fertile valley of Drachenstead and by the Mountains of Simonsberg with their high marked top distinguished for the trick played to the East India company about twenty years ago.

An adventurer having melted down a considerable quantity of Spanish dollars into a mass and mixed them up with sand and rubbish, applied to the honourable body to know if they thought the mine he had discovered was worth the working.

The Company, intoxicated with the hope of gain paid him down to a sum of money to promote his discoveries and in the meantime they converted the mass into a chain to suspend the Key of the Castle by, where it remains still this day, in token of their Credulity. (Robinson 1994: 255).

She repeats the story in a letter to John Barrow in 1797:

The road from Stellenbosch leads thro' a pass formed between the above mountain and Simon's Berg, called Bange Kloof, or the tremendous passage.

This last Parnassian Mountain with its high forked top has also its Helicon but no Apollo nor the Muses. The only inspiration it has yet caused has been the thirst of Silver. A Man from whom it has derived its name, with an intention to make his fortune at the expense of the folly and ignorance of the Dutch East India Company, melted a number of Spanish Dollars and produced a Mass of Silver of which he said he had discovered the Mine. A Bargain was immediately struck and a great sum paid down to Simons, who was to conduct the Mine and supply the Company with whatever quantity should be wanted, and in the mean time the Mass was converted into a Chain to suspend the Keys of the Castle Gates as an ocular proof of their riches, and it *still* remains in the same service, a memorial of Dutch credulity, for Simons never found the Mine, nor the Company their expected riches. (Fairbridge 1924: 39).

The second account comes from the same John Barrow that Lady Anne Barnard had written to, and who in his *Travels in the Interior of South Africa* published in London in 1801, says that during the governorship of Simon van der Stel (the late 17th century), there was a man "... intent on making his fortune by imposing on the credulity and ignorance of the Company's servants, metlted down a quantity of Spanish dollars and presented the mass to the Governor as a specimen of silver from a rich mine that he had discovered in the mountain (Simonsberg, which perpetuates the name of the Governor), meanwhile the mass of silver (which was mixed with gravel) was ordered to be manufactured into a chain to which the keys of the Castle gates should be suspended ... The chain was made and still remains." (Barrow 1801: 59).

Barrow's account is clearly derivative of Barnard's but then attributes the date of the episode much earlier, probably due to a confusion between the earlier exploratory foray mentioned by Kolb and Valentyn and the later activities. Both accounts mention the silver being melted down to form a chain for the Castle keys (at Cape Town), but as we shall see, the archives clearly mention other objects. Of course some may have been kept back for a chain and not reported, but apart from the location and rough date given by Barnard, there is little reason to trust the veracity of her story. Nevertheless, her version, or at least the version she related, has been the accepted one in popular memory. Burman's account of the silver mine in 1966, the first and only one researched in any detail, re-affirms Muller's guilt, but almost by default, because of the integrity of all the others involved—namely the 'Great and Good' of the Society (Burman 1969: 66–68). But what really did happen?

The later silver mine project started in 1740 when a soldier of the Company, Frans Diederik Muller, claimed to have discovered silver in Groot Drakenstein, a claim which prompted the Governor of the Cape at the time, Hendrik Swellengrebel, to make a visit to establish the truth of this claim. He was persuaded by Muller that the mountains were rich in ores, but rather than take on direct responsibility for mining operations, the VOC granted a charter to an association of citizens (*burghers*) led by a local dignitary, Olof de Weth in 1743. The petition for a charter was applied to the Political Council in Cape Town on 22nd February 1743 and requested exclusive mining rights over a large area for a wide array of minerals: gold, silver, mercury, copper, lead, tin iron, cobalt and bismuth. In return for Company labour, equipment and supplies, the association would give the VOC 6.6% of the proceeds and sell the remainder to them at the going rates (de Wet 1984). The Political Council provided their consent and granted the charter, with an amendment three days later to include Frans Diederick Muller, as deputy foreman (*bergwerker*) with the same rights (*ibid.*).

The newly formed association, *Octroojeerde Society der Mynwerken aan de Simonsberg*, which was granted the charter, collected 1800 rixdollars from its 22 shareholders and work began in March 1743 with Muller directing the operations on the ground. The mine was optimistically named *Goede Verwachting* ('Good Expectations'). The Society met at Cape Town in November of the same year having already spent nearly all the money, most of it on equipment and supplies. They each put in another 30 rixdollars and appointed a board of directors from their number to meet every three months with a report from Muller and to oversee all matters relating to the mining. On the board were: Hendrik Swellengrebel, Rijk Tulbagh, Olof de Weth, Jan Louwrens Bestbier, Jacob Cloete, and Jan Phillip Giebbelaar with Nicolaus van Dessin as treasurer and Johannes Louw Pieters as deputy cashier (CA C2773). This list of names is very informative—not only does it include local burghers such as de Weth, Giebbelaar, and Bestbier, it also included the most high ranking members of the VOC government at the Cape, including the Governor, his second and secretary of the Orphan Chamber,

Table 2.3. List of shareholders in the Simonsberg Mining Society. (*Source*: SAL, Eric Rosenthal Local History Collection, MSB 974 2(2))

Shareholder	Status	Role
Gustaaf Wilhelm van Imhoff	Governor-General of VOC	—
Hendrik Swellengrebel	Governor of Cape	Director
Rijk Tulbagh	Chief of Advisory Council	Director
Olof de Weth	Burgher	Director
Jan Louwrens Bestbier	Burgher	Director
Jacob Cloete	Burgher	Director
Jan Phillip Giebbelaar	Burgher	Director
Nicolaus van Dessin	Secretary of Orphan Chamber	Treasurer
Johannes Louw Pieters	Burgher	Cashier
Rudolf Siegfried Alleman	Captain of Garrison	—
Josephus de Grand Prez	Secretary of Council of Policy	—
Pieter Rheede van Oudtshoorn	Fiscal	—
Frans le Serrurier	Predikant	—
Jacobus Moller	Naval captain (Simonstown)	—
Jan van Schoon	Chief Surgeon	—
Jacob van Rheenen	Burgher	—
Jan Jops	Burgher	—
Jan de Wit	Burgher	—
Willem Morkel	Burgher	—
Andries Brink	Burgher	—
Hendrik van der Merwe	Burgher	—
Willem van As	Burgher	—

as well as local officials (*heemraaden*). The list of other shareholders is equally impressive and included the Governor-General of the VOC in Batavia, Gustaaf Wilhelm van Imhoff (Table 2.3; Burman 1969: 67–8; see Eric Rosenthal Local History Collection, MSB 974 2(2)).

Considering this was a private venture, almost everyone in the higher ranks of the VOC payroll was clearly hoping to cash in. This was not unusual, for although the Company prohibited its servants from engaging in private business, it was so widespread as considered to be normal at the Cape (Penn 1999: 109). Indeed, one of the shareholders, Alleman had previously been entangled in an official complaint against an abuse of his position by another VOC servant, Estienne Barbier who was later to become a voice for burghers against the corruption of the VOC (Penn 1999). Between 1743 and 1748, the shareholders of the mining society invested thousands of rixdollars in return for nothing but quartz. For 1743 and 1744, they regularly paid out 30 rixdollars each, and between 1745 and 1748, this doubled to 60 rixdollars. The money went on supplies for the construction of numerous buildings and on wages and rations for the workers. The exact accounts of the operation are given in the financial statements of the Association (C2774/2–3), but the costs were high. Just the wages alone must have come to over 10,000 rixdollars—for example, each soldier was paid 9 per month, sailors 6 and a smith 7 according to the first contract, while Muller himself was drawing 40 rixdollars per month after 1746. The rations for one three month period came to nearly 120 rixdollars, which when calculated for the whole period, suggests nearly 8000 rixdollars was spent on food, although given the increasing population of the mine works, this is probably an under-estimate. Finally the supplies, which were delivered to the mine, either from Cape Town or local burghers must have matched if not exceeded the ration costs.

The number of soldiers and sailors varied over time, with most of the men being replaced at one time or another, although there were also several desertions. The work started with about ten Company men, mostly soldiers with one sailor and a smith, but most of these were replaced after a year, only three of the original staying. Of these, only one man could be identified as lasting the whole course, the *stijger*, Johan Leendert Voogt. In 1746, five men from a nearby garrison (at Klapmuts) came to help as well as six more from Cape Town later in the year—though again, these may have replaced other men. In the same year, a total of 18 slaves also arrived to work on the mines. Two masons come to work there that year too, and the following year, two carpenters, along with six more labourers. On average during its peak, it would seem that the mineworks were probably home to around 16–22 company men and 12–18 slaves, making the population around 30–40 people in total.

Muller spent the first two months building quarters and a smithy, and only in May began working the mine. Throughout 1743 and 1744, he spent nearly half that time on construction work, and only 15 months on the mines. By May of 1745 he had built himself a house (and presumably quarters for his men), a smithy, two small ovens or furnaces (*oventje*), and completed a processing facility for the ore (*bochwerk*). Early the following year, the ore-processing building needed repairs. In late 1746, he began a second phase of construction, working on a smelting house and 'water building' (*waater muragie*), which were completed over a year later in early 1748, progress having been delayed by damage from rains. He also started to build a coal store (*koolhuis*) and smokehouse (*roosthuis*) in 1747. This new phase of building activity is indicated in the delivery records to the mine which reveal a marked increase in deliveries of planking and beams from late 1746 onwards. In total then, three major constructions were built at the mine works—an ore processing facility, a smelting house and a water mill. In addition, there

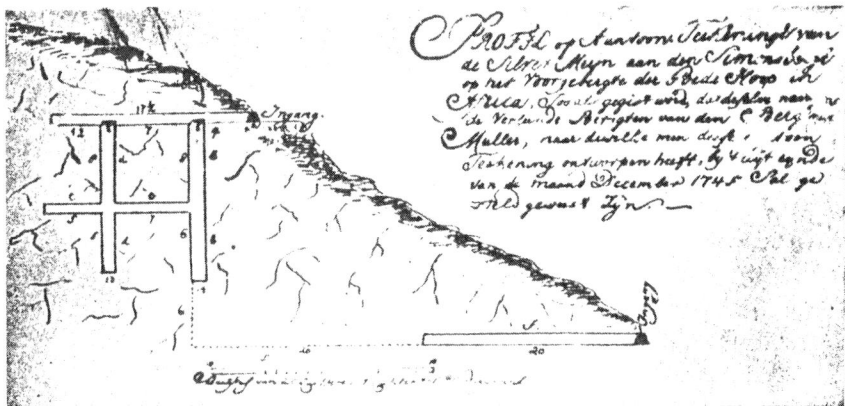

Figure 2.7. Contemporary drawing of the upper silver mine works from 1743. (*Source*: South African Library MSB 974/2)

were the two small furnaces, the coal store and smokehouse, a smithy and a dwelling house. There were probably other structures built too however—storage blocks, enclosures for the livestock and quarters for the Company men and the slaves.

The progress on the mines was equally variable. There were two main phases of mining, an early phase focused on the upper level at the interface of the granite and sandstone, and a later phase working lower down the slopes closer to the mining quarters. In Muller's reports to the Society, he gives a detailed breakdown on the upper mines' progress (in *lachter*—an old mining unit which varies but is about 2.04 m). This upper mine consists of seven different shafts or tunnels on three levels (Figure 2.7); the topmost level where work commenced and where the main entrance to the mine lay, was called *Jacob Straat* and worked for over a year and to about 35 m into the mountain side. Two vertical shafts were dug down from this, *Jonker Hendrik* and *Jonker Willem*, between late 1743 and late 1745 and penetrated to a depth of 25–30 m. Running between these and parallel to *Jacob Straat* above, were two if not three more tunnels, *Timmerman*, *Ryke Gang* and *Witten Spaad Gang*, and which were worked between 1744 and 1745, for about 15 m each. To ease the removal of ores from these mines, it was decided to cut a deep tunnel (*diepe stollen*) lower down the slope which would connect with one of the vertical shafts (*Jonker Hendrik*)—this was never completed but reached 40 m into the mountain side. At the beginning of 1746, it appears that the upper mine works were more or less abandoned and work commenced on new shafts much lower down the mountain side.

Information on these new mines are much less precise—Muller mentions discovering six new sites in total, but only appeared to have worked on three of them, which he called *Isabella*, *Sancta Helena* and *Sancta Elisabeth*. *Isabella* was the highest and had at least four tunnels, then *Sancta Helena*, with *Sancta Elisabeth* being the lowest and closest to his house. According to Muller, these mines lay about 180 m below the upper mines. Little detailed information was given in his reports about the new mines progress or depth, indeed he changes his measurements from *lachter* to *clafften* (which is a similar length, about 2 m), but he does mention they were subject to flooding which caused serious problems. Moreover it seems over time, Muller shifted his teams lower and lower down the mountain—perhaps partly because of the labour involved in moving the mined ore downhill. *Sancta Helena* was the only one he seemed to persist with after the middle of 1747, by which time, it had progressed about 24 m deep.

Throughout, Muller maintained that the ore he was mining, contained silver, and later copper and finally gold. He did vary in his optimism however, sometimes writing encouraging of the richness of the deposits, sometimes of their paucity. He never seemed to imply however that there were no precious metals to be had—only that the ores were not consistently productive. For the upper mine, he claimed silver ores, while for the lower ones, chiefly copper, though toward the end, he said silver and finally gold was coming out of one tunnel, the *Sancta Helena*. In September 1748, three members of the Society visited Muller at the mine and testified to Muller's claim of gold, just as in 1745, a four-member inspection team had testified to silver. Given that nothing ever came out of any of his ores, Muller was either deluded, incompetent or a liar. Perhaps it matters little which of these he was—perhaps all three. Certainly it is hard to believe this was a complete confidence trick, and my belief is that he did believe in the mines, at least at the start. As the failure of the mines became apparent, he probably became more and more desperate, and probably did lie to the Society to postpone retribution—and in the deluded hope he could redeem himself and strike it lucky. Ultimately, if he was incompetent and deluded, then no less were all the shareholders of the Society, and when realization dawned that they had invested so much money into a complete failure, they needed a scapegoat.

Muller was brought back to Cape Town, and in October 1748, appeared before a committee of the Society, which included Swellengrebel, Tulbagh, van Dessin, van Oudtshoorn, Alleman, Cloete and de Weth. Also present was a goldsmith (Matthys Lotter) and two silversmiths (David Vickers and Hendrick Fuchs) who both testified that neither gold or silver were present in the ores; a memorial from Anthony Grill (presumably a metallurgist) in Amsterdam, to whom a sample had been sent equally confirmed the worthlessness of the ore. There was obviously a period of deliberation, for it was not until a year later in December 1749 that the Society passed a resolution explicitly implicating Muller with fraud, particularly in relation to the silver claimed to have been found in 1745. It was suggested he had salted the ore; the silver from this ore had subsequently been used in making a baptismal font, drinking cup and two dishes, donated to the church at Swellendam by Swellengrebel (C2773). It appears Muller was sentenced to banishment and in 1751, ended up in Batavia (Java), yet by 1753, he had returned to Europe.

In the end, although Muller's name was defamed at the Cape, he seemed to have got off fairly lightly. No mention is made of his wife, but she may have gone with him to Batavia and thence to Holland. The VOC in Batavia were certainly not happy that he had been sent to them, and were even unhappier when they learnt that the Mining Society had distributed all his assets among its shareholders—though given who these shareholders were, this was probably a token gesture. Certainly the shareholders lost out in this venture, but perhaps not as badly as one might assume. As well as recovering what assets they could—equipment, materials and presumably the buildings and land on which the mining settlement lay—many of them were also profiting from the operation by supplying the very materials in the first place. For example, Jan Phillip Giebbelaar provided them with bricks (and the labour of his assistant, Martin Melck), while Johannes Louw Pieters supplied the thatch, which roofed most of the buildings. Other local burghers provided other supplies and though not on the list of shareholders, they would have profited from the operation nonetheless. Certainly an operation such as this must have stimulated the local economy somewhat in the 1740s, and at least two of the Society shareholders profited directly from this. Although an interesting story, I want to now look at this episode in Cape history from another angle; using archaeology with the archives, I want to try and enrich this short episode in history through a material culture study, and ultimately, stand back again and place this episode in the context of 18th century global capitalism in terms of the Netherlands.

LANDSCAPES OF LABOUR

The site of the mine tunnels and the ruins of buildings associated with the mine works have probably been known in local memory since the events themselves—most people in the local community of Pniel

Figure 2.8. Entrance to the upper mine works. (*Source*: Photograph by author, taken in 1999)

know about them and many, of their location. The mineshafts themselves are an important place in local history and the outer face of the main upper mine entrance (*Jacob Straat*) is covered with local grafitti, mostly people's names (Figure 2.8). There are two other mineshafts lower down the mountain, which probably correspond with *Isabella* and *Sancta Helena*. The ruins of buildings are perhaps less well known, and unless exposed in bush fires (which occur now and then), are completely hidden in undergrowth and trees. On my first visit to one of the sites in 1999, I had literally walked past the main ruins only a few metres away because of this vegetation cover—it was only a chance bush fire that opened them up for investigation in 2000. By 2001, they were already disappearing in new vegetation. Plans are underway to manage the vegetation growth and open the sites up for visitors.

The geology of the Simonsberg is primarily granite, capped with quartzitic sandstone and most of the mine shafts are cut into the granite, save the uppermost, main shaft which lies at the interface with the granite and sandstone. (Swanevelder 1987: 1–4). The soils on the mountain slopes are shallow, stony and sandy, and thus acidic with low water-retaining potential. They support little but the native mountain *fynbos* vegetation, although in the wetter and more protected mountain *kloofs* (ravines), some native tree species can also be found. Lower down the slopes, the soils improve with well-drained loams. Vineyards have displaced much of the natural vegetation on the lower slopes, while higher up, non-native Scots Pine woods and other alien species (e.g. black wattle) cover much of the remaining surface—these have probably been planted in the last century as early photographs show the slopes covered in low vegetation.

There are two sites of ruins, a major complex high on the slopes of the Simonsberg at the upper limit of the current vineyards (Site 2) and a smaller group much lower down and close to the lower edge of the vineyards (Site 1). Both sites are associated with the mine works, but only Site 1 has been archaeologically investigated prior to this project (Figure 2.9; Vos 1992). Just as later reports of the silver mine venture show large inconsistencies with contemporary records, so the archaeological survey produced results that were often hard to match to these contemporary records. This was frustrating, especially as the difficulties were most problematic when it came to trying to match direct correspondence between documented buildings and archaeologically recovered ruins. Yet a much more fruitful relationship between archives and archaeology is possible if one moves away from this kind of analysis to look at more thematic issues. My main focus in this section will be on the relationships between people on the site and how these were articulated through material culture and the landscape of the mine complex. I want to explore the working and living landscape of the sites on the Simonsberg. Unfortunately there are no comparable studies of mining settlements to draw on in South Africa, but then perhaps this is seeking too close a parallel. The archaeology of colonial mining is quite developed in other countries, especially North America and Australia, but then most of these studies tend to be on later mining settlements of the nineteenth or early twentieth century (Bell 1998; Hardesty 1998; Lawrence 1998). Here the set up is usually very different—either corporate industries or individual subsistence miners and in these contexts, the relations of labour and capital are very different, as are the subsequent landscapes created. In many ways, the best parallels to the eighteenth century Simonsberg mining settlement are to be found in other VOC outposts, such as the redoubt at Oudepost or the wood-cutters lodge at Paradise (Schrire and Cruz-Uribe 1993; Hall et al. 1993).

At a broad scale, there is clearly a separation of activities on the Simonsberg into three areas: the mine shafts up the mountain side, the miners settlement on the upper slopes (Site 2) and finally the ore processing buildings lower down (Site 1). The mine shafts are sited quite

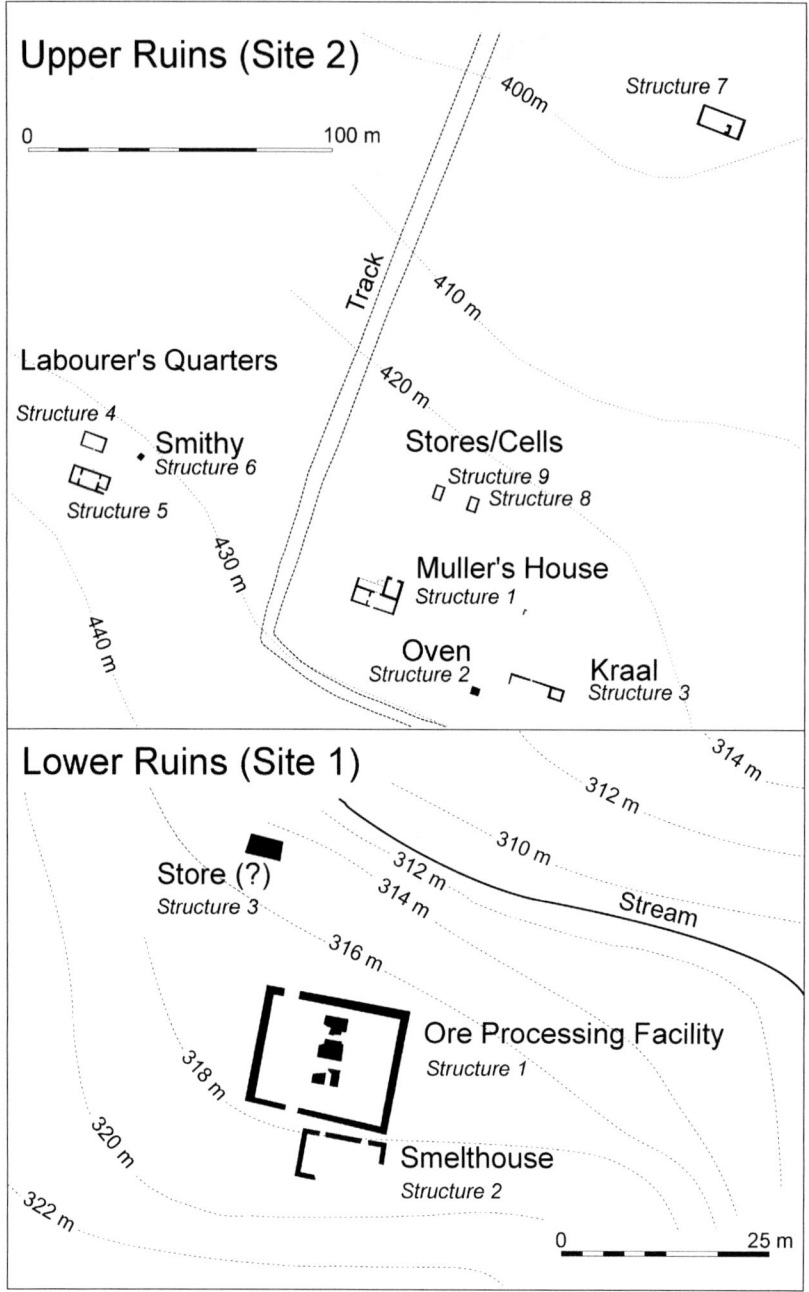

Figure 2.9. Sites 1 and 2 on the Simonsberg.

high up the mountain side, and the topography of their location really precludes any adjacent siting of buildings. The upper mine building complex could not have been practically much closer; but however dictated by topography, the experience of this separation of the mines from the buildings must have been prominent in the minds of the workers—today, it is nearly an hour's walk between the two. Although there was probably a more direct and cleared route in the mid 18th century, it would still have taken perhaps three quarters of an hour and most of that, on foot. A track running up toward the mine from the main site may have only gone half way at most. The journey carrying equipment up the slopes and mined ore back down would have been arduous enough, but to spend the whole day working in the mine shafts themselves must have been immeasurably more strenuous. One of Muller's reports to the Society also mentions shift-work suggesting, at least during some periods, the mines were worked day and night (C2773, Report from Muller to the Society, 30 September 1744). In the darkness of the mines, it perhaps mattered little—lighting would have been essential and the blackened niches in the shafts visible today were undoubtedly used for candles or makeshift oil lamps. Supplies to the mine mention both linen for candle wicks and candle fat, which was probably used in the houses as well as the mines.

Some of the work was done by blasting the rock—drilled holes in the rock face today testify to failed or aborted charges and the supply manifests to the mine list gunpowder and sulphur. However, much of the work was manual and involved digging with picks and spades, clearing and sorting the rubble out by hand. It was undoubtedly dangerous work—there is mention several times of injury or illness, though no details are given. In late 1744, six miners had been taken to hospital, three of whom were badly injured; in late 1746, one of the slaves called Frans had also been taken ill and on the 30th of May 1748 the surgeon, Jan Cats, was fetched to tend to one of Muller's best men, Johan Hendrik Voogt who had hurt his leg and an unnamed servant who had broken his arm.

If the actual work was not hard enough, it seems to have been exacerbated by Muller's tyrannical approach to running the mine. Several complaints were lodged against him, the first on 23rd July 1743, made by four of the Company soldiers working the mine (De Wet 1984: 261). They left the mine for Cape Town to complain that Muller had ill-treated them with "blows and abusive language" and paid them in sheep rather than cash and charged them high prices for food. Two members of the Society were sent to the mine to inspect the works and judge on the complaint, but they found against the men in favour of Muller (de Wet

1984: 279). The following year however, there was another complaint
by a different soldier, Stephanus Eckert, who left the mine without
permission and showed up in Cape Town complaining of having been
beaten and fined by Muller for no reason (C2773, correspondence from
Van Dessin to Muller, 30 November 1745). Then in October 1746, a lime
burner working at the site called Martin Melck—later one of the most
wealthiest men in the district—brought "a heap of complaints" about
Muller to the Director, mostly about Muller's "ugly abusive words". In
a letter back to Muller, the Society member Bestbier referred to Melck
as a "brutal person" but still warned Muller to start watching his language. The letter implies there had been many complaints about this
(C2773, correspondence from Bestbier to Muller, 1 October 1746).

   These three, recorded complaints of beatings and abusive language
probably indicate such incidents may have been frequent, and if Muller
mistreated the Company men, it is as likely he was as bad if not worse
to the slaves. The records mention that Muller also had two whips delivered to him in August 1746, and some of the small cellular buildings
on the site may have been used for confinement, as well as storage.
Life at the mine was clearly made more difficult by Muller's behaviour
and many found the conditions intolerable. The high turnover of mine
workers may or may not be related to this, but certainly within a year
only three of an original group of 14 were still there. More indicative of
bad conditions are the several recorded instances of 'desertions'; three
new workers who were replacing the original group all seemed to have
deserted in late 1746. Paulus Albregts, ran away but was later appre-
hended in Cape Town and sent back to the mine in December 1746.
Two others, Jan van Hoofden and Jan la Mort deserted in November
that year, Hoofden with stolen money, and no mention is made of their
capture. Finally in late 1747, another worker went missing, Dirk van
Leeuwen, and no mention is made of him after that. It was perhaps
not uncommon for Company men to desert at the time, indeed fugitives
(*drosters*) of one sort or another—servicemen, criminals and slaves—
formed a distinct but changing featured of the colonial frontier throughout the 18th century, often forming themselves into gangs threatening
the local burgher population (Penn 1999). No mention is made of any
slaves deserting from the mineworks.

   If the written transcripts attest to a hard working life, and a separation between the labourers (Company men and slaves) and the foreman (Muller), the archaeology is equally vocal on this separation. Of
the buildings at the main site, there are two possible structures that
could be Muller's house. The records mention the *bergmeester's* house
many times (indeed it is the only one mentioned) and even describe

Table 2.4. Composition of 18th century assemblages associated with main domestic structures in site 2 by minimum number of vessels/objects. (*Source*: Author's data)

	Mullers House (Structure 1)		Labourers Quarters (Structures 4 & 5)	
	No.	%	No.	%
Glass bottle	8	15.7	2	9.5
Glass drinking vessel	6	11.8	1	4.8
Porcelain vessel	33	64.7	8	38.1
Stoneware vessel	1	2.0	2	9.5
Coarse earthenware vessel	0	0.0	2	9.5
Tobacco pipe	3	5.9	6	28.6
Total	*51*	*100*	*21*	*100*

its size, which matches closely with Structure 1. Structure 1 was excavated and revealed a well laid out building with three main rooms, a *stoep* and a lower, strong room at a lower level. This structure was also associated with a rich material culture assemblage which included fine Chinese porcelain, lead crystal drinking goblets, wine and case bottles, much of it deriving from a midden behind the house. The only other dwelling houses on the site were positioned some distance away, Structures 4 and 5 to the west and structure 7 to the north. Surface pick-up of dense midden material around Structures 4 and 5 had a very different composition consisting mostly of coarse porcelains, stonewares and earthenwares as well as much higher quantities of clay pipe (Table 2.4). This suggests that these were probably the labourers and/or slave quarters, and their proximity to a smithy/furnace (Structure 6), is an interesting affirmation of their status. Structure 5 in portioned into three bays, as in any typical cottage at the time and was probably the quarters for the soldiers, while Structure 4 was open plan and may have more likely housed the slaves (see below).

The best comparison to Simonsberg is the site of Paradise on Table Mountain. Paradise was a small VOC outpost established for the collection of timber during the late 17th century and was run similarly to the silver mine with a foreman (the Master Woodcutter), VOC soldiers and some slaves, until the late 18th century when it was, for a brief period, occupied by the same Lady Anne Barnard who wrote of the silver mine scandal. Archaeological excavations at Paradise during the 1980s found evidence only for occupation during the 18th century but showed a developmental sequence of four phases between *c*. 1720 and

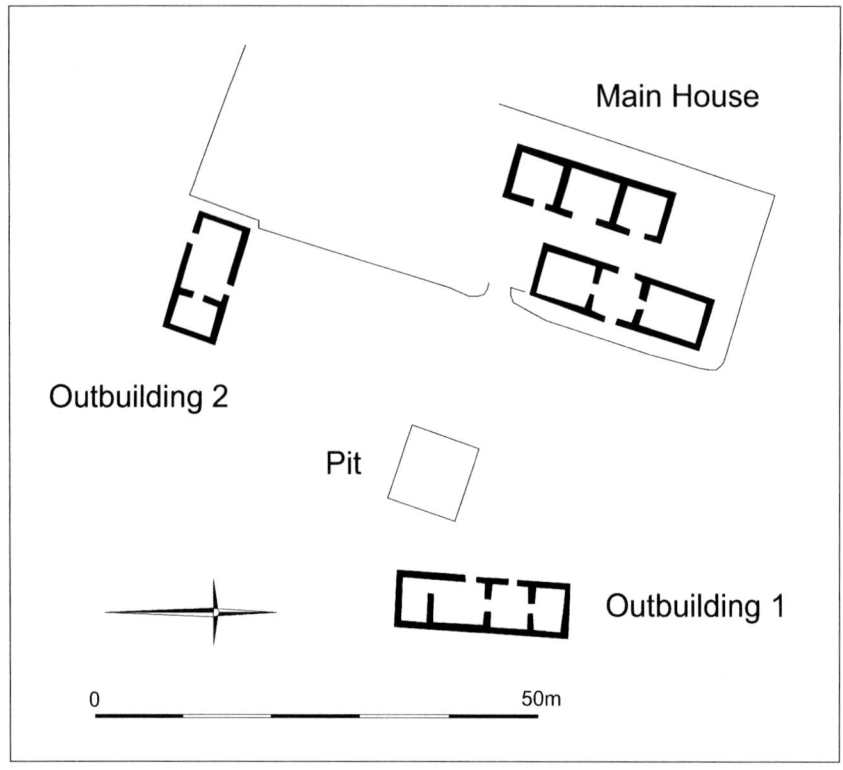

Figure 2.10. VOC Woodcutter's lodge at Paradise on Table Mountain. (*Source*: Adapted from Hall et al. 1993)

1795 (Hall et al. 1993). The site consisted of a main house on a terraced platform, with two outbuildings and a stone-lined pit (Figure 2.10). The main house was almost certainly the residence of the Master Woodcutter and developed from a single, three-bayed house to a T-shaped house and finally two separate three-bayed houses or an H-shaped house. Outbuilding 1 was some distance from the main house and started as a single-celled square house, which over time developed into a four-bay long house. This was interpreted as the soldiers quarters. The slaves were not considered to have had any separate lodgings but to have slept either with the soldiers or in the main house. Outbuilding 2 and the pit were not intensively excavated, but have been suggested elsewhere to be a Gardeners cottage and a fowl run respectively. Without excavation, it is hard to be sure what these other structures were, but Outbuilding 2—a two-roomed building with a cobble-floored stable and clay-floored store/living room—was probably another dwelling, while the pit was possibly used for water storage.

In comparison with the Simonsberg settlement, there are certainly close similarities—the separation of foreman and soldiers, and even the form of the houses are not dissimilar. The cellular origin of Outbuilding 1 is also particularly interesting given the number of cell structures on the Simonsberg, which have been interpreted as stores but they may equally have been small accommodation blocks or even confinement cells. In terms of the material culture, phase 2 of the main house and phase A of the outbuilding at Paradise are more or less contemporary with the silver mine and show a very similar breakdown of items, especially ceramics and glass (Table 2.5). The major difference is that Simonsberg has more porcelain and less earthenware, though this is probably a product of the fact that at Simonsberg only Muller's house

Table 2.5. Summary of ceramic and glass vessels from Paradise and Simonsberg. (*Source*: Hall et al. 1993 and author's data)

	Paradise (2/A)		Silver Mine	
	MNV	%	MNV	%
Pottery				
Porcelain	**182**	**64.54**	**44**	**89.80**
Oriental	182	100.00	44	100.00
Blue & white	100	54.95	29	65.91
Blue & white & enamelled	8	4.40	2	4.55
Brown	28	15.38	4	9.09
Enamelled	9	4.95	2	4.55
White	4	2.20	—	0.00
Undiagnostic	6	3.30	—	0.00
Provincial	25	13.74	4	9.09
Japanese	2	1.10	3	6.82
European	—	0.00	—	0.00
Stoneware	**25**	**8.87**	**3**	**6.12**
Oriental	4	16.00	—	0.00
European	21	84.00	3	100.00
Earthenware	**75**	**26.60**	**2**	**4.08**
Coarse	69	24.47	2	18.18
Tin-glazed	3	1.06	—	0.00
Refined	3	1.06	—	0.00
Glass				
Wine Bottle	10	45.45	5	38.46
Case Bottle	6	27.27	3	23.08
Stemware	3	13.64	3	23.08
Tumblers	3	13.64	2	15.38

Table 2.6. Summary of vessel forms from Fort de Goede Hoop and Simonsberg. (*Source*: Abrahams 1998 and author's data)

	Fort de Goede Hoop		Simonsberg	
	MNV	%	MNV	%
Porcelain				
Plate	270	32.30	13	29.55
Bowl	204	24.40	17	38.64
Cup	114	13.64	4	9.09
Saucer	144	17.22	7	15.91
Bottle	9	1.08	2	4.55
Dish	46	5.50	1	2.27
Jar	12	1.44	—	0.00
Platter	30	3.59	—	0.00
Other	7	0.84	—	0.00
Total	836	100.00	44	100.00
Coarse Earthenware				
Lid	36	22.5	—	0.00
Tripod cooking pot (kookpot)	21	13.12	2	100.00
Tripod cooking pot (kookkan)	19	11.87	—	0.00
Saucepans/Skillets	10	6.25	—	0.00
Colander	5	3.12	—	0.00
Dish	31	19.37	—	0.00
Saucer	4	2.5	—	0.00
Small storage pots & drinking vessels	20	12.5	—	0.00
Brazier	14	8.75	—	0.00
Total	160	100	2	100.00

was excavated, which skews the composition to finer ceramics (also see below). No real differentiation was found between the foreman's house and the soldiers quarters at Paradise in terms of the ceramic wares unlike Simonsberg, although the difference here is based on a very small sample for the labourer's house. Nevertheless, the general similarities between the two sites is good, although in many ways the ceramic assemblages—at least in terms of wares, are probably similar on most sites of this period (see Chapter 3) so too much stress should not be placed on this. The case is much the same when analysed by vessel form. On the Simonsberg, service vessels predominate the assemblage, mainly plates and bowls, but with a sizeable number of cups and saucers, with bottles, dishes and jars all very few (Table 2.6). No data on vessel forms is given for Paradise, but a large group of 18th century ceramics from the destructions layers over the Fort de Goede

Hoop in Table Bay do provide a baseline comparison (Abrahams 1998). Here, plates and bowls dominate the porcelains, as on Simonsberg suggesting this was a fairly typical ratio, though this site also has a better representation of coarse earthenwares (Table 2.6). While porcelain dominated even the Fort assemblage, the earthenwares provide an idea of the missing kitchen wares from Simonsberg, though porcelain (chiefly the coarse type) would have been used for food preparation and storage as much as for service.

Some idea of the food can be gained from a document dating to 1744, which gives the typical rations over a three month period for all the labourers: 26 sheep, 1 half-aum of brandy, 10 half-aums of wine (1 aum = c. 155 litres), 9 muids of flour (1 muid = 3 bushels or 24 gallons), 100 lbs of rice, 3 bushels of salt, 6 lbs of tobacco, tea, coffee and pepper (C2770). In other delivery letters, sacks of rice and flour are listed as regular deliveries, while other commodities like tea was rare (and expensive). Meat was presumably kept on the hoof; sheep are mentioned in the above document and elsewhere in delivery documents, but cattle were equally prominent. In late 1746, the mine is recorded as owning 20 cattle, which more than tripled in less than a year, up to 72 head of cattle in 1747. Cattle would have been used as traction for wagons, but also presumably for milk and meat—of the 72 cattle listed in 1747, at least 60 were heifers. Archaeological evidence of food was severely limited due to the acidic nature of the soils, which did not preserve bone, and thus offers no complimentary data. The comparable site of Paradise discussed above did prove more productive and showed a dominance of sheep in the meat diet (66%), with lesser amounts of beef (10%) and then various other fauna in smaller amounts, including pig and chicken as well as various wild species (Hall et al. 1993: 52).

However one reads the archaeological evidence, there is certainly some clear demarcation inscribed into the spatial organization of the mining settlement between Muller and his labour force. It is also interesting to note that Muller was married during this time; in correspondence to Muller, he is congratulated on his upcoming marriage which took place in August 1745 to Catharina Geertrug van Staaden. A year later his wife is mentioned in another letter (C2773, correspondence from Bestbier to Muller, 10th August 1745; 31st October 1746). No doubt his wife Catharina was living with him in his house, and it may have been her presence which is responsible for certain unusual features on the site, particularly as they relate to Mullers house. In the first case, at some point this house was modified from a two-bay structure to a three-bay one; the original house was in the typical vernacular style, one large room with a smaller room to one side, but—in what must have been a very short time after construction—the house was modified into a three room symmetrical house, defined by a wide central room with a brick floor and two flanking side rooms (Figure 2.11). This central room might be defined as a *voorhuis*, a reception room that was used for receiving and entertaining guests, an architectural fashion which was just becoming prevalent at the Cape in the grander town and country houses. I discuss this in much more detail in Chapter 3, but it is related to new styles of consumption of material culture, and ones that were closely bound with gender (see Chapter 3). It is tempting to think this change in Structure 1 reflects the changing nature of the household and occurred in relation to Muller's marriage. In the same way, the large number of porcelain pieces can be seen in the same light.

The presence of other women on the site is hard to find in the archives, which only mention the men. If there were women present, they may have most likely been slaves—the only possible reference to female slaves comes from a delivery order, which lists six dresses, along with six trousers, and twelve blue shirts for the slaves, implying perhaps that there six male and six female slaves (C2773, correspondence from van Dessin to Muller, 31st May 1747). These female slaves, as well as being engaged in hard labour at the mines, may have also been exploited sexually by the Company men, for certainly such relationships were not unknown. The slave lodge in Cape Town also served as a brothel, which soldiers and sailors frequented in the evenings. Despite the presence of a few women however, the settlement was probably predominantly a masculine space, either VOC soldiers, sailors and artisans or male slaves. The VOC men were technically all professionals and therefore used to a relatively disciplined life. They would mostly have come up from the Castle at Cape Town, though one group is mentioned as coming from a nearby garrisons at Klapmuts.

The landscape of the mining settlement was obviously different to that at Cape Town, especially the Castle (see above), but the discipline was undoubtedly similar. Working for the VOC was tough and from the very beginnings of the settlement in the 1650s, employees complained of the conditions and the work, and desertions were not uncommon, as already mentioned (Worden et al. 1998: 30–32). But however bad it was for the Company men, it was worse for the slaves. The slaves as a group are as marginal as women in the archives—while most of the Company men and Society shareholders are mentioned by name, only one group of slaves are listed by name. This group arrived in September 1746, the second of three groups of six to arrive that year. The first group are

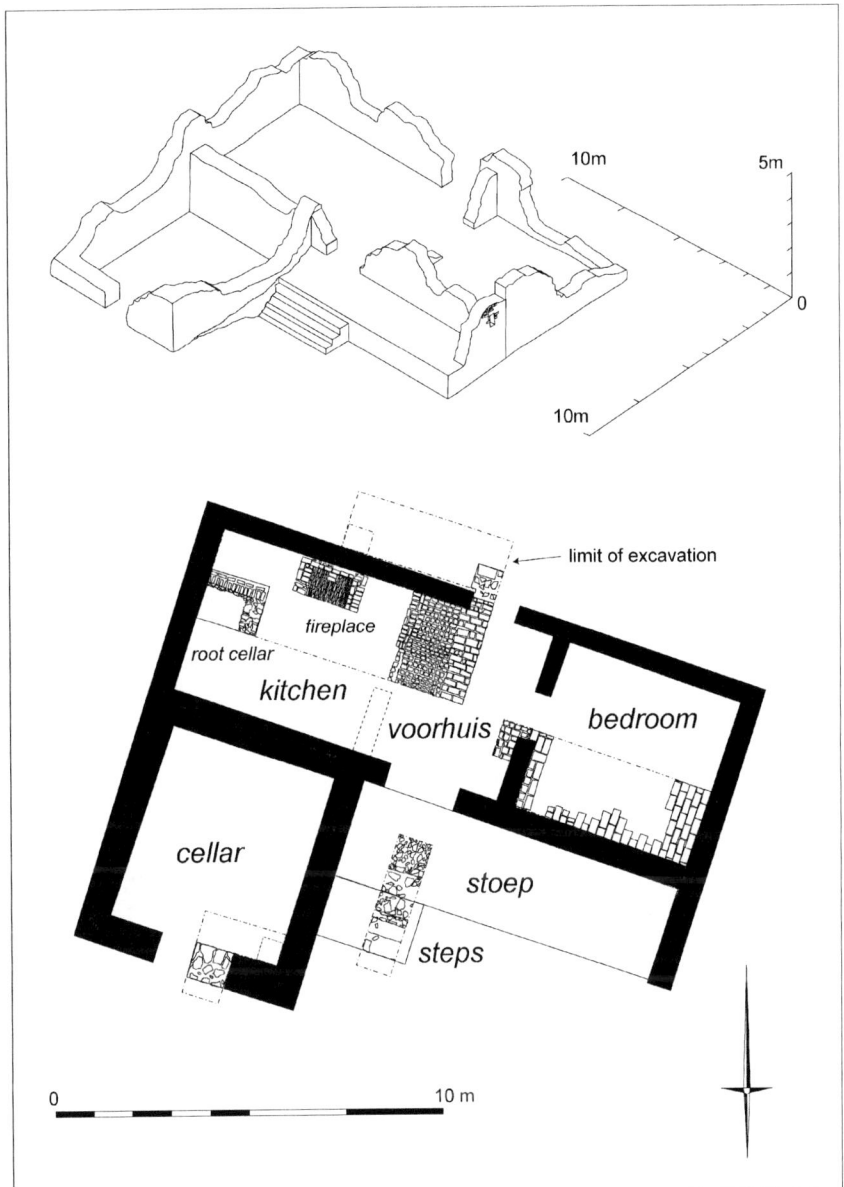

Figure 2.11. Muller's house on the mining settlement.

referred to simply as 'volk', and were possibly enslaved or indentured Khoisan, while the last, are referred to as 'six males'. The middle group however were named: Lappang, Letta, Kattier, Frans, Christiaan and Kajomas (C2773, correspondence from Bestbier to Muller, 15th September 1746). Frans was the one taken ill, presumably soon after his arrival (see above). The slaves were probably all Company slaves, from the Slave Lodge at Cape Town (see Chapter 4). One of the key items of material culture in the Lodge that expressed the hierarchy and power there was clothing, especially copper buttons, which acted as a kind of currency among the community (Shell 1994: 184). Thus the delivery of clothes to the slaves at Simonsberg mentioned above was part of a very tightly controlled economy of what items of material culture, slaves had access to. Their movement from the Lodge to the Simonsberg would have been a radical change in environment for them. On average, 450–500 slaves were quartered at the Lodge at any one time. Most slaves there were used for general labour and there was little gender differentiation in terms of their work (Shell 1994: 73). Indeed, at another silver mine, both male and female slaves were set to work around the clock (Shell 1994: 200). However, there was differentiation based on the origin of the slave; essentially, creoles (Cape-born) and mulattoes (mixed descent) were more highly valued and given better positions than newly imported slaves. As Shell notes, "the most unpleasant tasks of all—collecting salt, mining, grave digging, and removing the town's excrement—were invariably reserved for those full-breed slaves from the most unpopular areas." (Shell 1994: 188–9). Being sent to the Simonsberg was not a privilege, but a job for the lowest slaves in the hierarchy.

These slaves would have helped with the mine working as well as the ore processing and construction; their relationship to either Muller or the Company men remains unrecorded, but they probably lived, as well as worked close to the Company men, possibly in Structure 4. At another slave mine, mention is made of the slaves, men and women, living in a small, undivided hut (Shell 1994: 200). At Paradise it was suggested the slaves did not have a separate quarters and this may have been the case—certainly it is true that on most farms or town dwellings during the 18th century, there were no separate slave quarters (see Chapter 3), but it is possible a VOC operation may have been more likely to segregate the slaves, especially if they were present in high numbers. A minimum of 12 slaves were working on the Simonsberg at any one time and it is more likely they were housed separately.

The silver mine settlement on the Simonsberg thus incorporates some interesting tensions, but most particularly between the VOC and

Muller and his wife. Muller's house and possessions appears to be an attempt to recreate a normal, even aspiring domestic unit in an otherwise industrial setting, although a similar case might be argued for Paradise. Moreover, this aspiration is not unrelated to Muller's efforts to segregate himself spatially—and socially—from his workforce, which was clearly a source of major complaint by the latter. These tensions clearly illustrate on a micro-level, the wider ambiguities of the VOC in relation to colonialism and settlers. While the silver mine was a private enterprise, it was nonetheless heavily backed by the VOC through unofficial channels of sponsorship and the provision of a workforce. Muller and his wife may have viewed themselves as free burghers, and Muller as a private entrepreneur, yet the presence of the VOC through his workforce and sponsorship of the operation must have constantly rendered this status as ambiguous. However much Muller and his wife tried to articulate a distinct identity for themselves, they were enveloped in the world of the VOC, and Muller's house seems like a domestic oasis in an industrial landscape of labour. However, the silver mine does not just express the significance of the role of the VOC at the Cape, but equally in relation to global trade networks.

THE ROLE OF SILVER IN THE INDIAN OCEAN TRADE

The wreck of the *Geldermalsen* with which I started this chapter exemplified the nature of commodities being shipped back to Europe—mostly tea and textiles but also of course, porcelain. The kind of goods acquired in the east did vary over time though—a point I discuss further below. However, the cargo such ships carried with them to the East changed little: essentially it was gold and, more usually, silver in the form of bullion or coin (Schöffer and Gaastra 1982). Wrecks of other Dutch East Indiamen traveling in the other direction indicate this. In 1656, the *Jacht Vergulde Draeck* was lost off western Australia, on its way from the Cape to Batavia; its cargo included *c.* 40,000 coins as well as clay pipes (Green 1977). Nearly a century later, similar cargoes were held by the *Hollandia* and *Amsterdam*. The VOC vessel the *Hollandia* was one of two new 150-foot ships built in the Oostenburg shipyard in Amsterdam in 1743. Once completed, it sailed to Texel to pick up provisions, a full crew and several passengers—including the Governor-General's brother, Hendrik Frans van Imhoff; in July that year, it started its maiden voyage outward bound for Batavia, only to be wrecked off the Scillies in the English Channel. Unlike the

Geldermalsen, there were no survivors (Cowan et al. 1975; Gawronski 1992). During salvage operations, more than 35,000 silver coins were recovered, mostly Spanish-American *reales*, as well as wine bottles and clay pipes. We do not have cargo manifests for the *Hollandia*, but we do for another VOC ship which was wrecked a few years later in 1749, also en route to the East and also caught in the English Channel. The *Amsterdam*'s cargo list included 28 chests of silver, as well as thousands of bottles of wine; when this wreck was investigated, around 16,000 silver coins and 1200 bars of silver were recovered as well as wine bottles and clay pipes, which were also found on the *Hollandia* wreck (Marsden 1972; 1978). Significantly, most of the silver from the *Amsterdam* was Dutch, not Spanish-American like the *Hollandia* a few years earlier. Is this significant? Before we can answer that, we need to understand the importance of silver in the Asian trade.

The VOC trade with the east was of course founded on acquiring various commodities such as spices and porcelain for the European market; but one of the key problems in this trade is that while there was plenty the Dutch (and other Europeans) wanted to acquire from the East, there was very little that the communities there wanted in return that Europe had to offer. Of these commodities, which included textiles, lead and ivory, by far the most important were precious metals, especially silver (Gaastra 1983; Glamann 1958; Prakash 1994a; 1994b). Now the New World trade was providing silver in large quantities from mines in Bolivia, Columbia and Mexico, and while much of the silver came via Spain and Portugal, the Netherlands still managed to acquire a dominant position in the silver bullion trade. However, despite having this access to silver, it was not always enough or readily available for use in the Asian trade and its flow into the East Indies was thus restricted; the VOC preferred to acquire silver from elsewhere, namely from within the Asian sphere itself. Thus the VOC decided to engage in intra-Asian trade—that is acquiring commodities which they did not necessarily want but which could be used to trade for those goods (such as spices), which they did want. This trade network was already pre-existing and the VOC merely tapped into it (Chaudhuri 1985); nevertheless, it was this decision that gave them the edge over their European competitors, chiefly England and later France (Prakash 1994a).

The key link in this intra-Asian chain was Indian textiles. To get the spices such as pepper, cloves, nutmegs and mace from Indonesia, it needed Indian textiles to trade against, but to get Indian textiles, it needed precious metals, chiefly silver and gold. These it obtained primarily from Japan, by trading in turn against Chinese silks and textiles. It was a complex trade network, which the VOC handled deftly and the

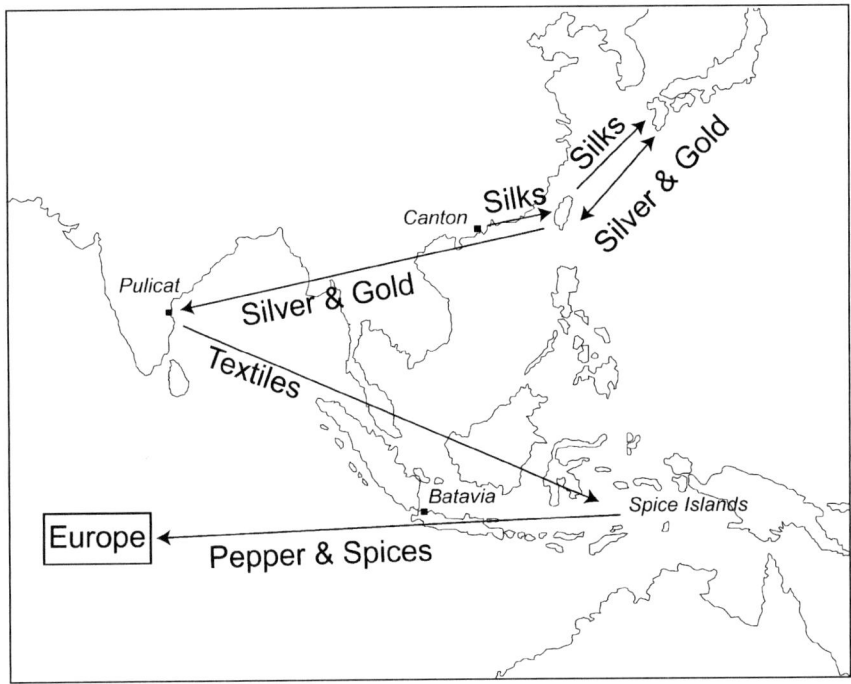

Figure 2.12. The East Asian trade network in the 17th and early 18th centuries.

hub of this network was India, especially at Petapuli on the Coromandel coast and Surat in Gujarat where the trade in textiles was focused (Figure 2.12). However, by the end of the 17th century, this trade network was disintegrating; in the first place, the European consumption of spices had dropped and became significantly less important in exports back to Europe, in favour of silks and textiles. Glamann in a pioneering study showed how a major shift occurred in the mid 17th century of the import trade into the Netherlands with textiles increasing rapidly as spices and pepper dropped (Glamann 1958: 13–14). Tea, the major commodity on the *Geldermalsen*, also rose, but it—along with coffee, only became a major part of the trade after the 1740s. Second, in 1668 Japan banned all export of silver, and while they still exported gold, its value decreased, thus severely constraining the purchasing power of the VOC in the Asian trade. During the 18th century, the VOC was thus forced to rely predominantly on its own stock of silver being shipped out from the Netherlands, a fact which is clearly revealed by calculated figures for the export of precious metals (Gaastra 1983: 451; see Figure 2.13). At

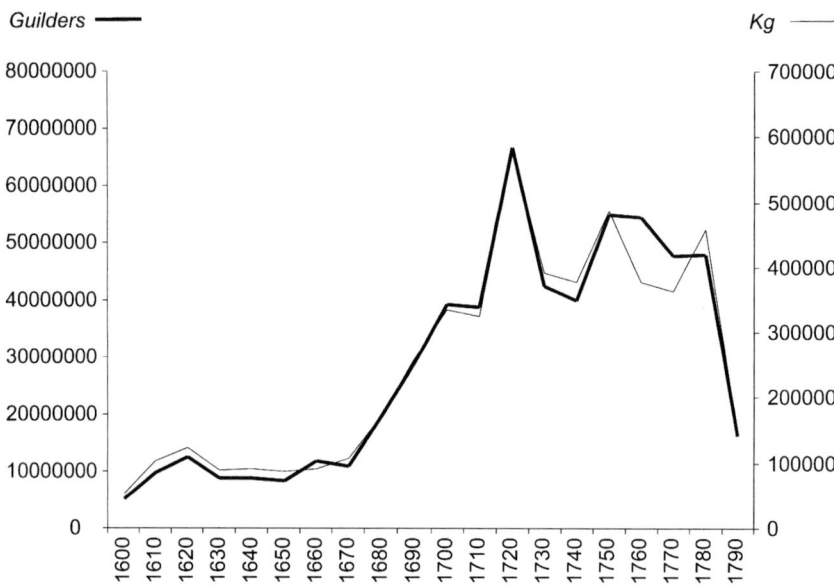

Figure 2.13. Export of precious metals from the Netherlands to the Asian trade. (*Source*: Based on data from Gaastra 1983)

first, this silver came from the reserve stocks held by the Dutch banks, but by the 1740s, even these were near to depletion; consequently, the VOC went straight to the mints to acquire their silver (Marsden 1978: 134). This largely accounts for the different sources of silver coinage on the *Hollandia* and the *Amsterdam*; within five years, Dutch reserves of Spanish silver had to be replaced by Dutch silver currency.

Ironically, as the trade focus shifted from spices to textiles (and later tea and coffee), so silver and gold became even more important in the Euro-Asian trade. By the mid-18th century, the demand for silver was perhaps at its peak and the VOC really felt the pinch; in 1748/9, the Board could only supply half the silver Batavia requested (Gaastra 1983: 464). It is in this broader context of Dutch capitalism and the global trade that we need to finally place the silver mine on Simonsberg. The potential of the Cape producing silver for the Asian trade would have had a major impact on the fortunes of the VOC in this sphere. The silver mine operation on the Simonsberg came after a long hiatus of several earlier attempts to find silver and other precious metals at the Cape, including on the Simonsberg itself, and needs to be seen in this context (Burman 1969; Heller 1949). The potential for extracting minerals and precious metals at the Cape was never a major element of VOC policy but at the same time they were not an organization to ignore it altogether, especially given its value in the Asian trade. Exploration parties were instructed to be on the look out for potential mineral sources, although they were hardly experienced in such matters.

Some stones were tested close to the Fort in Table Bay as early as 1654, but it was only in 1669 the Company sent out experienced miners and assayers from Europe to assess the potential of the Cape Peninsula, and for several years they worked in Table Valley—on Devil's Peak, Lion's Head, Wynberg and along the Steenberg. Despite cutting deep shafts, nothing was ever discovered though various claims were made at different times for gold, silver, and copper. The first mining 'rush', if one can call it that, was when reports came of copper deposits in Namaqualand. Some Namaqua had brought samples of copper ore to the VOC, and in response an exploration party with three miners was dispatched north in 1684 to assess the nature of the source. When they returned with more samples, they were smelted and proved to be rich in copper, prompting the Governor at the time, Simon van der Stel to make a personal visit to Namaqualand in 1685, whereafter mining operations started. However, given the distance from the Fort in Table Bay, the costs of mining and transporting the ores soon proved to be uneconomic, and the operation was abandoned.

Encouraged by the possibilities however, prospecting was initiated closer to the Fort again—at Witteboomen in 1686 and at the Steenberg in 1687, miners sunk shafts, but the results were not promising. Eventually, the VOC gave up and no further attempts were made. It was then, nearly half a century later that the Simonsberg mines were started. Despite the multiple failures of the late 17th century, the Simonsberg was considered a sufficient gamble; of course by now there was a new Governor, indeed perhaps they were few people in the VOC at the Cape in 1740 who had been around in the 1680s to recall the failures first hand. More importantly however, this operation was officially a private venture even if the VOC was effectively sponsoring it. The potential for silver could not be quite given up, for if silver had been found at the Cape, it would have undoubtedly transformed the Dutch Asian Trade, especially at precisely the time when it was in severe decline. The Simonsberg Mines—*Goede Verwachting*—remain a testimony not so much to a confidence trickster or Company gullibility, but as a symbol of Dutch Capitalism and the key currency in a trade upon which the VOC and the Netherlands founded their wealth.

Status and Settlement in the Cape Colony | 3

THE SETTLEMENT OF THE SOUTHWESTERN CAPE, 1657–1717

As mentioned in the last chapter, the first free farmers to settle at the Cape occupied plots of land adjacent to Table Bay in the Liesbeeck valley in the late 1650s. This was a mixed success, indeed over half of these first burghers gave up and tried to make a living in the growing settlement around the fort (Guelke 1976: 29). When it was realized that the agricultural base of the colony had to be expanded if the colony was to function properly as a refreshment station, in 1679 the VOC decided promote further settlement into the interior. The land east of the settlement around Table Bay was a barren, sandy waste—the Cape Flats, now home to thousands of people who had been forcefully removed under Apartheid and the Group Areas Act. To find the next available farm land, one has to cross this wasteland to the foothills of the 'Hottentot Hollands', the southern tip of an extensive mountain range running north-south: the Drakenstein. It was here that the new Commander at the Fort, Simon van der Stel, whose position was later promoted to Governor, offered freehold grants of land on a first come, first served basis in 1680. The first grants authorized lay along the Eerste river valley, and then in 1687, more grants were issued along the upper Berg river valley but on a more selective basis. Settlement continued to expand north along the Berg river and to either side along its tributaries during the early 18th century until 1717 when the policy of issuing freeholds came to an end (Guelke 1976; Guelke 1989; Guelke and Shell 1983). Although settlement expansion did continue after 1717 through leaseholds, the VOC had clearly decided to make it policy to discourage any further settlement. Enough land was being farmed and produce supplied that any surplus would start to be detrimental to the Company (Guelke 1976: 31). The population at the Cape was not sufficient to mop up this surplus and nor were the ships passing the Cape; some was exported east, but the export market at this time was not strong. To encourage continued expansion and production without a market was thus foolhardy.

The first settlers of the late 1650s, as mentioned, were ex-VOC employees having completed their service who chose to stay at the Cape as burghers; those of the 1680s however, were quite different. Although ex-servicemen still formed a proportion of the new settlers, Simon van der Stel also encouraged freed slaves ('free blacks') to populate the new frontier settlement zone. Moreover, between 1685 and 1707, the VOC tried to promote emigration from the Netherlands by offering free passage; few availed themselves of this, except for one group—French Huguenots seeking a new life. They formed by far the largest section of the free community in this new settlement, and most arrived in 1688. These Huguenots who came to the Cape had escaped religious persecution in France after the revocation of the Edict of Nantes in 1685 (Botha 1919a; Boucher 1981; Coertzen 1988; Franken 1978). Huguenots, (i.e. members of the French Reformed Church) had seen their political power rise and fall since the 15th century in struggles with the Catholics for royal favour, however by the mid-17th century, this struggle was radically affected by structural changes in French politics, between parliament and the king. Under the Catholic king Louis XIV, national unity was a prime goal, and this meant religious unity too. All kinds of means were tried to convert Protestants to Catholicism, but after the 1660s there was an increasing restriction on religious practice and by the 1680s, military threat was employed. Finally in 1685, the Edict of Nantes—proclaimed in 1598 guaranteeing the rights of Protestants to practice their religion—was revoked. Practically, this meant that all places of worship (called 'Temples') were destroyed, all ceremonies and assemblies prohibited and all ministers were to leave the country. Their congregation however was not permitted to emigrate and moreover their children had to be baptised as Catholics, thus forcing them in effect to either abjure Calvinism or live as a Protestant without being able to practice in any way. Unsurprisingly, many left, necessarily illegally and were aided by illicit emigration agencies; in total it is estimated that around 20,000 Huguenots fled France (about 20% of the Protestant population), the most popular destination being the United Provinces (i.e. the Netherlands) followed by Britain. A smaller proportion moved on, including those numbering around 200 who came to the Cape. The main body of those fleeing consisted of the professional and bourgeois classes and subsequent lack of employment was a major factor in forcing them to emigrate to places such as the Cape.

With the establishment of new settlements some distance from the Fort, a new level of governmental institutions were required; the new area of settlement of the Eerste and Berg rivers was administered as a separate district from the Cape and named after its principal settlement, Stellenbosch (later 'and Drakenstein' was added). Its jurisdiction came under a chief administrator and magistrate (*landdrost*) and a council (*heemraad*), duplicating the same structure of VOC government at yet another level. Later, as settlement expanded, further districts and local administrative posts were created. Part of the job of this district government was the provision and maintenance of public amenities such as roads and bridges, education and religious service. However, particularly in the early years, a major role was securing the safety of the settlers against raids from the indigenous Khoikhoi through the establishment of a local militia. So far, I have made it sound like the settlers moved in to an empty land, which they carved up between themselves; but there were people already there, the indigenous Khoikhoi, whom these new settlers displaced, in almost 'silent' violence. Their story is very hard to recover and while one might think archaeology would be more vocal than the documents, sadly this is not the case, except in rare instances such as Shrire's work at Oudepost (Schrire 1987; 1988; 1995). The indigenous people at the Cape prior to European contact have been the subject of archaeological research for a long time (but see Deacon and Deacon 1999), but work on post-contact groups, especially the Khoikhoi, is almost non-existent—as if they themselves no longer existed after 1652. A large part of this relates to the problems of identifying post-contact Khoikhoi sites of course, but some of it must also relate to the research objectives of archaeologists. Nevertheless, there has been an increasing amount of revisionist history over the past few decades, which has sought to bring the story of the Khoikhoi after 1652 out of this silence (e.g. Elphick 1985; Elphick and Malherbe 1989; Boonzaier et al. 1996; Marks 1972).

There is some ambiguity over the differences in the various groups living at the Cape at the time of colonization. The term Khoisan is sometimes used to cover this ambiguity, but commonly a distinction is made on both linguistic and social grounds between hunter-gatherer groups called the Soaqua or Sonqua (i.e. the San, or as they were called originally, Bushmen) and nomadic pastoralists of various tribes of whom the two major ones at the southwestern Cape were the Cochoqua and Gorachoqua (known collectively with other groups as the Khoikhoi, but originally as Hottentots). Elphick has suggested that the differences between San and Khoikhoi were very fluid, based primarily on whether they were stock herders or not, and that ownership of stock might fluctuate over time (through theft, disease or drought for example), even within any particular community (Elphick 1985). Certainly the Khoikhoi looked down on the San as socially inferior. Archaeological evidence has not supported Elphick's model, at least in a pre-colonial context but for the later 17th and 18th century, it may be more applicable. Certainly the affects of the European-Khoikhoi trade drastically altered the structure of indigenous pastoral societies and their relations to the San, dispossessing many of their livestock and livelihood, and they may have taken up a more hunter-gatherer lifestyle as a consequence.

Trading with the Khoikhoi was established as early as the 1590s when Dutch and English ships regularly stopped off at Table Bay between Europe and the East Indies; in return for meat—chiefly mutton and beef—the Khoikhoi acquired tobacco, copper and iron from these passing ships (Elphick and Malherbe 1989: 8). Tobacco was accepted as an alternative to their local narcotic, dagga, while copper and iron were already a familiar part of their material culture through inland trade—copper as jewelry and iron for arrows and spearheads. Realizing that iron was used as potential weaponry against themselves, when the Dutch established their post at Table Bay in 1652, they ceased to trade this item. The VOC official policy was to stabilize and pacify trading relations with the Khoikhoi and exchange tobacco and copper for sheep and cattle; the Dutch however, needed the Khoikhoi more than they needed the Dutch, and nor did the Khoikhoi want to trade their best livestock. For the Dutch, the supply of meat (especially beef) was never enough for their needs.

Inevitably this caused the VOC to venture further inland for new trading partners. Three scouting parties were sent from the fort *de Goede Hoop* in to the interior to barter for stock: in 1657, 1659 and after some brief hostilities (see below), again in 1660, all passing through the Berg River on the way (de Wet 1987: 13–14). Beyond these official trips, occasional hunting parties also probably visited the area, but otherwise there is no further recorded European incursion into the valley until the first settlers arrived in the late 1680s. Van Riebeeck was never particularly happy with the Board of Director's policy and repeatedly requested permission to enslave the Khoikhoi and take their livestock; this they refused so Riebeeck occasionally held some of the Khoikhoi chiefs hostage as ransom for livestock (Elphick and Malherbe 1989: 11). Rather than start conflict with the indigenous people to acquire the necessary meat, the Board decided the colony should provide for itself by granting the first freeholds for farmers, but this only exacerbated relations with the Khoi who felt the Dutch were not only stealing their pasture land but barring them access to waterholes. In 1659, the first Khoikhoi-Dutch War broke out as Khoikhoi raided these new farms and took most of the livestock, but avoided the fort. Peace was made the following year where in return for letting them keep the raided livestock, the Khoikhoi ceded to the VOC rights over the land in the Liesbeeck valley.

As settlement expanded and the colony grew more self-sufficient, the Board of Directors in the Netherlands were less and less concerned with relations with the Khoikhoi, leaving the Company men out there more of a free hand. The second Khoikhoi-Dutch War was instigated by the VOC and between 1673 and 1677, four expeditions were sent out, specifically to target who they thought was their greatest threat, a chief in the north called Gonnema of the Cochoqua. When it was over, not only did Gonnema agree to cede an annual tribute of 30 cattle to the colony, but more importantly, in the process many of the Khoikhoi had become Dutch allies. Consequently, the VOC requested tribute from them and increasingly intervened in their internal affairs, and as they became more and more involved in Khoikhoi politics, so they started to reverse the balance of trade, particularly the prices and conditions under which this trade occurred. Furthermore, in the early years of the 18th century, the burghers were permitted to barter with the Khoikhoi, and in the absence of any obvious controls, the Khoikhoi were subject to even further abuse. As the political structure and economic base of Khoikhoi life disintegrated, so the people started to come and seek work for the Company at the Fort or for Burghers on their farms, which only further accelerated this disintegration. Originally, this may have only been seasonal, but by the 1690s, many were permanent, living in their own huts on their employers land (Elphick and Malherbe 1989: 17). In 1672, those Khoikhoi working on farms or for the Company were assigned recognized legal status as subjects of the colony, not a chief.

The Khoikhoi suffered a major blow in 1713 when a smallpox epidemic hit the Cape; while it killed hundreds of servicemen, settlers and slaves, it much more severely decimated the Khoikhoi. Figures are unknown but whatever the numbers, they were probably large (Elphick and Malherbe 1989: 21). Nevertheless, resistance continued, indeed, throughout the 18th century there were numerous small conflicts, mostly now between the ever expanding frontier farmers and the Khoikhoi, which led to the establishment of a small commando force, at first run by the VOC but soon taken over by a burgher militia (Marks 1972: 69–73). The conflicts largely consisted of stock raiding—on both sides, but for the Khoikhoi, this was also a political act of resistance; as they told a Company commando in 1739, their aim was to "...chase the Dutch out of their land as long as they live in their land, and that this was but a beginning but they would do the same to all the people around here." (quoted in Marks 1972: 71). Raiding was a common part of Khoikhoi society even before 1652; it was a mechanism for maintaining balance between communities between their needs and means for stock herding. Arbitration to prevent raid and counter-raid from spiraling out of control was also a major role of the chiefs and sustained their political position as well as an articulation of masculinity; when the Dutch started to intervene as arbiters after 1677, they compromised the power of the chiefs leading to social de-stabilisation, and one can see the continuance of raids throughout the 18th century as a means of contesting this arbitration as well an attempt to preserve a way of life.

Colonial settlement in the early 18th century was thus very much a moving frontier north and east, which involved the successive displacement of Khoikhoi from their pastures, and a transformation of their relationship to the VOC and settlers from one of independent trader to dependent labourer. In the next section, I want to explore this process in more detail by focusing on the colonial settlement of the Dwars Valley, and examine how this occurred and what subsequent dynamics were established within the settler community.

SETTLEMENT IN THE DWARS RIVER VALLEY, 1690–1795

Reading Maps

Among the earliest maps of the area, several dating from c. 1690–1710, show the valley and I want to point out two things: the prominence given to one farm, and the presence of Khoikhoi kraals. One farm stands out for special attention on at least two maps—the farm of Zorgvliet in the upper part of the valley (Figure 3.1). In 1705, a minister working for the VOC, Francois Valentijn visited the farm, and his description certainly corresponds with its prominence on contemporary maps:

> ... here is one of the most ornamental and noble estates that can be imagined, which, although not very large, need yield place to no estate in Africa, and to few even in Holland. It is owned by the Landdrost *Johannes Meyer*, who has shown himself here, as in many other matters, to be a man of judgement and unusually methodical, since he has made this piece of land so fine, that one does not know whether art or nature has the upper hand here, since hardly anything can be imagined for the adornment of an estate which he has not wonderfully taken into account in laying it out.
>
> The house, which because of the heavy squalls is not too high, lies in a pretty and ornamentally laid out wood of lovely oaks, so that one barely sees it until one is close by. Then one comes into the most beautiful vineyards, and from these into 2 or 3 separate gardens, each among the finest to be seen

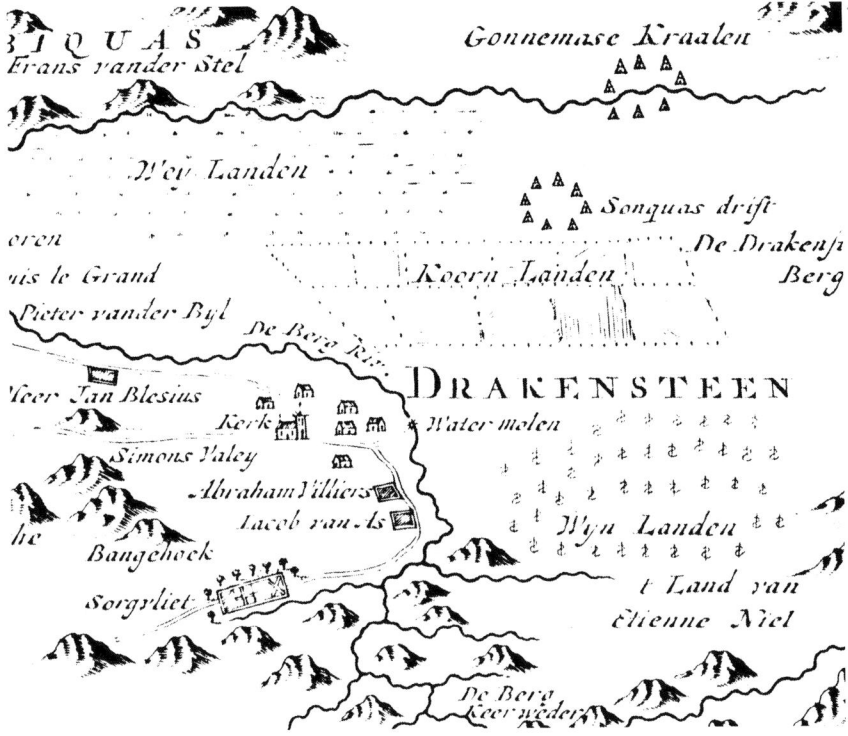

Figure 3.1. Detail of 1690 map of Drakenstein. (*Source*: Cape Archives 1/1159)

anywhere thereabout, in which are the choicest fruits, fountains, a fishpond
in the center of a flower-garden, many aloes cut into all sorts or ornamental
pyramids, choice flowers, and all kinds of rare shrubs and plants imaginable.
These he has known to bring together very skillfully and properly in such a
small space; and to them an incomparable pavilion of laurel lends unusual
adornment, with an artificial hill beside it, very ingeniously made, with a
grotto of all sorts of minerals set together in which hundreds of colours can be
observed, with a quantity of flowers growing out between them; and further
the hollows and clefts of this artificial hill are set with all sorts of porcelain
figures, animals, castles, etc., so finely disposed that all who have seen this
estate must admit never to have seen so much beauty brought together in so
small a space. It is called Zorgvliet, and far surpasses the place after which
it is named, both in art and in the fine opportunities offered by nature and
from which it benefits. A silver-mine was also opened here, but has not been
further exploited owing to the great cost. (Valentyn 1971: 158–161).

The silver mine is of course, that discussed in the last chapter, but
I want to discuss this farm here. I have quoted Valentyn at length for a
number of reasons. First, the description of the house and, particularly

the gardens clearly had an impact on Valentyn, and possibly many of his contemporaries. Martin Hall has discussed Valentyn and other descriptions of gardens at the Cape, and suggested that gardens were symbols of culture against nature, the "... representation of human power to contain and transform wild nature, symbols of the essence of colonial settlement and transformation." (Hall 2000: 89).

Zorgvliet certainly seems to have represented the colonial dream, indeed it is even said to have surpassed its namesake near The Hague, a villa owned by Jacob Cats who retired there after a career in Dutch politics as the Pensionary of Holland (Israel 1995: 748). During the late 1620s and 1630s, there was a fashion for building 'arcadian retreats' in the Netherlands, villas expressing mercantile wealth and patrician status. Zorgvliet was built for Jacob Cats in the early 1650s (ibid.: 871), and it was particularly noted for its fine gardens (ibid.: 886). Valentyn called the owner of the Cape Zorgvliet, Johannes Meyer, although the recorded name on the property deed is Johannes Mulder. He came to the Cape as a soldier of the VOC and he was appointed the first *landdrost* of the district in 1685, as a salaried Company official (Visagie 1987: 25). Mulder had his chambers and a residence in Stellenbosch (the site of the current Theology faculty at the University), but acquired Zorgvliet in 1692. According to the deeds, the original owner was Caspar Willers, granted the freehold in 1692, but no mention is made of the transfer to Mulder; the first recorded transfer is on the death of Mulder in 1732. Interestingly, it may have been Mulder's wife rather than himself who was responsible for the beauty of Zorgvliet—and possibly its name. His wife, Jacoba Kichelaar (or Kicheler) whom he married in 1682, was from The Hague and may have been more personally familiar with the 'original' Zorgvliet, as Mulder was from Amsterdam.

Zorgvliet is interesting because after Mulder's death, it seems to have declined in importance in the valley, while others had increased. Mulder and Kichelaar had no children and the property was bought by another burgher in the locality, Johannes Louw. Indeed, the importance of Zorgvliet is probably directly related to Mulder's ascribed status in the district, for during the 1690s and early 1700s, there were two major families which increased their landholdings by acquiring other properties through consolidation: the families of Abraham de Villiers and Jacob van As. I examine these further below in the context of developing social differentiation within the Dwars community, but both names are also shown on the map (Figure 3.1). It is no doubt significant that while Mulder's estate is marked simply as Zorgvliet, the de Villiers and van As estates are marked after their personal names, reflecting perhaps the

fact that Zorgvliet was more renowned as a place than for its owner—
as Valentijn attests. Another reason though may be that Zorgvliet was
perhaps claimed by the VOC and given to Mulder; the lack of any transfer records from Caspar Willers to Mulder is odd, though such gaps are
not unknown.

The second thing on the map is the Khoikhoi kraals, showing their
proximity to the expanding settler front. Little is known about the indigenous settlement of the Dwars valley—no previous archaeological
work has been conducted here and it has often been assumed that the
area was simply unoccupied—a common theme in colonial histories. Indeed there is a strong belief among the present day community in the
valley that no ancestry exists with the indigenous Khoi. Yet it is more
than likely that groups of Khoikhoi or even San came through this valley at various points in the recent past; a chance find while walking
on the upper edges of the present day vineyards on the Simonsberg
recovered a stone flaked artefact which attests to their presence. Beyond that however, our knowledge of settler-Khoikhoi interaction in
this particular locale remains undefined at present. We can however,
suggest certain likely scenarios given what is known from the wider
area. Certainly many of the Khoikhoi would have come into some contact with Europeans already, before the first settlers arrived; scouting parties sent into the Drakenstein area in the late 1650s and early
1660s to trade for stock, taking with them as goods, copper, tobacco and
tobacco pipes (de Wet 1987: 13). When the first settlers arrived, they
too probably tried to barter, although private trade was prohibited by
the Company until 1700, a right revoked in 1702 and then reinstated in
1704. There is evidence of frequent bartering with the Khoikhoi in the
adjacent valley to the Dwars, Oliphantshoek (present day Franschoek)
during the late 17th and early 18th centuries. Indeed, it was a Khoikhoi
chief who reported the settlers to the VOC for engaging in illegal
bartering in 1696, and another who complained of their violence in
1700 (Meyer 1996: 11). Already by this time, it seems the settlers had
acquired more stock than the Khoikhoi. Throughout the early decades
of the 18th century there are occasional records of conflict, sometimes
resulting in death, on both sides. Based on these various recorded interactions, Khoikhoi kraals can be placed in at least two adjacent areas in
the years around 1700—one north between the Simonsberg and Paarl,
and one east at Oliphantshoek, though these are not marked on the
map. The only Khoikhoi kraals there, tellingly, are placed at some distance and on the edge of any colonial settlement. The khoikhoi kraals
in the Drakenstein may have been temporarily working for some of the
settlers, as was common practice by this period, and though they were

officially free and working on a contract basis, in the worst cases they may have been treated no better than slaves (Penn 1999: 135)

One particular incident in especially interesting because of who is involved. In 1702, the settler Abraham de Villiers lodged six complaints against a Khoikhoi called Kleine Kaptein: for killing his dog, stealing a lamb, heifer, pig and ox and finally threats of arson and theft. In return however, Kleine Kaptein accused de Villiers of burning his houses and shooting his livestock. In the event, it seems Kleine Kaptein had to pay the costs of the case: three calves, to the *landdrost* (Meyer 1996: 13). This Abraham de Villiers moreover, was the same one who was to become a major landholder in the Dwars; at the time he was on a farm in Oliphantshoek, but in the same year as he reported this incident (1702), he seems to have moved to the Dwars, buying up a farm there. It is possible the move was motivated by the absence of Khoikhoi in that valley, but for whatever reason, his fortunes changed rapidly. In the next section, I want to go into more detail regarding the European settlement of the Dwars Valley, and look at the changing patterns of land ownership, wealth and status to see how social differentiation developed within the settler population and how this manifested itself in material culture.

A Tale of Two Families

The exact dates of the various settlements in the Dwars Valley are not always known, as the title deeds of the freehold grants were often issued several years after the land had already been settled. Nonetheless, the first settlers arrived in the valley sometime between 1688 and 1690. Upon arrival, these settlers were supplied with a few months provisions as well as tools and wood with which to build temporary homes and start farming (Coertzen 1988: 84–85; Malherbe 1997: 5). The settlement of the Drakenstein region generally was much more controlled than the previous settlement of the Eerste river valley to the south; there, land was granted on a first come, first served basis and could be staked anywhere. When a VOC commissioner came out to assess the state of the colony between 1684–5, he was horrified by how Simon van der Stel had not attempted any kind of organization. His main critique was that the settlers had established their plots parallel to the river, thus cutting off the free land behind them from any water source—a potential problem should future settlers occupy this free land. The commissioner, Hendrik Adriaan van Reede, suggested plots should run at right-angles to the river to prevent this, thus the free plots which might be claimed later, would still have access to water.

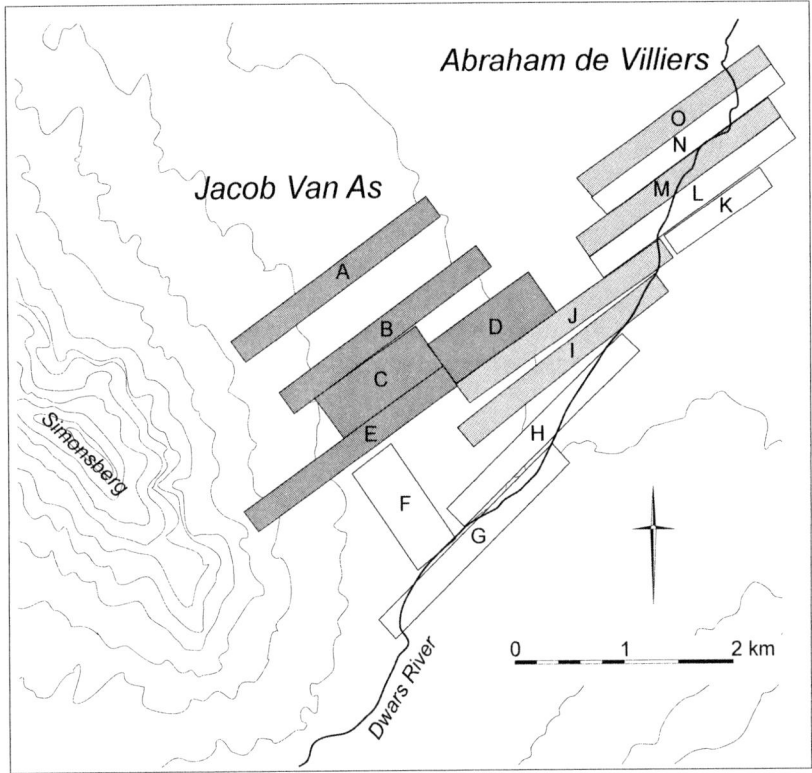

Figure 3.2. 17th century land grants in the Dwars valley showing farms owned by van As (dark shading) and de Villiers (pale shading) in 1716 (*Key*: A=Eenzam, B-E= Nieuwendorp, F=Goede Hoop, G=Languedoc, H=Rhone, I=Boschendal A, J=Boschendal B, K=Lubeck, L=Zandvliet, M=Lekkerwijn, N=Eenzamheid, O=Meerust).

(Guelke 1989: 74; Guelke and Shell 1983: 266–9). The plots laid out in the Dwars valley and others in the lower Drakenstein, clearly have the stamp of van Reede's suggestion (Figure 3.2), and they were surveyed prior to allocation at a standard size of 60 *morgen* (125 acres). This policy however, did not last long and subsequent freehold grants to the north were given in the same, laissez-faire manner as the Eerste river valley.

Although van Reede had a point, the fact is, much of the land behind these plots was held by the VOC and was generally not suitable for farming anyway. Indeed, under van Reede's scheme, these new plots often contained marginal land, unsuitable for farming while plenty of good arable land lay fallow, as pasture. In short, while Simon van der

Stel's scheme resulted in the most efficient use of the available land by leaving it to the settlers, van Reede's approach reflected the same, imposing geometry on the landscape as seen in other VOC programmes such as the Fort or the layout of Cape Town and the Company Gardens (see Chapter 2; Guelke and Shell 1983: 268). Indeed, early VOC policy on agricultural plots was largely based on the Roman grid system, although it was soon abandoned as impractical (Zandvliet 1998). This explains why there was so much empty land left by the settlers of the late 1680s—mostly Huguenots, a situation which more or less remained until the 19th century when it started to be taken up.

Looking at the pattern of land holdings in Dwars valley suggests that the major way in which individual families expanded their property was primarily through buying up or consolidating with already existing plots rather than taking virgin ones. Of course a major reason for this was because after 1717, no further freeholds (*eigendom*) were granted, but other land may have been acquired on loan (*leening*) and after 1732, as rental/quitrent (*erfpacht*; Botha 1919b). Quitrents required formal registration, but tenure of such land was only temporary and did not encourage major investment. From 1743, a tenant could convert their tenure into an effective freehold by having the loan in perpetuity, but it was not until 1813 that Perpetual Quitrents were introduced, i.e. a leasehold which could be sold and transferred like freeholds. Thus it is not until the 19th century that we see the empty land in the Dwars valley carved up. The process of settlement development and the emergence of a colonial 'landed gentry' in the Dwars happened fairly quickly after intitial settlement—within perhaps half a century. This is reflected in the general pattern of the economy when settlers could get very large returns on relatively little investment compared to wealthy landowners; within half a century, this had leveled out, and poorer farmers were more likely to remain poor while the wealthy ones could sustain their position (Guelke and Shell 1983: 270–275). I want to explore how this happened in the case of two families in the valley, the two who were clearly important enough to be marked on that map: the de Villiers and van As'.

Abraham de Villiers was one of three brothers from a wine farm in Bar-sur-Seine, in Champagne, Burgundy, all of whom originally settled in a tributary of the next major valley to the southeast, Oliphantshoek in present day Franschoek (Boucher 1981: 233–4). Abraham and his two brothers, Pierre and Jacob, sailed out in 1689 on the ship Zion and arrived in the Drakenstein the same year, taking three plots adjacent to each other which they named respectively: Champagne, Bourgogne and La Bri. These three brothers were actually singled out in a letter from the VOC in Netherlands to Simon van der Stel as having good knowledge of wine-growing, and this, as well as wheat formed the major basis of their agricultural output (Coertzen 1988: 111). Abraham eventually sold his farm of Champagne at Olifantshoek and re-located to the Dwars valley buying up many of the farms there, the first being Meerust in 1702, followed by Boschendal (1710) and then Lekerwijn (1716). Before he died in 1720, Abraham was the largest landowner in the valley holding three farms at nearly a quarter of all the freehold land—a total of 500 acres (240 morgen). A few years before his death, he sold his largest farm, Boschendal, to one of his brothers, Jacob who left his farm of La Bri in Oliphantshoek to join Abraham in the Dwars valley. The two brothers were probably close, and both had married sisters, Susanne and Marguerite Gardiol—also Huguenots who had arrived at the Cape the same year as the de Villiers. Upon Abraham's death, the other two farms stayed with his wife Susanne who, although she remarried, moved to Cape Town with her new husband, where she already owned a house. After she died in 1729, the properties passed to his brother Jacob.

Although the peak of landholdings by Abraham de Villiers occurred in the mid 1710s, the subsequent splitting of his accumulated property reflected the fact that he had no sound male heirs. The transfer of Abraham's wealth is an interesting example of the 'patriarchal façade' that Hall discusses in the context cape colonial society (Hall 1995; Hall 1997; Hall 2000: 110–114). Although Abraham had no able male heirs to inherit his properties (his only living son was disabled and died a bachelor in 1732), he wanted to ensure they would remain in the de Villiers family. As Hall points out, it is quite clear that descent through the female line was widely practiced behind the patriarchal façade of male control of assets. Under Cape-Dutch law, couples married in community of property with inheritance being partible—that is, the widow inherited half the estate and the children divided the other half between them. Women—especially widows—were thus substantially empowered, a feature further enhanced by the male to female ratio imbalance (see below). Nevertheless, the husband always controlled all the assets while alive and should a widow re-marry, the new husband would gain control of her assets. Partible inheritance thus made marriage an ambiguous alliance—on the one hand a man could marry a wealthy heiress and acquire rapid status and power, but on the other, a woman retained half the property in the event of being widowed.

Soon after the death of Abraham's wife, Jacob almost immediately passed two of the three properties on to one of Abraham's daughters, Marie de Villiers, although it is the daughter's husband (Johan

Schabort) listed as the owner, not her. These properties however—
Meerust and Lekkerwijn, eventually passed back to a male de Villiers,
one of Jacob's sons, Jan. Jacob himself died in 1735, outlived by his
widow Margeurite by many years who died in 1749, and the one property he had retained, Boschendal, was passed to this same son Jan
in 1736, who later acquired the other two from his aunt. Such shift-
ing of properties between family members was very common throughout the 18th and early 19th century and often reflects attempts to
keep property in the family through the female line behind the patriarchal façade of male control of assets. Indeed, this kind of strategy has been suggested to have enabled an elite to emerge and maintain their position; partible inheritance did not encourage an equitable
re-distribution of wealth (Guelke and Shell 1983: 279–80). Ultimately,
Abraham's properties were kept within the family and helped to sustain
an emerging family dynasty, which continued to dominate the farms in
the valley and beyond. Before I carry on their story, I want to turn to
the other major landholding family, for their two destinies were to be
entwined.

Jacob van As was the son of a freed slave, Mooi Ansiela or Angela
who originally came from Bengal. Angela was manumitted in Cape
Town in 1666, still young but with three or four children, one of them
being Jacob van As, possibly the son of a Johannes van As from Harlin-
gen in Friesland. In 1669 Angela married an ex-VOC soldier, Arnoldus
Basson, and they had several children together during the 1670s. When
Simon van der Stel opened up the Drakenstein with new freeholds in
the late 1680s, the free burgher Basson and his family left Cape Town
to settle on two farms in the Dwars valley in 1689, although they kept
land at Table Bay (Naidoo 2000; Malan 1999). The two freeholds were in
the names of Basson and his step-son, Jacob van As. Between 1690 and
1692, three more farms were granted close by, one to Willem Basson,
son of Angela and Arnoldus. In the same year as moving there, Jacob
married, to Maria Clements a Swedish immigrant from Stockholm; his
half brother Willem Basson, married Maria's sister, Helena. Arnoldus
Basson died in 1698, and after her husband's death, Angela did not de-
cide to stay in the valley. When further land was opened up after 1699
to the north, she and most of the family seemed to move on, except for
Jacob; he stayed and steadily accumulated all the farms nearby, including his parents' and half-brother's. By 1701, he owned five plots, which
he consolidated into one large estate, Nieuwendorp, at 625 acres (300
morgen), making him the largest landowner in the valley, even before
Abraham de Villiers. By 1702, Jacob's wife Helena must have died for
in that year he remarried, to Helena van der Merwe.

By the time of Jacob's death in 1713, he was a very wealthy burgher with loan farms to the north as well the estate at Nieuwendorp; according to his inventory, his wealth seems to have been based on a mixture of livestock, wine and wheat, and he also owned eleven slaves, mostly males. This estate was passed to his wife under the same law of partible inheritance discussed above; he had two children by his former wife Maria, and one with his second Helena, but under the terms of the inventory Helena was given sole control. Within a year of his death, his widow remarried, to Christiaan Maasorp (or Matzdorp), himself a widower, and whose previous wife had been Jacob's half-sister. The new couple did not stay long at Nieuwendorp however, and in 1716 they sold the whole estate, thus ending the brief period of the influence of the van As family in the valley. Although Jacob had three children, none seemed to remain in the valley; the two children by his first wife disappear from the records but his third with Helena, does seem to have been partly successful. He was Willem van As and he married a Dutch woman and had eight children; he acquired a farm in the region, Hazendal, and must have retained an interest in the Dwars valley, for he is listed as one of the shareholders of the silver mine company (see Chapter 2).

The stories of these two great landowners in the Dwars valley are interesting for a number of reasons. First, one was a first generation European settler, who came from an established family of winegrowers in France while the other was the son of an ex-slave from Bengal. Both clearly had large, extended families, but while one family largely remained in the valley and the locality, the other seemed constantly on the move, dispersing throughout the Cape as new opportunities arose. Thus while Jacob van As became the first and largest landowner in the valley, it was Abraham's kin who remained to become the most powerful family in the 18th and 19th centuries. Indeed, their stories entwine after the deaths of their two founders, for in 1724, the large estate of Nieuwendorp was bought up by Jacob de Villiers, the son of Abraham's brother of the same name, Jacob. In acquiring Nieuwendorp, this second generation de Villiers doubled the family landholdings so between the different members, they now had nearly half the valley at 1125 acres (540 *morgen*). Jacob was more successful with male heirs than his brother Abraham, and had many children, including seven boys and five girls; apart from his son who was named after him, Jacob had two other sons who became important landowners in the valley, Jan and Abraham. Jan de Villiers was particularly successful and owned many properties, including inheriting the major farm of Boschendal in 1738, while his brother Abraham acquired the farm next to Nieuwendorp, called Goede Hoop, in 1735. Both these brothers married

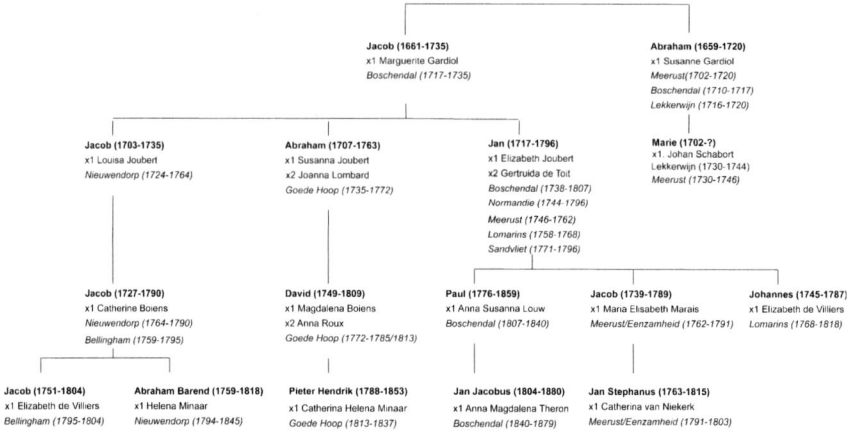

Figure 3.3. De Villiers genealogy in relation to properties in the Dwars valley.

sisters, Elizabeth and Susanna Joubert respectively, whose aunt, Louisa Joubert had married the elder brother Jacob. Moreover, the Joubert sisters' mother was Susanna de Villiers, one of the elder Abraham's other daughters (Figure 3.3).

There are some recurring features in these stories, particularly as regards marriage. In the first case, it is common to see two families creating strong alliances by not one but two or more marriages between them. The first generation de Villiers married two sisters, while the second generation married three times into the Joubert family, another wealthy Huguenot clan (Coertzen 1988: 116–117). Similarly Jacobus van As and his half brother Willem Basson married the daughters of a Swedish immigrant. However, there are also differences; while the de Villiers and other Huguenot families tended to prefer marriage among their own, no doubt because of language and cultural factors, the Basson and van As families were clearly more flexible (Table 3.1). In fact, in the first decade of settlement, the Huguenots were very intent on retaining their cultural identity, a cause promoted by their pastor Pierre Simond who constantly liased with the VOC (by whom he was paid) on their behalf. This desire for independence was not in the interests of the VOC and they became increasingly angered by Simond and the Huguenot community for resisting integration into the wider burgher community, so much so that there were official requests from the Governor for no more French settlers, but rather Germans or Dutch. When Simond finally left the Cape in 1701, the Huguenots lost their major spokesperson, and integration eventually occurred so that within

Table 3.1. Marriage Patterns among the first freeholders in the Dwars valley. (*Source*: Huguenot Museum, Franschoek)

Huguenots	
Intra-marriage	7
Extra-marriage	1
Unmarried	2
*Others**	
Free blacks	3
Huguenots	1
Other European	3
Unmarried	4

* Mostly Dutch or north Europeans, but includes two of mixed descent.

a century of settlement, among the third to fourth generations almost no-one could speak French (Coertzen 1988: 94–97).

In stark contrast to the initial non-integrationist stance by the Huguenots, mixed marriages to free blacks was much more common among ex-VOC servicemen—although they were never very common in general, always less than 5% of all recorded marriages (Guelke 1988: 464). Not only did Basson marry Angela, one of Angela's daughters by another, unknown European, Anna de Koning, also married an ex-VOC servicemen (and a Swede again) in 1678, Olof Bergh. Olof and Anna were very successful and amassed a large fortune, which included one of the most prestigious farms in the colony, Constantia, established by Simon van der Stel and famous for its wine (Malan 1999). There were two other farms in the Dwars run by a free black and ex-Serviceman, one of which, Zandvliet, has an interesting story attached. The freehold to this was granted in 1687 to Hans Silberbach and his spouse, Angela, a freed slave born at the Cape; they transfered this property to Christoffel Snyman in 1692 who was himself, like Jacob van As, son of a freed slave. Born to Catherina van Palliacatt and a VOC soldier of the same name, Christoffel's father left to return to Europe and he was raised by his mother and stepfather, another free black called Anthony of Bengal. Anthony died in 1683, when Christoffel was only 14 years old, and it may be they moved with Silberbach and his wife to Zandvliet in the late 1680s. It has been asked whether free blacks helped each other out, perhaps recognizing a certain kinship (Malan 1999: 67); it has also been pointed out that in some areas around Table Bay, there were small enclaves of free blacks settling on adjacent farms forming a community (Cairns 1985). It certainly seems as if a similar bond formed in the Dwars valley between free blacks—not only between the Snymans and Silberbaghs, but Christoffel was later a godfather to Jacob van As third son, Willem.

Although Christoffel is listed at the owner of Zandvliet from 1692, Silberbach still apparently lived at the farm, as in 1697 he was caught up in a fatal altercation with a Huguenot neighbour, Ari Lecrevent which resulted in the latter's death. It seems likely then that the Silberbachs and the Snyman's were living together, and after Christoffel Snyman got married in 1690, Silberbach may have agreed to transfer ownership to him. Snyman actually married into a Huguenot family, one of the few examples from the first generation of settlers, and not just any family but one of the more renowned—the de Savoye's. What is interesting however, is that the head of this family, Jacques de Savoye, was embroiled in a major conflict with the pastor Simond, which fundamentally seemed to relate to a difference between the two men regarding their relation to the VOC; Simond saw himself as defender of the Huguenot community against the VOC, while de Savoye was on much better terms with the Company, and might thus, be seen as more integrationist than Simond (Coertzen 1988: 135–136).

The other feature to note from these stories is the speed with which widowed spouses remarried; the fact that it was very common is not necessarily a reflection of lack of feeling for the deceased, but rather perhaps a social necessity. That such a practice was widespread can be seen from Guelke's statistical analysis in reconstructing the demography of the European settler population (Guelke 1988). One of the key aspects to this demography was the imbalance in gender ratio for the first half century of settlement: in Drakenstein in the 1690s, there were more than three men for every woman, which by the early 18th century, had dropped to about two men until the late 18th century, when the ratio was nearly equal (Guelke 1988: 461; Guelke and Shell 1983: 196). This is a fairly typical ratio for a colonial settlement. It is thus not surprising that re-marriage was common, especially for women, and again, the percentage of women re-marrying is very high in the early years of settlement, decreasing over time as the gender ratio balances out (Guelke 1988: 455). In the new world which the early settlers were inhabiting, there was practically no social networks to fall back upon—these resided either on the other side of the world in Europe or within the structures of the VOC. Thus the very construction and maintenance of family networks was a priority, and this was done through alliances by marriage and the production of heirs. Indeed, a similar situation has been suggested for Batavia where in particular, alliances between families formed the social glue and were more important than patrimony (Taylor 1983: 71).

That marriage was one of the key social ceremonies at the Cape might be inferred from Mentzel's description from the mid-18th century, which discusses them as the main context for feasts or parties (Mentzel 1925: 105). Otto Mentzel was one of the most important contemporary commentators of life at the Cape in the mid 18th century whose book *A Geographical and Topographical Description of the Cape of Good Hope* (1785–7) provides many details of daily life and customs. Marriages were clearly considered a major occasion for sustaining social networks, not simply through the marriage itself but as importantly, through the people and families attending the marriage ceremony which significantly, took place at the bride's parents. By the end of the 18th and early 19th century, the situation seems to have changed little—various English writers snobbishly commented on what they regarded as the overly socialized and public nature of marriage ceremonies, especially during a time when in Europe, the marriage was becoming less of a public affair (McKenzie 1993: 71–3). Even the VOC thought that weddings could be excessive, as they made explicit in the sumptuary laws, which were introduced to the Cape in the mid-18th century—though the ceremonies of VOC officials were themselves highly lavish affairs, especially funerals which were an occasion for the greatest pomp (Ross 1999b: 21–29).

Both the de Villiers and van As saw the need for this, but they approached it in different ways. The de Villiers' sought to consolidate their wealth and position in one area by marrying into other local families often through more than one marriage. Though many de Villiers spread out to settle new farms, the family core in the Dwars valley remained solid, creating an ever-strengthening network of alliance and kin in the valley. In contrast, the Basson's and van As' tended to disperse and move on, and while several of its members became landowners in other areas, they did not retain the same large family network in one close area as the de Villiers, even though there is some suggestion they formed a close association with other free blacks in the valley. The differences are partially accounted for perhaps by the social background from which the two families came—one from a French emigrant population with already shared values and experiences, the other from a mixed population whose only real commonality was the VOC—either as serviceman or slave. But this difference should not be over-stressed, as many Huguenot families also followed the pattern of the Basson's and van As', as we shall see below. Indeed, I do not want to overplay the contrast here, and certainly do not want to suggest one was more successful than the other in terms of building up property and status; clearly as the examples of Jacob van As and his half sister, Anna de Konning show, this is not the case. Moreover, research on the material consumption of free black households compared with other burghers suggests no real difference either (Malan 1999). Rather, the point is that other cultural values may have inflected family histories and thus in turn, their influence within one particular locale. Since the focus of this book lies with the Dwars river valley, it is the de Villiers family that I will look at it more detail, but through a close-textured analysis of just one property, the farm Goede Hoop, using both archives and archaeology.

DE GOEDE HOOP: ANATOMY OF A SETTLER FARM, 1688–1897

The Emergence of a New Landed Gentry: The Production Base

The freehold of Goede Hoop farm was only granted in 1708, but the land itself was portioned out in 1688 to the Huguenot Pierre Jacob with his wife Suzanne de Vos and their three children. This family came from the northwestern coast of France from Vieille-Eglise near Calais, and probably sailed out on the ship *De Schelde* early in 1688, finally arriving in Table Bay after a voyage of over three months. It was a longer than usual journey because of bad weather, but there no deaths or sickness' on board (Boucher 1981: 252–3; Coertzen 1988: 80). The family, with others journeyed on to the Drakenstein where plots of land were already assigned; as well as the plot of land of 125 acres, they received basic supplies to get them started (Table 3.2). The family would have had to clear their plot, build a house and prepare the land for cultivation, and with very little help. They may have joined with their neighbours to help each other out, they may even have hired some local Khoikhoi, but they would have had practically no money and very little assets to pay for hired labour (*knechts*) or buy slaves. The plot is one of only a few others in the valley that is rectangular, for most of the plots were long, narrow strips (see Figure 3.2), but it had good frontage onto the Dwars river. Unlike the de Villiers, this family and its alliances did not seem to be successful, indeed they may have been more the norm among the Huguenots.

In 1690, after requests from their pastor Simond, the VOC distributed money from a special fund of *c*. 6000 rixdollars among the new

Table 3.2. List of Supplies granted by the VOC to Pierre Jacob and family. (*Source*: Coertzen 1988)

1688

Food and utensils
8 bags of wheat, 10 measures of fish oil, 3 lbs of pepper, 4 measures of olive oil, 6 vinegar, Iron pot

Tools and Hardware
2 spades, 2 shovels, large plane, 2 axes, 2 handsaws, 2 chisels, 3 drilling bits, 2 spark irons, 2 hammers, 2 files, 1 trowel, 3 knives, 1 threshing tool, 2 sickles, 2 pangas, 55 lbs nails, 2 jute bags, 1 lb canvas cotton, 2 measures olive oil

Plus quarter shares in:
3 lbs of lead, 1 fathom cable rope, flintlock stone, 2 flintlocks, 2 gunpowder, 10 oxen

1689
10 bags of wheat
quarter share in a plough

Total debt: 560,24.4 guilders

settlers according to their needs. Pierre Jacob received the third largest amount from this Batavian fund, 640 guilders (1 rixdollar = 3 guilders), suggesting he was in very dire straits compared to his neighbours (Coertzen 1988: 84). Pierre Jacob died three years later in 1693 and his wife and children worked the farm alone for the next few years. In 1698, Suzanne remarried, to the son of another Huguenot on a neighbouring farm, Boschendal—Nicolas de Lanoy, both of whose parents had also died previously, thus bringing the two farms under one owner for a brief period. Both families were from the same locality around Calais, journeyed on the same ship out to the Cape and may have known each other quite well by this time (Boucher 1981: 263–4). However, Nicolas died a few years after his marriage, in 1703, his wife Suzanne following him a few years later in 1708. There is an inventory of Suzanne de Vos showing the assets of the combined estates of Goede Hoop and Boschendal from 1710, when both properties were split and transferred to new owners, and these assets do not seem to have expanded much from the original list of provisions provided by the VOC 20 years earlier (Table 3.3). Indeed, Nicolas de Lanoy's father had received the same provisions and also a large amount (400 guilders) from the same Batavian fund, which had helped Pierre Jacob. As late as 1719, both settlers still owed the Company over 421 and 552 guilders respectively (Coertzen 1988: 86). According to Kolb writing in the early 18th century, such debts among settlers were very common (Kolb 1968: 48–49).

After Suzanne de Vos' death, the farm of Goede Hoop was bought by Hans Heinrich Hattingh in 1710, who also owned the nearby farm

Table 3.3. Inventory of Suzanne de Vos for the farms of Boschendal and Goede Hoop, 26th May 1708. (*Source*: Cape Archives MOOC 8/2 3/G)

Slaves
(none)

Livestock
11 draught oxen, 3 cows, 3 heifers, 2 calves, 1 horse, 1 foal, 20 Sheep

Agricultural Produce
11 $^1/_2$ Muid[1] spoilt rye, 1 Muid of rye, 1 Muid of Wheat

Agricultural Hardware
1 old broken plough, 1 old wagon, 1 old saddle, 1 trough, 2 old shares, 2 old couters, 1 old plough chain, 2 old pickaxes, 2 old spades, 2 barrels, 2 vats, 1 old churn, 4 old vats, 1 half *Legger*[2], 2 old half *Leggers*, 1 old *Mompijp*[3], 2 half *Leggers* with contents (wine)

Household Furniture and Hardware
3 chairs, 1 table, 1 bed, 1 feather mattress, 2 pillows and 1 blanket

1 water bucket, 2 iron pots, 2 chests, 1 *heugel*, 1 three-legged pot/stand, 1 griddle

---

[1]Muid = 92 kg; [2]Legger = 582 litres; [3]Local brew (cask)

of Lekkerwijn; this farm was originally settled by a Huguenot who was killed in dispute with a neighbour as already related above, but he left behind a widow—Marie de Lanoy, Nicolas' sister and four children. In the same year that Nicolas married Suzanne de Vos, Marie married Hans Hattingh, thus when Hattingh bought Goede Hoop, it was in some way, kept in the family. However, Marie died in 1714, having had three children by Hattingh, who soon after remarried. Hattingh had sold Lekkerwijn in 1712, but kept Goede Hoop until 1728 when it was sold to a newcomer, Bernadus Biljion; he only stayed at Goede Hoop for a short period, and in 1735, the property was bought by a de Villiers in whose family it remained for the next hundred years. Why the de Lanoy's and the Jacob's were not successful enough to make a stay in the Dwars valley is perhaps impossible to know, nor may we understand why Abraham de Villiers, who also received the same start-up supplies and 570 guilders from the Batavian fund, was so successful that by 1710, he could buy up the de Lanoy's plot of Boschendal. However, a major reason does seem to lie in the basis of agricultural production, as discussed below—between staples (livestock and cereals) and luxuries (wine). Certainly the de Villiers exemplify the emergence of a landed gentry in the region and it is the manifestation of this at one particular farm—Goede Hoop—which I want to study in depth.

Goede Hoop, like other farms in the valley, lies on fairly fertile ground; situated at the foothills of the Simonsberg, the soils consist of alluvial sands and loams overlying granite, which outcrops in places

Table 3.4. Capital stock of the various owners of Goede Hoop for the 18th and earlier 19th century. (*Source*: census data)

Year	Slaves	Livestock (head)	Cereals (kg)	Wines (litres)
1708*	0	41	184	582
1717*	9	1009	6440	0
1724*	9	441	20240	873
1728	3	29	0	0
1734	1	268	0	0
1735*	1	932	14720	11058
1771*	10	38	5520	17460
1773	6	126	0	52380
1785*	21	118	0	52380
1787*	24	280	0	14550
1809	11	25	5152	14550
1811	12	251	0	15423
1812	10	156	0	19788
1814	7	68	0	17169
1835	7	0	0	36084
1836	4	0	0	36084
1842	—	44	0	36084
1843	—	44	0	27354

* Includes other farms

(Swanevelder 1987). Today, vineyards have displaced much of the natural vegetation on the lower slopes and valley bottom, and the climate in the region, with its cool, wet winters (May-August) and warm, dry summers (December-March), is good for wine production. From Suzanne de Vos' inventory, she did have some wine, but it does not seem to have formed the major use of the land at Goede Hoop; rather cereal production and animal husbandry seems to have been the mainstay of agricultural production, and this is exactly what the VOC wanted. However, this changed. Using census information over the 18th and early 19th century, we can follow the fortunes of Goede Hoop's owners (Table 3.4). The census returns (*opgaaf rollen*) for the area run from 1708 to 1845 and were taken annually by officials (fieldcornets) and collated for the whole district by the *landdrost*; the data selected here just cover the years at the start and end of each new owner. One thing needs to be borne in mind when reading this data, and that is that the quantities shown, list the capital stock of the *owner* not the farm. Many of the owners had other properties in the district with stock and all this is included in these returns—these are marked by an asterisk in the table. Nevertheless, as an indication of the prosperity of the owner and by association, the farm, they are useful statistics, which moreover reflect the changing emphasis in agricultural production over the 18th century—from cereals and livestock to wine.

The key change in the table clearly occurs in 1735 when the property is transferred to Abraham de Villiers, and wine production almost doubles and cereal production halves. De Villiers also owned two other properties to the north, and part of the figures undoubtedly reflect these, but it is likely large scale wine-production was instigated at Goede Hoop under him; certainly by the time his son acquired the property forty years later, cereal production seemed to have more or less ceased and viticulture dominated the farm output, producing over 50,000 litres of wine per year from a stock of 50,000 vines. The area today continues this monoculture, with vineyards dominating the valley and the region, which is known as the Cape winelands. The labour that was needed to carry out this transformation was probably a mixture of slaves and Khoikhoi; only slaves are listed of course under the capital stock and there were six working at Goede Hoop in 1773. While this may have been sufficient for much of the year, during harvest time de Villiers probably hired local Khoikhoi, a common practice. As late as 1814, two Khoikhoi are listed in the census living on the farm, and in 1835 a family of eight were there; also in that year, the return states that eight people in total were employed in agriculture and five in commerce (there were seven slaves at the time), giving some indication of the numbers needed to run a farm with 60,000 vines to tend.

Although wine was not originally a product the VOC wanted to encourage, its success meant that it formed a major part of their revenue. The production of all this wine was primarily for the domestic market at the Cape; although the VOC exported the famous Constantia wines to Europe, most Cape wine was not considered good or cheap enough for international export (Ross 1989: 254–5). Nevertheless, the domestic market was sufficiently strong to see continual growth throughout the 18th century as Ross had demonstrated, with particularly high production rates in the later part of the century and into the early 19th century (Figure 3.4). Mentzel discusses the prominence of wine in social drinking, both in the cheaper taverns where it was sold in 4 pint flasks and the more respectable bars in 1 pint bottles (Mentzel 1925: 86). Wine was not just consumed in taverns though but also at home where he says it was always available, along with tobacco, and was usually drunk at meals and social entertaining (*ibid.*: 105–6). The statistical data showing the strong domestic market for wine and Mentzel's text are both further supported by archaeological assemblages where wine

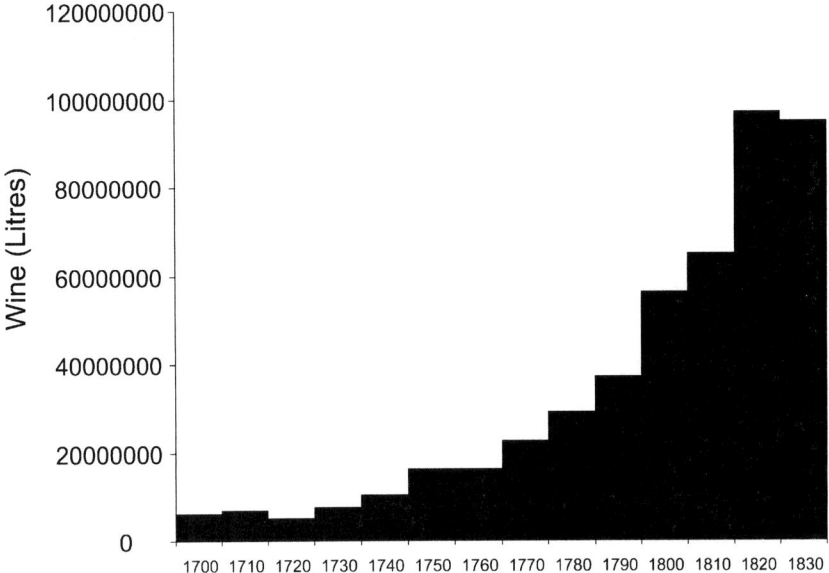

Figure 3.4. Wine export from the Cape. (*Source*: Adapted from Ross 1989)

bottles, tumblers and stemware all attest to its common consumption. It is commonly found at all types of sites from the Simonsberg silver mine settlement and woodcutters lodge at Paradise discussed in the last chapter to the elite estates in the country side such as Elsenberg or Goede Hoop (see below). Wine continued to play a major role in Cape society, indeed from the 19th century it even started to be exported abroad in larger amounts. The major increase in wine production towards the mid-19th century at Goede Hoop (see Table 3.4) reflects a new growth in the export trade to the international market, stimulated initially by the introduction of preferential tariffs within the British Empire to which the Cape by this time belonged. Not only wine, but wheat and livestock also had a healthy internal market during the 18th century and saw steady growth throughout the period (Ross 1989: 248–54).

Slavery was certainly the real basis on which the de Villiers—and indeed most farmers at the Cape—made their money. I will discuss slavery in much more detail in the next chapter, but even though slaves were the essential part of the labour force, it was the decision by the de Villiers to specialize in wine production that seems to have distinguished them from their predecessors. The first owners of Goede Hoop, Pierre Jacob and his wife Suzanne de Vos, had no slaves and a very modest farm split between livestock, cereals and wine; their household

Table 3.5. The inventory of Maria Walters, wife of Bernardus Biljon, for Goedehoop, 27th of February 1732. (*Source*: Cape Archives MOOC 8/5: 53)

Slaves
2 males

Livestock
88 cattle, 100 sheep, 2 horses

Agricultural Produce
—

Agricultural Hardware
1 old oxwagon, 1 churn, 1 barrel for preserving butter.

Household Furniture and Hardware
1 big shelf, 1 small shelf, 1 chest, 2 square tables, 3 old chairs

2 old buckets, 3 iron pots (of which 2 are old), 1 iron brazier, 1 iron gridiron, 1 iron fire tongs, 1 old copper tea-kettle, 1 old copper fish-kettle, 1 copper mortar, 1 coffee pot, 6 porcelain teacups and 6 porcelain saucers, 6 porcelain slop bowls, 12 pewter table plates, 3 old pewter dishes, 2 pewter bowls, 1 old pewter infusing pot, 6 pewter spoons, 1 old flintlock-musket

possessions were few and basic (see Table 3.3). Even the owners in the early 18th century had few possessions—Bernardus Biljon and his wife Maria Walters, whose returns list only livestock for the farm, had acquired a little more than the Jacobs and the de Lanoy's in 1732— two slaves, and a few more domestic utensils (Table 3.5). But when Abraham de Villiers' first wife died in 1736, the inventory for the farm Goede Hoop shows a completely different picture; here is a family whose consumption of domestic material culture is much closer to what one would expect of a landed gentry (Table 3.6). If the basis of the de Villiers wealth came from wine and slave labour, how that wealth was articulated through consumption is equally interesting and is what I want to focus upon next.

Gentrification and Cape Dutch Architecture

The present homestead at Goede Hoop is dated 1821 and the wine cellar, 1832, these changes occurring under Pieter Hendrik de Villiers' ownership, Abraham's grandson, who took possession of Goede Hoop in 1813. There are other buildings in the farm *werf*, one behind the homestead (an annexe and former labourer's/slave quarters), one next to the wine cellar (old millhouse) and one to the east (stables) associated with an enclosure and sheds (Figure 3.5). I will discuss these buildings later, especially as they represent the zenith of the farm in terms of its owners

Table 3.6. Inventory of Susanna Joubert, wife of Abraham de Villiers for Goede Hoop, 29th of July 1736. (*Source*: Cape Archives MOOC 8/5: 119)

Slaves
7 males, 1 female

Livestock
3 horses, 80 cattle, 400 sheep

Agricultural Produce
1 legger of wine, 2 empty leggers

Agricultural Hardware
3 halves of wagons, 1 churn, 2 barrels for preserving butter, 2 ploughs with their accessories, 1 set of iron teeth for a harrow

Household Furniture and Hardware
1 clothes cupboard, 2 beds with their accessories, 1 four-poster bed, 6 chairs, 1 small table, 1 chest with tools, 3 empty chests, 1 cellar with jars, 1 writing desk, 5 shelves, 1 mirror

4 iron pots, 2 tea-kettles, 2 cake tins, 1 3-foot chimney chain with iron crown (for hanging pots over the fire), 3 three-legged stand, 2 copper pots, 2 dozen pewter plates, 2 dozen porcelain plates, 2 tin trunks, 10 empty bags, 2 dozen spoons, 5 pewter dishes, 1 dozen knifes, 2 dozen forks, 1 coffee pot, 1 clothing iron, 2 sets of tea service, $1/2$ dozen earthenware dishes, 3 infusing vessels, 2 butter bowls, 3 (wooden) ladles, 2 dozen napkins, 6 tablecloths, 1 dozen slop bowls, 4 buckets.

---

aspirations in material consumption, but I want to begin with the farm as it was in the 18th century. The evidence for reconstructing the development of Goede Hoop farmstead is based on both architectural survey of the standing buildings and limited excavation, carried out in 2000 and 2001. When Pierre Jacob arrived at Goede Hoop with his family in 1688, one of his first jobs would have been to build a house; this would have probably been a small timber structure, as many of his neighbours (including the de Lanoy's at Boschendal) are recorded as living in such buildings, called *kapstylhuise* or *timmerage* (Malherbe 1997: 5). However, over time, more substantial structures would have been erected, either completely in stone or with stone footings and mudbrick walls, and it is these first stone structures that we have any real evidence for at Goede Hoop.

Test pit excavations around the present homestead uncovered the remains of two earlier buildings on the site, dating to the 18th century (Figure 3.5). The excavations were only limited so there is no information on the internal space of the buildings, but both structures had stone footings and a stamped mortar and brick (*grock*) floor. The upper structure lies mostly under the annexe behind the present homestead, while the lower one lies between this and the present homestead. This

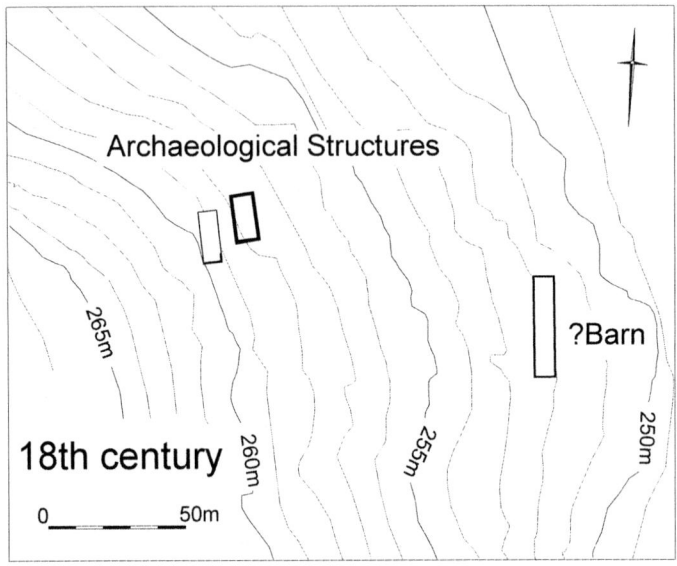

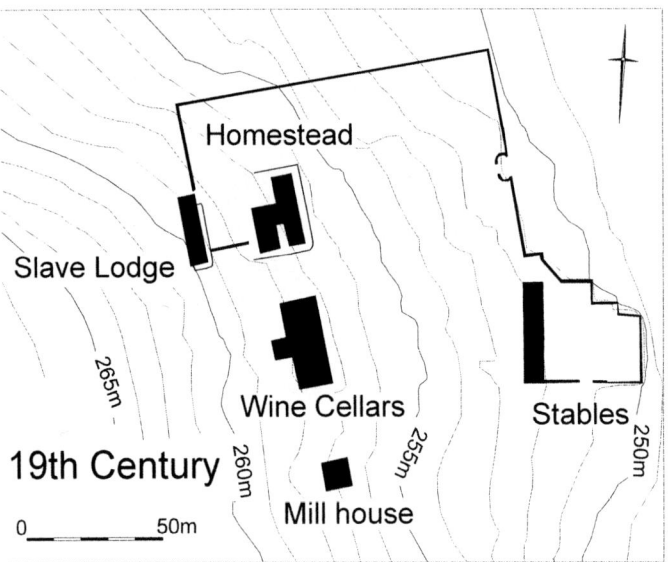

Figure 3.5. The development of Goede Hoop werf.

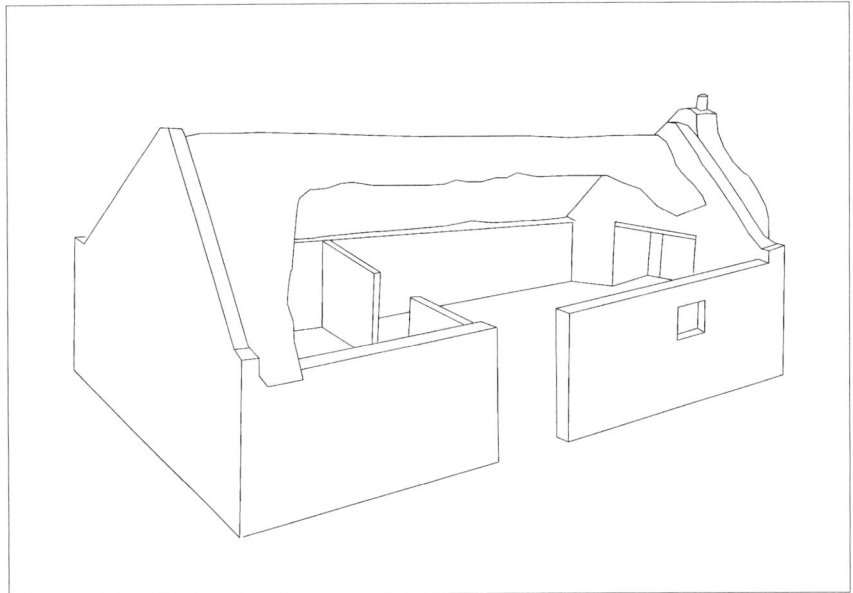

Figure 3.6. Plan of a typical Cape two bay house. (*Source*: Adapted from Walton 1995)

latter one, based on our test pits and an augur survey is estimated to have been about 12 m long and 6 m wide, and may be slightly later than the one behind it, as cultural material lay beneath its floor layers. It is likely that the upper one was the first substantial dwelling on the farm. The inventory of the third owner of the farm does give an indication of the building there in 1732—although no details are mentioned, the possessions are listed by room, of which there are two: a kitchen and a 'room on the right hand side'. This suggests a simple rectangular two-bay structure with the doorway in the kitchen. Such a structure was very typical in the early 18th century at the Cape, as studies have demonstrated and indeed was probably the basic house style throughout the Cape for the first century of settlement (Figure 3.6; Walton 1965; 1995).

These buildings were eventually leveled to make way for the construction of the present homestead in the early 19th century. It has been suggested that the annexe was the original farmhouse, but given that traces of an earlier structure lie beneath it, this should at least be qualified. The annexe was either built at the same time as the T-shaped homestead, in the early 19th century, or a little earlier, perhaps even when the second buried structure was erected. This structure, which lies between the annexe and the present homestead was probably built in the later 18th century as part of an enlargement of the homestead; in many ways, it is reminiscent of the final phase of development at Paradise in the late 18th century, with two parallel houses suggested to form an H-shaped complex (Hall et al. 1993: 46). This would place this development toward the end of the first de Villiers' ownership, or the start of his son's; either way, the changes would seem clearly related to the growth of the farm under the de Villiers, and its successful production of wine. Given the limited excavations, it is impossible to say what this new farmstead looked like in detail, but it was probably part of wider architectural changes sweeping the Cape in the mid-late 18th century, which saw the emergence of the Cape Dutch style. A sketch of Goede Hoop drawn between 1800–1803 by Samuel Daniell, and therefore before the construction of the later T-shaped homestead, shows a symmetrical house with central door, pairs of flanking windows and a stoep; there is also the suggestion of a central gable over the front door, though it is ambiguous. This is almost certainly the buried structure, in the last years before it was pulled down (Daniell 1820; Figure 3.7).

Figure 3.7. Sketch of Goede Hoop c.1800 by Samuel Daniell. (*Source*: Daniell 1820, engraving no. 13)

Early studies of Cape architecture tended to stress a rapid evolution from such a simple rectangular structure or longhouse to the more grand Cape Dutch houses with their characteristic front gables and T-, L- or H-plans (de Bosdari 1953; Fransen & Cook 1980; Obholzer *et al.* 1985; Trotter 1903; see Figures 3.8 & 3.9). The premise here is that the Cape Dutch 'style' goes back to the very beginning of the 18th century, with its roots in the Netherlands. Yet as more recent studies have shown, this is misleading for the classic symmetry of Cape Dutch architecture with its central hall (*voorhuis*) is a mid 18th century creation, and one which developed indigenously in relation to wider social changes (Brink 1990; 1992). Many contemporary commentators describe the floor plans of these new residences, as often, do inventories (Malan 1990; Mentzel 1925: 112; Thunberg 1986: 42; Woodward 1983). Yvonne Brink quite rightly critiques earlier architectural historians for looking at the development of Cape Dutch style in essentialist and originary terms, explaining it through basic elements (such as the gable) derived from a mother country. Indeed, the past emphasis on Cape Dutch style reflected a very partial view of architectural history, 'whitewashing' the past both literally and metaphorically (Hart & Winter 2001: 85–6), while marginalizing vernacular styles (Hall et al. 1988: 91; Walton 1995). In contrast, Brink has argued for a greater emphasis on local variation and articulation of this style in relation to its social context, and her studies have used the importance of the *voorhuis* to track this process.

The *voorhuis* was the first room or reception space one met upon entering a typical town house in the Netherlands, similar to the hall in English interiors. Between the 16th and 18th centuries in Europe, it reduced in size and position, becoming a smaller, narrower passageway or room off to one side (see Figure 2.1, Chapter 2). At the Cape, the *voorhuis* as it survives in existing buildings occupies a central space, articulating the overall symmetry of the house, and it has been assumed that this tradition goes back to the earlier houses. However, there is no evidence for this; indeed, it is more likely the earliest houses with a *voorhuis* were in the Dutch style. Examples of such arrangements at the Cape are rare and often contested, such as a house in Bo-Kaap, Cape Town (e.g. Townsend & Townsend 1977; Walton 1995: 115; also see Chapter 4, Figure 4.17). However, most houses at the Cape probably did not even have a *voorhuis*, for these were probably simple two- or three-bayed rectangular houses, as suggested for Goede Hoop. It was only after the 1730s that houses with a central *voorhuis* started to become more common, especially in the countryside, as Brink has demonstrated in her statistical survey from 18th century inventories (Brink 1992: 50–51).

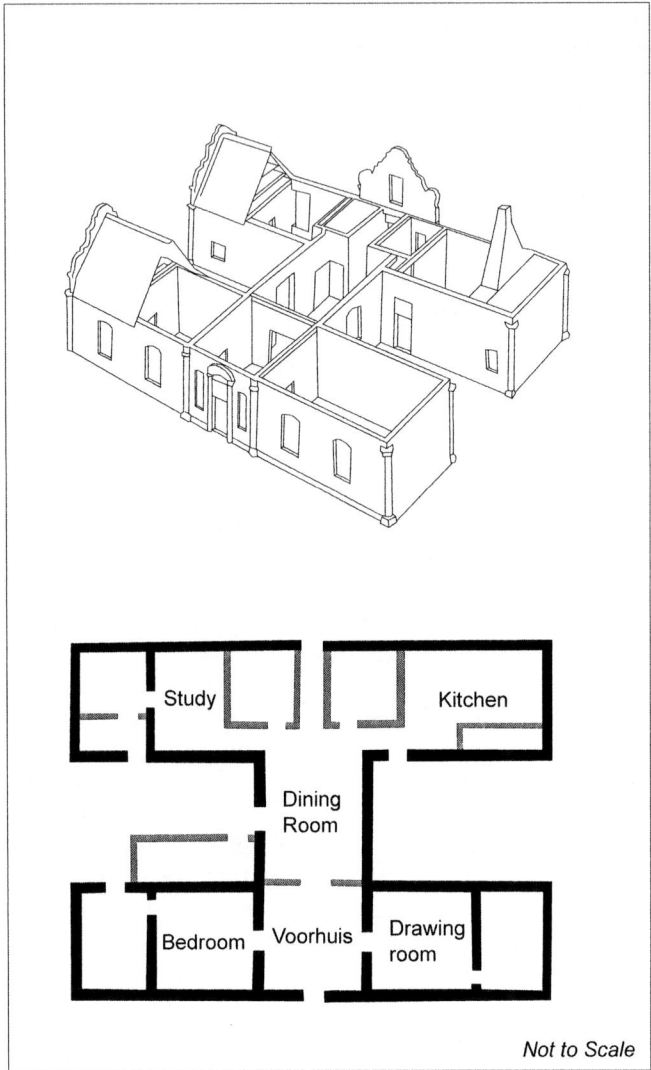

Figure 3.8. Boschendal Manor House. (*Source*: Adapted from Fransen & Cook 1980)

Brink interprets these changes in inventory descriptions with architectural changes, specifically with the *voorhuis* being increasingly placed centrally and associated with a T-shape plan rather than the more traditional Dutch urban style; moreover, she suggests that the simple, bayed rectangular structures did not really have a *voorhuis* but

Figure 3.9. The gabled front of Boschendal. (*Source*: Photograph by the author, taken in 1999)

belonged to a different, more vernacular tradition of European architecture (Brink 1992:47). Brink's arguments for major changes occurring in architectural style after the 1730s is very convincing, and has certainly been demonstrated archaeologically at one site, Paradise, discussed in the last chapter. However, I am not so sure that single pile, rectangular houses could not have had a *voorhuis*; indeed, Muller's house, as modified, on the silver mine settlement also discussed in Chapter 2 would seem to be an example, albeit rather abnormal. Here the *voorhuis* leads simply from the stoep straight out to the back. Of course it might be denied this is a *voorhuis*, but then this begs the question. The chief issue here really lies in changes in architectural design, which drew on the existing vernacular as well as elements of Dutch urban housing, and culminated in the Cape Dutch Style; moreover, this probably does happen later than conventional architectural history has suggested, not in the late 17th century but, as Brink's study indicates, in the mid-18th. At Paradise, the original single pile rectangular house was re-built as a T-plan house in the mid-18th century (Hall et al. 1993), reflecting this change; at other places, a completely new house may have been built, the old house converted to an alternate use. The latter was perhaps the

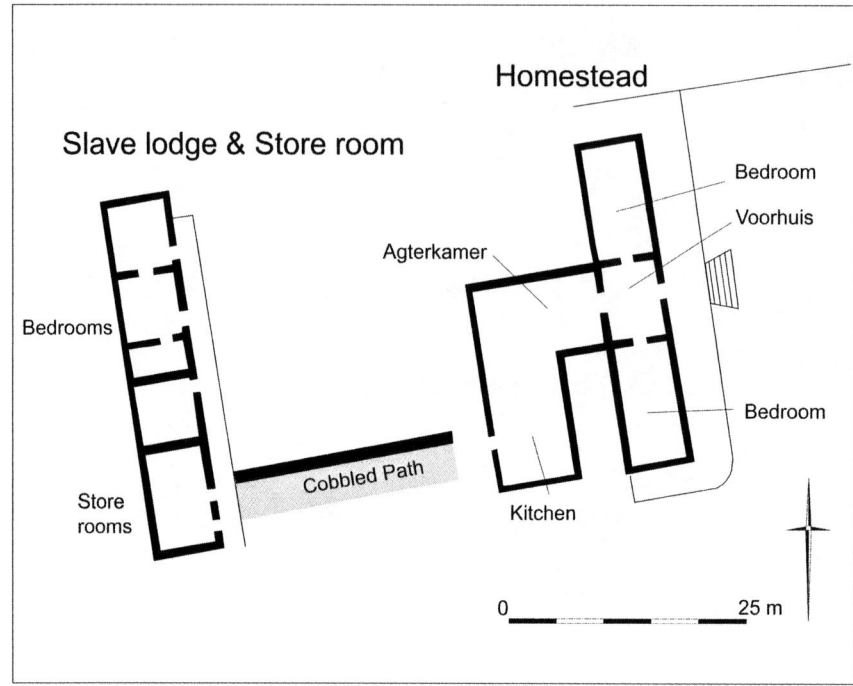

Figure 3.10. Goede Hoop Homestead in the 19th century.

more common choice, as there are many examples of such farms today where an older, rectangular building exists alongside a later T-shape house (e.g. Hall et al. 1988; Diener 1993). This certainly seems to have happened at Goede Hoop, at least in part, as discussed above. It is time now though, to discuss the latest major changes to Goede Hoop as they appear today, and which date to the early 19th century.

The *werf* of Goede Hoop lies at the northwest corner of the freehold plot, its vineyards stretching southeast down to the river. Just outside the main *werf* lies the graveyard for the farm, and next to it, a more recent structure erected probably at the very end of the 19th century. The current layout of the *werf* has a (modified) T-shaped homestead facing out over a sweeping front lawn, and bounded by a thick stone wall enclosure, defining three sides of the *werf*. The interior layout of the homestead exhibits the classical features of Cape Dutch architecture: a central *voorhuis* with rooms either side, with *agterkamer* (back room) and kitchen behind (Figure 3.10). The front façade displays the usual symmetry of windows and central gable over the front door.

Symmetrical with this front entrance is the gateway through the *werf* wall, from which runs a track down to the main road through the valley. The northern enclosure wall as it is today may have originally been further out, based on test pit excavation, and if so, would place the homestead and gateway more centrally (see Figure 3.5). Behind the homestead lies the annexe, which in local memory, has been called the slave lodge. Certainly in the early 20th century it was used as the servants quarters as well as storage space and referred to as the 'coloureds cottage' (Dressler, pers. comm.). I will discuss the slaves more in the next chapter, but it needs to be said that separate slave quarters were not common on farms at the Cape, as most lived in the main house or in outbuildings; however, some of the wealthier farms with large numbers of slaves did provide separate accommodation, especially in the early 19th century, such as Boschendal, and it is not unlikely the annexe was used as a slave lodge after the homestead was rebuilt.

Adjacent and south of the homestead is the wine cellar, and south of that, a small house generally presumed to have been a mill house. Census returns from the 1840s mention a watermill on the farm and it is likely this is that building, thus making it more or less contemporary with the construction of the new homestead and cellars. The only other buildings on the *werf* are the stables and its associated courtyard to the east; these are interesting because they lie on a very different alignment to the main structures and are potentially older than the rebuilt homestead, cellars and millhouse. In fact they share a very similar alignment to the buried structures discussed above. An examination of the architectural fabric of the stables and courtyard revealed that they have a complex history or repairs and additions and may even have stood as a ruin for a period. In all likelihood, this (with possibly the annexe) may be the oldest standing part of the farm, and dating to the mid-later 18th century. It may have served as an agricultural outbuilding, being sited away from the main homestead, and probably also where some of the slaves may have resided, until the annexe was used in the early 19th century.

From the archaeological and architectural investigations, it seems clear that the early 19th century re-modelling of the *werf* at Goede Hoop was the final, realized articulation of the Cape Dutch style. While incorporating elements of the old farmstead—chiefly the rear structure as a probable slave quarters and the distant courtyard building as stables— it nevertheless built many new elements such as the homestead, cellars and millhouse, as well as the enclosing wall. It was these new elements that transformed the *werf* into an ordered, symmetrical space reflecting the ideology of an established, landed gentry. The same process occurred

Table 3.7. Dates of gabled houses in the Dwars
valley. (*Source*: Fransen & Cook 1980)

Farm	Date on gable
Bellingham	—
Zevenrivieren	1790
Rhone	1795
L'Ormarins	1811
Boschendal	1812*
Goede Hoop	1821
Zandvliet (Delta)	1831
Lekkerwijn	1834
Bethlehem	1840
Meerlust	1849
Zorgvliet	1860

* Family history claimed a sketch once existed depicting an
earlier house with a gable dated to 1746

on farms throughout the valley and neighbouring areas, at differing
times, but certainly most of the present structures standing today only
date to the early 19th century (Table 3.7), though some may have had
earlier versions of the standing buildings, such as Boschendal (Fagan &
Fagan nd). The question of why these changes occurred still needs to
be addressed, and for this we need to look at the larger context—but
before this, it is important to see these changes against the impact of
Britain on the Cape colony in general and Goede Hoop in particular.

British Culture and Goede Hoop in the 19th century

It is an irony that the final remodeling of the Goede Hoop werf and
its buildings in the style of Cape Dutch, took place *after* the Cape colony
became a permanent acquisition of the British Empire—although we
have already suggested that this was in fact the second Cape Dutch style
homestead on the site. However, as Ross suggests of the late flowering
of the Cape Dutch style, it may have been a reinforced expression of
burgher identity against English ethnic affiliation (Ross 1999b: 80). In
1795, the Cape colony had been annexed by Britain; at this time, the
Netherlands was gripped by the same political ideology as the French
revolutionaries and was known as the Batavian Republic. As an ally of
the new French Republic in its war against Britain, its colonies became
fair game for Britain, who felt legitimated to take them over to secure
its Empire in India and the east. When Britain and France made peace
in 1803, the colony reverted back to the Dutch—but not for long, for as

Napoleon rose to power in France, so the return of war forced the British to re-annexe the Cape in 1806. The period between 1795 and 1806 is known as transitional because of this pendulum of power change, but thereafter, the colony remained part of the British Empire until 1961, although it achieved effective autonomy in 1910 (Freund 1989). The 19th century was thus the century of British imperial control of the colony, and, albeit gradually, it stamped its own shape on life there. At first, many of the lower ranking officials in the government remained the same as under the VOC and Batavian governments, but after 1820, the British presence was more and more significant—not only in the administration but also in the population, especially with the influx of new settlers bound for the eastern Cape (Peires 1989; Scott & Deetz 1990; Winer 2001; Winer & Deetz 1990). These new settlers created the impetus for major administrative changes to the Cape in the mid 1820s, including the creation of an independent judiciary, a reformed civil service and the promotion of free trade. This effected a complete reversal of many key VOC policies, such as its monopoly on trade as well as preventing misuse of power by government officials for personal gain (Peires 1989: 495).

In the western Cape however, especially in the winelands, the effect of the change in government was primarily economic, at least to begin with. The reduction of duties on Cape wines entering Britain in 1813 resulted in an explosion of wine production, boosting the local economies of places like the Dwars Valley. By the early 1820s, Cape wine formed *c.* 10% of all wine consumed in Britain (Freund 1989: 331), and although there were lean years and changes to tariffs, the early 19th century witnessed ever increasing production for the export market. It was in this context that Pieter Hendrik de Villiers probably decided to re-build his homestead, including the construction of a wine cellar—previously, the wine had probably been stored in the slave lodge or annexe behind the homestead. It is more difficult however to know how much British fashions affected Goede Hoop—this was probably much more subtle and gradual. British visitors and immigrants certainly brought certain fashions with them, especially in architecture and interior furnishings. Double storeys, the narrowing of the entrance room into a passage and the use of corridors linking rooms were key differences to the Cape Dutch style (Lewcock 1963), while Georgian style furniture—lighter than the heavy Cape Dutch vernacular, was widely perceived as influencing interiors in Cape Town by English writers such as Lady Anne Barnard and Samuel Hudson (McKenzie 1993: 44–48).

How much new English fashions in the city of Cape Town were adopted in the countryside is difficult to gauge at present—even within

Table 3.8. Ceramic assemblages in Cape Town. (*Source*: Malan & Klose 2003 and Hall et al. 1990)

Sea Street (c. 1790–1830) N=Phase	1		2		3		4	
	MNV	%	MNV	%	MNV	%	MNV	%
Oriental porcelain	12	85.71	446	53.03	93	23.43	35	23.49
European porcelain	0	0.00	0	0.00	0	0.00	2	1.34
Oriental stoneware	0	0.00	10	1.19	3	0.76	0	0.00
European stoneware	0	0.00	36	4.28	16	4.03	5	3.36
Tin-glazed earthenware	0	0.00	10	1.19	0	0.00	0	0.00
Coarse lead-glazed earthenware	1	7.14	90	10.70	29	7.30	5	3.36
Refined Industrial earthenwares & stonewares	0	0.00	247	29.37	253	63.73	98	65.77
Total	*14*	*100*	*841*	*100*	*397*	*100*	*149*	*100*

Barrack Street (c. 1790–1900) N=Phase	4 (c. 1790–1840)		3 (c. 1840–1890)		2 (c. 1890–1900)		1 (1900+)	
	MNV	%	MNV	%	MNV	%	MNV	%
Oriental porcelain	27	64.29	13	9.77	0	0.00	6	8.33
European porcelain	0	0.00	3	2.26	4	9.30	3	4.17
Oriental stoneware	0	0.00	0	0.00	0	0.00	0	0.00
European stoneware	5	11.90	12	9.02	4	9.30	10	13.89
Tin-glazed earthenware	2	4.76	2	1.50	0	0.00	0	0.00
Coarse lead-glazed earthenware	0	0.00	0	0.00	0	0.00	0	0.00
Refined Industrial earthenwares & stonewares	8	19.05	103	77.44	35	81.40	53	73.61
Total	*42*	*100*	*133*	*100*	*43*	*100*	*72*	*100*

Cape Town, it was not necessarily a revolution transforming all households, but evidence from other aspects of material culture can help examine this process. At two sites in Cape Town with closed, stratified assemblages—Sea Street and Barrack Street, there is some evidence for a relatively slow transformation from Cape to English preferences in ceramics, most notably the reduction of Chinese porcelain in favour of Staffordshire industrial refined earthenwares and stonewares (Table 3.8). These industrial ceramics were already dominating domestic production in England by the late 18th century, although how widespread its consumption was is difficult to assess given the lack of archaeological research in this period in Britain. Even so, the Cape does appear to be slow in its uptake of industrial ceramics. This change seems to have occurred gradually over the early 19th century, with English industrial ceramics only dominating the assemblages from about 1830/1840 onwards (Klose and Malan 2000; Malan and Klose 2003). The ceramic signature at the Cape in the 19th century in relation to broader issues of consumption have been addressed in detail by Antonia Malan and Jane Klose in two recent papers where they highlight this delayed shift—however, given the slow changes occurring in other aspects of British influence at the Cape—from administration to legislation, this is perhaps not surprising (ibid.). They also relate the pattern at the Cape with a broader imperial pattern which is seen in other British colonies such as Australia and Canada, following Susan Lawrence's suggestion where there was a strong preference for bright, colourful wares (Lawrence 2003a; Malan & Klose 2000: 57;). Typical of colonial exports were hand painted wares in bright colours were a distinctive type among Cape, called *boerenbont* ('farmers gaudy'), and a similar term is often applied to these vessels in England, 'peasant ware'. Similarly, certain forms seemed to be fairly common, especially bowls (*kommetjes*) in bright painted or slipped colours, which may be a more specifically Cape phenomenon given their similarity to Chinese porcelain bowls. Indeed, other specific continuities might be inferred for the Cape, such as the popularity of blue willow transfer designs whose appearance was similar to Chinese porcelain—though their popularity was widespread, not just in the Cape.

The 19th century assemblage from Goede Hoop conforms to this pattern; although substantial stratified assemblages were not recovered, the material is unequivocally dominated by 18th century oriental porcelains on the one hand and 19th century refined industrial wares on the other (Table 3.9). Most of the material from Goede Hoop was

Table 3.9. Summary of ceramics from Goede Hoop *werf*. c.1740–1940. (*Source*: Author's data)

	MNV	%
Oriental porcelain	71	35.5
European porcelain	9	4.5
European stoneware	1	0.5
Tin-glazed earthenware	3	1.5
Coarse lead-glazed earthenware	3	1.5
Refined Industrial earthenwares & stonewares	113	56.5
Total	*200*	*100*

surface spreads and without stratified material it is difficult to track the change, but on the whole, the refined industrial earthenwares mostly date to the mid 19th century and after; there are very few if any early 19th century wares such shell-edge plates, creamwares or early transfer wares. It suggests the consumption pattern at Goede Hoop was following the Cape trend, and most likely its owners continued to use oriental porcelains until the mid 19th century. This certainly seems to fit with the architectural changes evident on the werf, when the farm is re-built in the Cape Dutch style as late as the 1820s and 1830s. Indeed, the material assemblages are not the only aspect that reflects changes to Goede Hoop; sometime in the mid-late 19th century, two new houses were built on the farm, one large house close to the main werf and another small cottage up behind the farm, next to some of the 18th century ruins of the silver mine complex. The large house may have been the residence of a partner of the owner of Goede Hoop in the mid 19th century, Paul Retief who must have arrived on the farm c. 1841–1842. With Pieter Izak de Villiers, he donated part of the farm toward the establishment of a mission station for ex-slaves in 1843 (see Chapter 4). The house is clearly influenced by English style in terms of its internal organization, but also mixed with Cape Dutch elements; the house is symmetrical with a central door leading into a wide hall with a room off each side. At the end of the hall is a long corridor running the width of the house from which one gains access to most of the rooms (Figure 3.11). At the

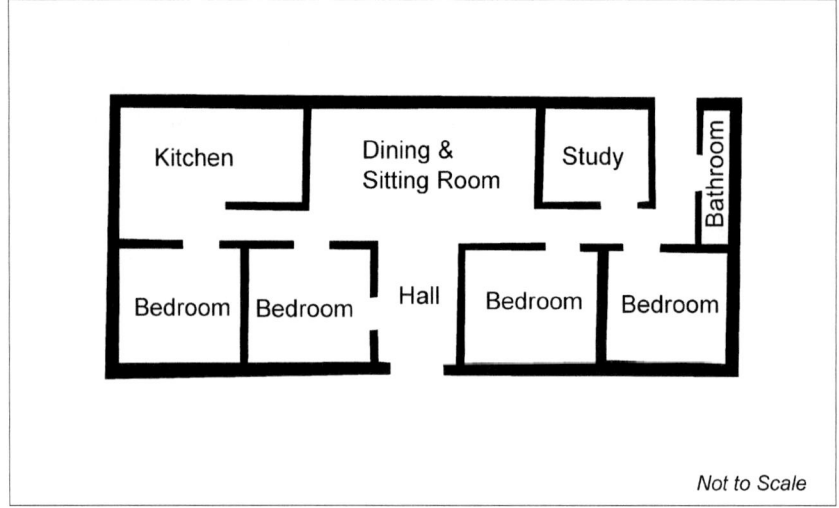

Figure 3.11. Paul Retief's House on Goede Hoop from the mid-19th century.

center back of the house, fed by the hall, however is a wide open room, more reminiscent of Cape Dutch configuration (i.e. *agterkamer*). The room functions are based on mid-20th century use, though they are probably more or less similar to those of the original later 19th century. The house was unoccupied until the late 1960s. Surface collection of ceramics around the house was minimal, indeed according to the last occupants, most rubbish was disposed of in pits dug into an orchard at the back (Dressler, pers. comm.). The few sherds of pottery recovered merely confirmed the 19th century date of the building.

The other 19th century house lies far from the werf and has all the appearance of a retreat; it may have been built for occasional use by the family or members of the family, as it is very small, consisting only of three rooms, though originally it appears to have only had two, one large front room and a smaller back room (Figure 3.12). Indeed, the garden is more impressive than the cottage; fronting the cottage and almost covering the same area is a tiered stoep on three levels, leading

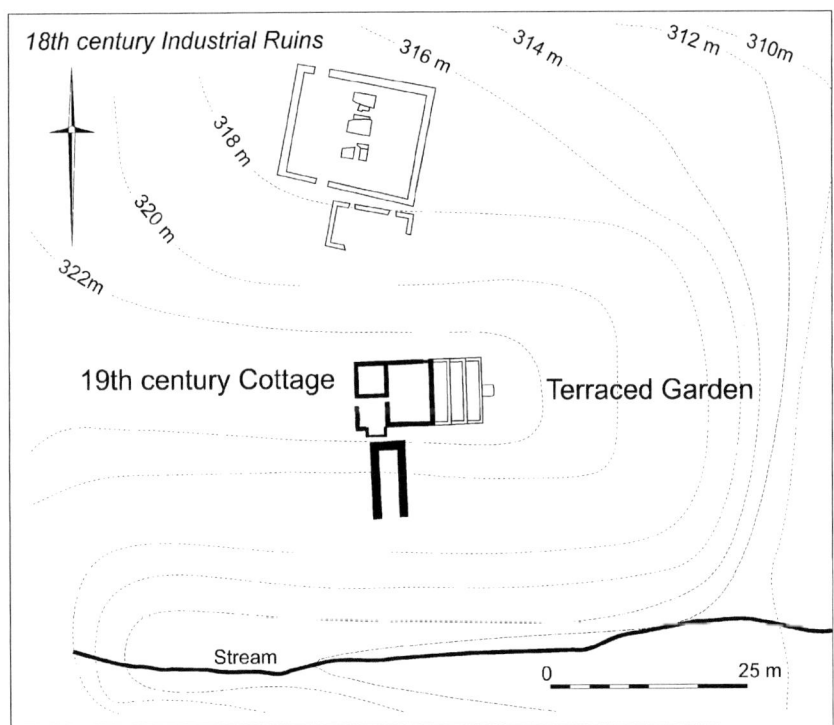

Figure 3.12. The Cottage on Goede Hoop from the mid-19th century.

Table 3.10. Ceramics from the Cottage at Goede
Hoop. (*Source*: Author's data)

	MNV	*%*
Oriental Porcelain		
Transfer-print	2	7.7
undiagnostic	1	3.8
European Porcelain		
Decal	1	3.8
Gilt	1	3.8
undecorated	1	3.8
Industrial Refined Earthenware		
Banded	2	7.7
Moulded	2	7.7
Slipware	3	11.5
Spongeware	1	3.8
Transfer-print	5	19.2
undecorated	4	15.4
undiagnostic	3	11.5
Total	*26*	*100*

down to a sweeping front lawn, which is also terraced on many levels. In
the garden, fig, rose and olive trees have been planted as well as a row of
oaks, on one of which have been carved three hearts with initials inside
and in another, remains of a tree house. Two porcelain dolls heads were
found associated with site further attesting to the presence of children.
The site today is now completely overgrown and wild, but it takes little
imagination to return it to its former state; moreover, the cottage was
clearly sited for its view, lying on a promontory with a vista of the Dwars
Valley. The cottage was probably built in the mid-19th century, largely
from stone robbed from one of the 18th century ruins and was in use up
to the early 20th century. During this time, it had at least two phases of
modification to the back, including the addition of another room with an
oven, and it was finally abandoned in the 1920s or 1930s. Excavation of
associated midden dumps from the house produced a small assemblage,
consistent with infrequent use (Table 3.10).

In short, the cultural effects of the Cape falling under British hands
was very much a delayed reaction, probably through both British Imperial design as well as local resistance. When the influence of Britain
was felt on a wide basis from the mid-19th century on, it clearly affected
material culture, such as architecture and goods, although this was by
no means a revolution. The Cape Dutch homesteads remained as they
were, and even when British ceramics replaced oriental porcelain, there

was some continuity in the selection of forms and decoration, even if many if the ceramics were very different. While the British were initially derogatory of the Dutch settlers or *boers*, this was largely linked to their own spirit of nationalism (Ross 1999b: 42–3). On the whole, there was little reason to accentuate any cultural or ethnic differences among the free population, since it served both sides, politically, to maintain common interests. The changes were more gradual and ideological, coming after the 1840s as new concepts of respectability and gentility—imported from England—slowly took hold at the Cape (Ross 1999b). Moreover, these concepts, though inflected along ethnic lines, applied more to the emerging class and racial distinctions of the later 19th century—between former master and slave—than between Dutch and English. This is a theme I take up in the next chapter. The issue I want to pursue here, really concerns the nature of consumption however, and how it helped to articulate burgher's identities in the rural western Cape—not so much as Dutch or British, but simply as burghers or citizens, distinct from the colonial authorities, whether they were the VOC or the British.

CONSUMPTION, MATERIAL CULTURE AND SOCIAL DIFFERENTIATION AT THE CAPE IN THE 18 TH AND 19 TH CENTURIES

Brink sees the emergence of the Cape Dutch architectural style as a gentrification of the vernacular on the part of the burgher community, asserting a distinct identity against that of the VOC (Brink 1992; 2001). Certainly tensions between the burghers and the VOC were quick to rise and they exploded in a major scandal in 1705–6, which ultimately resulted in the dismissal of the Governor at the Cape. The first two governors of the colony, Simon van der Stel and his son who succeeded him in 1699, Willem Adriaan, both built up large estates—Simon at Constantia, Willem Adriaan at Vergelegen. Constantia, as I have already mentioned was famous for its wines, but Vergelegen was impressive for other reasons: its grand architecture, which came to symbolize the excesses of VOC abuse of position (Markell 1993). Willem Adriaan van der Stel's estate at Vergelegen is unusual at the Cape because of its symmetrical layout—contemporary farms did not look anything like Vergelegen and it must have clearly made a vocal statement to the burghers (Figure 3.13). It was perhaps the only attempt to transplant European estate architecture to the Cape—the only other comparable

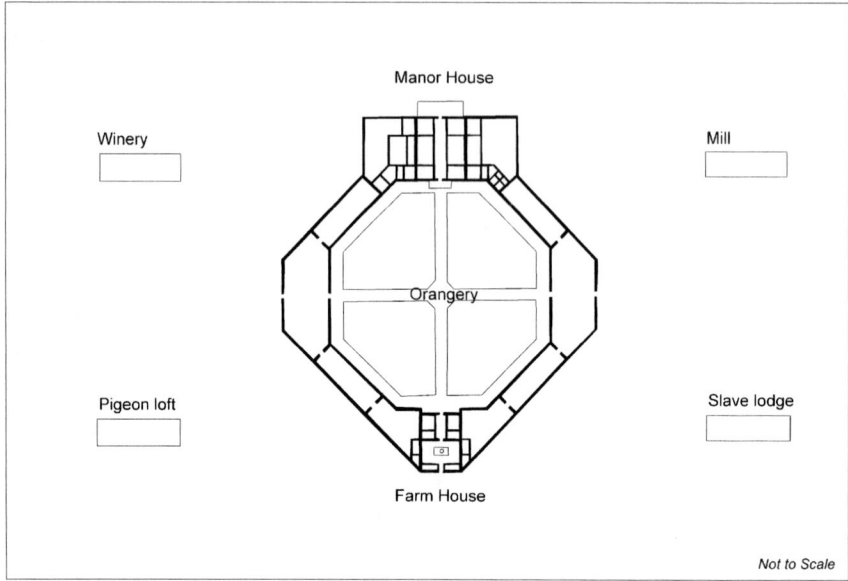

Figure 3.13. Vergelegen Estate. (*Source*: Adapted from a plan in the possession of Anglo-American)

model of power was the Castle at Cape Town, which was clearly an official VOC building, unlike Vergelegen. Indeed, the octagonal enclosure around the homestead even recalled the castle's fortifications (Markell 1993: 80). It was also exceptional at the time in providing a separate slave lodge, again a feature rarely if ever found on burgher farms in the 18th century but a major part of the VOC building stock.

Complaints originally arose about Willem Adriaan van der Stel and other company officials abusing their position to gain an unfair advantage in the market for their produce; legally the VOC had the monopoly rights on almost all trade in the colony, but also legally, VOC servants were not supposed to be engaged in this trade in a private capacity. As we saw in Chapter 2, this latter law was routinely abused, but equally, the VOC did not always enforce its monopoly rights and unofficial trading went on (Ross 1989: 245–6). Nevertheless, in 1705 however, a group of burghers signed a petition officially outlining their grievances against the Governor, which they sent to Batavia and the Board of Directors in the Netherlands (Schutte 1989: 303–7). In response, Van der Stel imprisoned the ringleaders and tried to prevent the petition from being sent; he failed and so acquired signatures to a counter-petition. Interestingly, among the signatories of both sides were Huguenots, more or less in equal proportions (Coertzen 1988: 96). When the Board considered the petitions of the two factions, they decided in favour of the burghers: Van der Stel was discharged and recalled back home. Why they did this is uncertain but it may have had as much to do with politics among the Board as fear of insurrection at the Cape. In any case, though the Governor was gone and his property sold, no legislation was passed to improve the burghers situation and the same system remained in place.

Ironically, the symbolism of power captured in architecture, such as at Vergelegen, was something the elite burghers themselves were to exploit when they wished to express their differential status. Although the style of Cape Dutch houses was very different to the highly formal geometry of Vergelegen, it ultimately tapped into the same European tradition. The adoption of certain neo-classical elements current in European refined architecture such as symmetrical facades, gables and increasing room differentiation were meant to signify the 'cultured' nature of this new rural elite; much the same process can be seen in Europe and the Anglo-American world where 'Georgianization' might be considered the equivalent (Brink 1992: 166–7; Leone 1988; Lucas & Regan 2003). Inside, the increasing use of certain rooms for public entertainment such as the *voorhuis* and dining room (*gaanderij*) and the display of objects such as porcelain in cabinets, mirrors and clocks accentuated this new style (Brink 1992: 173; Malan 1997: 281). In particular, the gable seemed to be a favoured symbol, perhaps because it was so easily translated into other materials, from the tops of cabinets to gravestones. Perhaps also, as Hall suggests, it symbolized the basis of wealth and its gendered tensions, between the male façade of inheritance and power and the female role in reproduction and the fertility of the family (Hall 1995; 1997). Hall has mapped the distribution of 18th century gabled homesteads with known ownership histories, and they clearly cluster in the Stellenbosch and Drakenstein districts—the Cape winelands. As he says, following Ross, they are related to successful agricultural production and an emerging landed gentry whose wealth was based on farming through a slave labour force (Ross 1983a). Moreover, all his examples ultimately distil to an elite group of just eight families of whom the de Villiers were among the most prominent (Hall 2000: 109–110).

It is fair to say that this new tradition was thus firmly related to the development of increasing social differentiation in the Cape colony within the burgher population, and it is perhaps no coincidence that this process occurred in the heart of the close-knit, Huguenot immigrant population. Such conspicuous differentiation of course needed an audience. Brink has highlighted the importance of hospitality in relation to Cape Dutch architectural innovations, suggesting that the role of the *voorhuis* as a reception area played into the increasing importance of receiving guests in the home. Indeed, the whole nature of display on these new Cape Dutch farms, was closely linked to the fact that it was meant for visitors, and Brink suggest the layout of the *werf* and the main homestead was such as to carefully control or stage the whole nature of visitation through successive points—the *werf* wall gates, the stoep, the front door capped by its gable, and finally the *voorhuis* (Brink 2001: 16). The role of material culture in relation to such differentiation was perhaps a fundamental part of Dutch culture in the 17th and 18th centuries. This can be related to the various 'Sumptuary Laws'—legislation that aimed to uphold status distinction by ensuring visible wealth did not exceed social position—which were issued by the VOC in the 18th century (Ross 1999b). Such laws were common in Europe at this time, and the VOC applied them with equal vigour in its colonies. More fundamentally however, such laws can be seen to express a profound ambiguity about conspicuous wealth, which was being ever expanded through the very processes, which organizations like the VOC were facilitating. Wealth was both a benefit and a bane, it could serve to improve life yet also corrupt it; such ambivalence toward material wealth, an 'embarrassment of riches' has been said to characterize Dutch culture at this time to an extreme degree (Schama 1991). Certainly it has been pointed out that Dutch society—and Dutch colonial society—was very different for example to that in England in the 18th century, not least in that social mobility was much more possible (Ross 1999b: 15). It was not until the late 18th and early 19th century however when the nature of consumption changed radically to make such laws—and embarrassment, superfluous (McKendrick et al. 1982; McCracken 1990).

In many ways however, it is in places like the Cape colony where various factors converged to enable this transformation to be performed in advance of Europe. One was its easy access to goods and services, which in northern Europe, were still very expensive and the preserve of only the elite—such as domestic servants and porcelain. Porcelain, as discussed in the last chapter, was widely used as both a kitchen and table ware at the Cape, but it was suggested that the VOC might have wanted to restrict its access and this may have even been the reason for setting up a pottery to produce European earthenwares (Jordan 2000). Another indication of its value is that much of it was usually kept in the more public rooms of the new Cape Dutch houses, and in special cabinets and over the 18th century, porcelain seems to have replaced pewter as display items in these spaces (Malan 1999: 56). As both inventories and archaeological assemblages attest, porcelain remained the dominant ceramic ware in 18th century households, typically comprising 60–70% of all pottery, although in one mid-18th century urban assemblage (Bree Street) it comprised nearly 90% (Malan 1997: 293). Another similar but rural site is Elsenberg, where porcelain was present in similar high proportions and included rare types not commonly seen at the Cape such as *famille rose*, an expensive porcelain more commonly exported to Europe (Halkett 1993). This site is interesting also because it was the residence of one of the richest members of Cape society in the mid-18th century—Martin Melck. He came to the Cape as a Company servant, but swiftly became a free burgher, even working for a period at the silver mine in Drakenstein (see Chapter 2). When his employee Johan Philipp Giebeler died, he married his widow thus instantly acquiring property and status. In 1761, Melck rebuilt Elsenberg in the classic Cape Dutch style, and through both architecture and material goods such as porcelain, he epitomized the new patterns of consumption at the Cape (Hall 2000: 89–90).

As well as porcelain, slaves too can be seen as an important factor in articulating new patterns of consumption. As well as used in agriculture, slaves—especially females—acted as servants in the homestead or townhouse. Their use for carrying out all or most of the domestic tasks of running the house would have freed up the time of their female owners for engaging in other pursuits such as social visiting or entertaining as well as business (McKenzie 1993: 78; Malan 1997: 287). In Europe, domestic servants were the preserve of the elite, and only gradually did they become more common in the late 18th and early 19th centuries with the emergence of an expanding middle class. At the Cape, particularly in the urban context of Cape Town in the late 18th and early 19th centuries, slaves may have increasingly be perceived in status terms through their role as domestic servants (Bradlow 1987; McKenzie 1997); Kirsten McKenzie, whose important study of the slave-owner Samuel Hudson I will discuss further in the next chapter, highlights the implied role of slaves for social display as much as labour in his writings, supporting the idea that, like porcelain, slaves were increasingly exploited as symbols of status (McKenzie 1993: 65–66). Perhaps something of how this process developed at the Cape may be gained by examining the gender ratios of slaves in households. Although one needs to recognize that both male and female slaves were often used for similar work, especially manual labour by the VOC, on burgher farms and households, females were preferred as domestic servants and in fact most female slaves on farms were used in this way (Shell 1994: 291, 328). Male slaves were generally more common in burgher

Table 3.11. Ratio of male
to female slaves at Goede
Hoop. (*Source*: census data)

Year	Male	Female
1732	2	0
1736	7	1
1773	5	1
18th c. mean	*5*	*1*
1809	9	2
1811	6	6
1812	7	3
1814	6	1
19th c. mean	*7*	*3*

households than females—typically up to seven males to one female in
the early 18th century (see Chapter 4). However over the 18th century
this ratio decreased, and especially after the mid-18th century it began
to equalize. Some of this pattern may be demographic, reflecting the
increase in Cape-born slaves, where gender ratios cannot be so easily
controlled compared to imported slaves, but even so, the *meaning* of
more female slaves is what is important, not the immediate cause. The
rise in females may be seen as reflecting a rise in the demand or need
for domestic servants.

The Van Sitterts whose inventories Antonia Malan has studied,
had a high ratio of female to male slaves—in the 1750s, between eight
and seven males to five and four females (Malan 1997: 284), which suggests that domestic servants were a prominent part of the household.
At Goede Hoop in the 1770s, there were five males to one female and
this was a much more normal ratio. However, even at Goede Hoop, the
ratio changed over time and would seem to correspond with the architectural changes which occurred in the early 19th century (see above);
combining limited census and inventory data, the later 18th century
average was five males to one female, while in the early 19th century, it
was seven to three (see above; Table 3.11). Using gender ratios as a mea-
sure of the importance of slaves as domestic servants is an interesting
possibility; however, it does need to be qualified, for at the same time
as the gender ratios were equalizing—from the late 18th century—so
were the traditional divisions of female slaves as domestic servants and
male slaves as labourers. From this time, male slaves were increasingly
also being used as domestic servants, especially in Cape Town, dressed

in livery (Shell 1994: 161–4). Similarly, female slaves were increasingly being used in agricultural work, especially in the wine boom years in the early 19th century.

The role of women in this transformation was quite pivotal; I have already discussed their role in maintaining property within the family through the law of partible inheritance and how Martin Hall has used this to engender Cape Dutch architecture. Antonia Malan has also raised their importance in the context in which consumption was largely carried out, especially in towns where the distinction between retail and domestic contexts were usually blurred (Malan 1997: 295). Social visiting often combined with shopping, and in a place where there were no shops, much of this was conducted at home and by the women of a household. The lack of shops was due to the VOC monopoly on trade and that private trade was illegal—though of course it occurred, but by default, took place in contexts such as the home. The relation between business and domestic affaires was often intermixed in Europe during the 18th and early 19th centuries (Davidoff & Hall 2002), however by the late 18th century, shops were a far more common context for retail purchase in Europe unlike the Cape, and the perpetuation of domestic contexts for retail at the Cape may have had quite unique consequences. The subject of consumption in the colonies in relation to the metropole is much larger than I can enter into here, but issues such as slave labour in the domestic context and easier access to luxury goods such as porcelain, may have played a major role in fostering a consumer revolution. A key part of this was the women's role in the household, whether as slave or mistress. Otto Mentzel gives clues to this, in describing a major change in burgher women's dress from the 1780s; when he was there in the mid century, he noted the plainness of women's clothes except for special occasions, but he refers to a letter from a friend many years later which states that the 'French fashion' was now in vogue (Mentzel 1925: 110–112). It suggests not only that the consumer revolution was at the Cape, but that women were in the vanguard of articulating this (also see Ross 1999b: 15). Indeed, reading Mentzel's descriptions, partial though they inevitably are, one gets a very strong sense that women are much more closely linked with domestic material culture, controlling its consumption and the etiquette surrounding social life in general. However one looks at it, consumption of material culture entered a new phase in the later 18th century at the Cape, and one which was by no means lagging behind the same revolution in Europe. It was merely expressed differently.

The rise of social differentiation in Cape burgher society was thus a multi-faceted phenomenon. It depended on the growth of large agricultural estates producing wheat and/or wine during the first half of the 18th century, particularly in the Stellenbosch and Drakenstein districts, but also to some extent in Table Valley (Ross 1983a). Such growth was closely linked into family alliances and dynasties, which retained properties and wealth within a small group of elite families. The status accruing from this wealth was increasingly articulated through specialised consumption of material culture, from architecture to porcelain, and in which women played a key role. Even by the mid 18th century, Mentzel whom we have mentioned several times already, perceived a social stratification at the Cape into four classes: wealthy town-dwellers who owned country estates which were run by overseers (*knechts*); wealthy rural farmers who lived on their estate; poorer but still independent farmers; and at the bottom, stock farmers (Mentzel 1925: 98–110). Mentzel even described the livelihood of these different classes, their average day, their property, possessions and consumption patterns. Of course one needs to read his generalisations with some caution and realize they are not always based on first-hand experience—certainly Mentzel mixed mostly with the first and perhaps second groups. However, as a general comment on the emerging social differentiation among the burgher community, they do reinforce the evidence from documents, architecture and archaeology. Such differentiation, as I have alluded to throughout this chapter, was however ultimately based on one vital element of Cape society: that more than half the population were forced to provide the labour for maintaining this lifestyle of these burghers. People who were taken from their homelands by violence or born into servitude. It was slaves who tilled the fields, slaves who built their grand estates, slaves who cooked their food, washed their clothes. Whenever one admires the beauty of Cape Dutch Architecture, one should not forget whose freedom was sacrificed in making it possible. For all Mentzel's comments on Cape burgher society, all he could say about these enslaved people were that they were "sulky, savage and disagreeable" (Mentzel 1925: 129).

The changes that happened in the later 18th century were only consolidated and entrenched in the 19th century. A key part of this involved an increasing separation of male and female spheres of action, specifically the increasing domestication of women and their association with the home, and the increasing exclusivity of men with public life and work (Davidoff & Hall 2002; McKenzie 1997; Ross 1999b). I will discuss this more in the next chapter, but the gender ideology of 'separate spheres', and the particular association between women and domesticity which was in place by the mid 19th century, remained a dominant theme well into the twentieth century of course until its contestation by the feminist movement. An English middle class woman writer living in the Dwars valley in the 1920s clearly retained the notion of 'separate spheres', but was also aware of the growing movement against it, as many of her peers were going out to work:

> The whole mistake in this modern attitude lies in the assumption that the work women are doing outside their homes is of supreme importance. (I am not referring, let it be understood, to the single or unmarried woman who is compelled to earn a living, or to the voluntary, unpaid work that so many good women do in their spare hours.) Is it really important, for instance, or of service to the world in any sense, to run a big dressmaking or millinery establishment which merely encourages women to buy unnecessary and expensive hats and frocks? To me it is deplorable to find in one such place as London a beautiful girl, whose brother was at Eton, serving as a mannequin. I cannot believe that if her brother was at Eton there was not any economic necessity for her position, and, if not, why was she not making better use of her time, apart from the unhygienic environment, than spending her youth and beauty in the close atmosphere of an artificially heated room when she might perhaps have been racing over the moors with a band of happy children? (Alston 1929: 27).

I have quoted this at length because it sums up the whole web of key concepts in the ideology of gender at the time, and so succinctly: women, work, consumption, class, maternity and hygiene. Although Madeline Alston was only a short term visitor to the Dwars valley, her attitude was one which was undoubtedly shared by many of the white, middle/upper classes of Cape society. The association between women and the household is effortlessly inflected by class and race in her writing, indeed, she goes on to highlight the importance of domestic servants to women in the colonies, especially those in Africa:

> I have no hesitation on saying that South Africa, and perhaps Kenya, Nyassaland and Uganda, are the only parts of the overseas Empire where women do not grow old before their time with over work. Why? The answer is that, although they have enough domestic work to keep them occupied and healthy, the native servants are the saving of them. The shoulders of women in South Africa do not grow bent from stooping over a wash-tub, nor from going down on the knees to scrub floors. Their skins do not dry up from standing over a hot fire. Their feet do not ache from standing over the week's ironing—most exhausting of operations. Therefore, if they choose, they have time to read, time to be sociable time to attend the training of their children, and to cultivate their gardens. A woman is not driven to burying all her talents among the pots and pans. Many take an active interest in politics, in social questions, and in education. They ride, play tennis, badminton, or golf. They perhaps paint or write. In a word, they have time to enjoy the beautiful things in life, including their children. Herein lies the difference between farm-life in South Africa and in Canada or Australia. (Alston 1929: 34–5).

Notice how 'natives servants' are not even classed as 'South African women', perhaps one of the most cruel ironies in colonial ideology; and if ever there was an example demonstrating the complexities of gender, race and class, this is it. That Alston can empathize with the labour involved in domestic work, can appreciate its effort, and yet only consider how her class and race are saved from it, and not how her 'coloured servants' were enslaved to it, is a salutary reminder of how strong such ideologies can be. Even though it is clear that Alston writes as an arch-supporter of British imperialism, her views were probably not that extreme. The separation of spheres was thus closely linked with the changes which happened in the late 18th century relating to issues of consumption, especially the significance of domestic servants, for female identities, both of slave and owner, were highly entwined in this mistress-servant relationship. However, a new key component of this relationship which emerged in the later 19th century was (female) leisure, which helped to sustain the separation of spheres. The 'retreat' at Goede Hoop built in the late 19th century with its panoramic view and garden appears to be one articulation of this new element, and though it may not have been a female space, it does seem to be a place of leisure. Significantly, it was also associated with children's material culture—two porcelain doll's heads were found and the remains of a tree house lie in one of the large oaks in front of the cottage. If consumption through Cape Dutch homesteads, domestic servants and display of fine porcelains became a means of articulating new burgher identities in the mid 18th century, from the mid 19th century, these identities were being re-shaped further, especially around the axis of gender and the pursuit of leisure. Such consumption patterns, in both the 18th and 19th centuries were only possible because of the labour force which built and cleaned the houses of these burghers as well as worked their fields to produce the wine and wheat on which their wealth depended. In the next chapter, I explore the lives of these labourers, and how they attempted to create their own identities, especially in the wake of emancipation.

Farm Lives | 4

From Slavery to Apartheid

The slaves in the Cape colony had very little opportunity to inscribe their voice into the historical archive; they did not leave letters, diaries or journals, they did not have inventories taken of their possessions, they did not officially own property—because they *were* property. This is how they largely appear in official documents—listed alongside property or goods in census returns, inventories and other archives, usually close to the top of the list. The order in which property is typically listed in these documents reflects the Enlightenment hierarchy or 'chain of being', from wives, to children to slaves to livestock to cereals/vines to objects. The only one missing from this hierarchy is of course, the (usually) European male owner. The slaves' position within a hierarchy of being is articulated further in more narrative texts, such as Mentzel's quoted in the last chapter, and I discuss these further below, However, there are rare instances where the slaves own voice is inscribed— namely in court cases, usually where they are being tried for some crime. Leaving aside the issue that, technically even here it is not the slave who writes the words, such testimonials only give us the voice of the slave in a highly contrived and abnormal situation. Usually it is the slave who is on trial, and the context in which they are placed means their words and language will be highly influenced by this context. Nevertheless, such testimonials are still an important resource in slave histories and provide a rare opportunity to hear a slave speak.

In this chapter, the slave history for the study area of the Dwars valley is examined through a variety of sources, from official administrative documents to oral history, from architecture to artifacts. Slave identity is, by definition, heavily inscribed by the other—the owner. This inevitably makes the task of understanding the slave's own sense of identity and that which they had of their owners, all the harder— yet it is one in which a study of material culture, more than anything, can help. Moreover, the period immediately after emancipation when a new field for expression opened up, offers a critical insight into how the slaves regarded their former status. Not that emancipation necessarily saw a complete transformation of the condition of these people—indeed, in many cases they did the same work, for the same people and in some cases even lived under more or less the same conditions. Emancipation did not transform Cape society overnight, and while it was an important change, it is important to recognize that the change in legal status did not automatically create a change in social or economic status. Emancipation is a complex issue, which still has implications for labour and social relations in the Cape today. This chapter, as well as being about slaves and their descendants, also takes a broader time span and moves the story further in time, closer to the present day.

SLAVERY AT THE CAPE, 1652–1834

The Atlantic Slave trade between West Africa and the Americas is the more familiar image most people have of slavery, and indeed it did form the major focus of slavery for European colonial powers in the 17th, 18th and 19th centuries, including the Dutch. However, the Indian Ocean trade also was very active in slavery, particularly in Asians but also in East Africans. There were indigenous slave-owning societies in East Africa, India, Sri Lanka and south-east Asia and when the Portuguese and Dutch entered the Asian trade network (see Chapter 2), slaves quickly became part of their trade commodities—but not for export back to Europe, rather for working on colonial stations and plantations within the Indian Ocean Basin (Armstrong & Worden 1989; Lasker 1950; Meillasoux 1991; Miers and Kopytoff 1977; Reid 1983). Thus within months of the post at Table Bay being established, van Riebeeck requested slaves for construction work; although it took some time, the numbers of slaves quickly became a major part of the colony's population with 1658 seeing the first major influx so that they formed half its numbers. This ratio was more or less to remain throughout the history of slavery at the Cape.

Slaves came to the Cape from three sources: specially sponsored slaving voyages primarily to Madagascar and Mozambique, VOC ships sailing to the Cape from the East Indies with Asian slaves, and finally slavers en route to the Americas from East Africa (Armstrong and Worden 1989: 112). The Madagascan trade was the chief source of Company slaves at the Cape and was already a well-established system through Arabian and Portuguese traders (Armstrong 1983). Slaves from India, Sri Lanka and Indonesia formed a smaller proportion, but were generally more highly valued (see below). As in most trade conducted by the VOC, Company individuals exploited the official venture

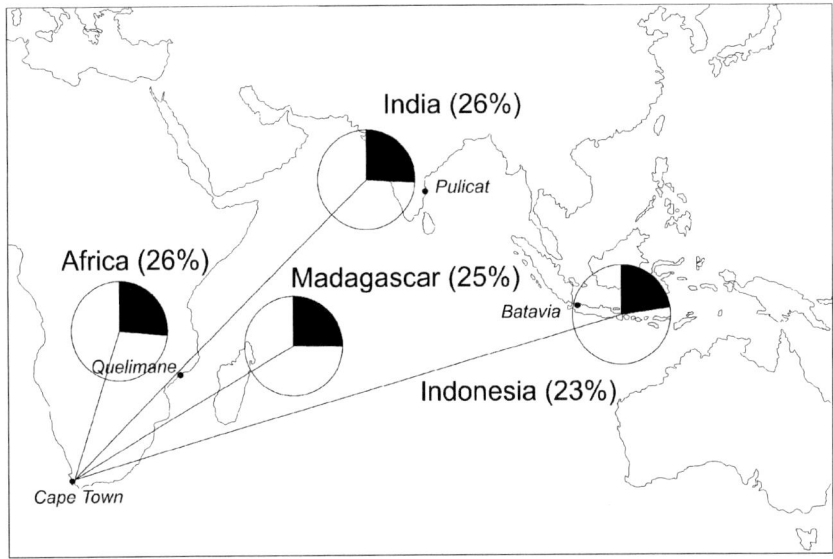

Figure 4.1. Origins of slaves. (*Source*: Adapted from Shell 1994)

for personal gain, and many private slaves also came from these shores. Slaves continued to be imported into the Cape until 1808 when the abolition of the slave trade was enforced by the new British administration, although some small-scale illicit trading probably continued for a while. Calculating accurate figures for slave importation is not easy, but it has been estimated that around 60,000 slaves came to the Cape during the century and half of the Oceanic Slave Trade (Ross 1999a: 23). Of these numbers, it is estimated that 26% came from Africa (chiefly Mozambique), 25% from Madagascar, 26% from India and 23% from Indonesia (Shell 1994: 41; Figure 4.1). However, over time these proportions varied, so that for example Asians were more common in the early 18th century and Africans/Madagascans in the latter part of the century.

Although slaves were continually imported throughout the period 1652–1808, there was a degree of self-reproduction among the slave population, chiefly among the slaves of burghers, which saw a radical increase after the mid-18th century (Shell 1994: 47). Cape-born slaves, called creoles, formed more than 50% of the slave population from the 1760s, and this proportion gradually rose over the later 18th and early 19th century (Figure 4.2). Evaluation of slaves by origin and descent was a very significant development at the Cape and was expressed in a number of ways including racial stereotypes, division

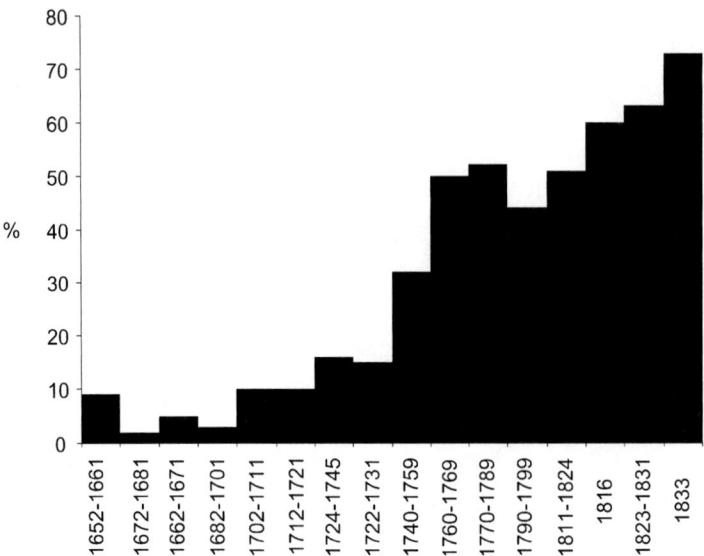

Figure 4.2. Increase in Creoles. (*Source*: Adapted from Shell 1994)

of labour and price. Because of being born locally and into the system, creoles were considered to be the most assimilated and therefore useful, fetching the highest prices—especially those born from mixed European with African or Asian descent. Indonesians and Indians were next in this hierarchy, prized for their skill as artisans, while Africans and Madagascans were seen as fit for little else but unskilled, manual labour (Shell 1994: 49–58). This mixture of slave origins and descent was both useful and obstructive to the slave owner; on the one hand, the ethnic and linguistic diversity ostensibly prevented the formation of a separate 'slave culture', but on the other, communication was often very difficult when a labour force may have spoken three or four different languages. The preference for and increasing dominance of Creole slaves in the population over the 18th century made this an increasingly less relevant issue, further enhanced by the development of a Creole language now known as Afrikaans. It first developed as a language between slaves and only gradually was adopted by people of European descent, so that today it is the first language of the country.

The increase in Creoles at the Cape needs to be seen in the wider context of sexual demographics. The male to female ratio of Company slaves was more or less equal until the later 18th century when males started to dominate. It is well known that the Company slave lodge also functioned as a brothel, chiefly for Company servants and the relatively high numbers of females certainly aided this function. Among privately owned slaves however, males were generally much more common—variously six to seven males to every female slave in the early 18th century, though the ratio evened out during the later 18th and early 19th century by which time it was closer to two males to one female, and only reached parity in the later 19th century (among the former slave population; Shell 1994: 72–77). The increasing numbers of female slaves over the later 18th and early 19th century is probably related to the increase in creole slaves—insofar as the VOC controlled the sex ratios of imported slaves, the unequal sex ratios could be maintained, but as a self-reproducing population of slaves developed in the later 18th century, so inevitably the sex ratios evened out. The main change however only really occurred after the abolition of the slave trade, when the numbers of female slaves rapidly increased as they became they only means of replenishing the slave stock (Figure 4.3). The question of why Creole slaves increased might be seen as just a natural demographic, yet the development is uneven—there does appear to be a major change in the mid 18th century marking a radical break from the past which is exhibited in a discontinuous leap in Creoles. In the last chapter, I argued that this was potentially related to other changes in Cape society and a burgher articulation of identity, expressed among other things, through the need for more domestic servants.

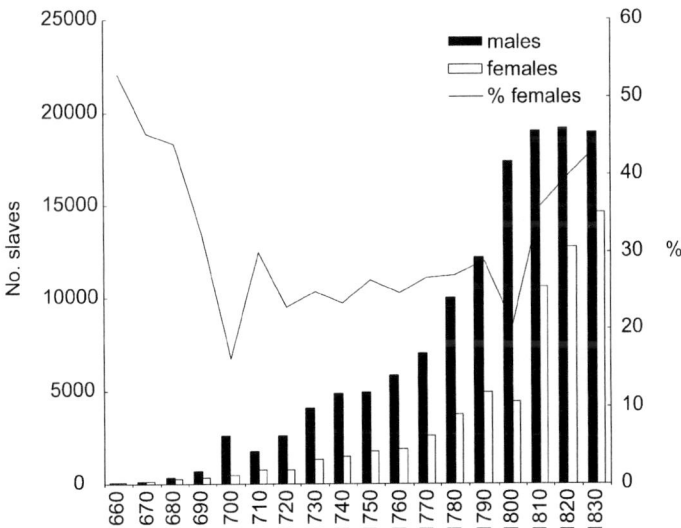

Figure 4.3. Gender ratios of slaves. (*Source*: Based on data from Shell 1994)

The difference between slaves who were owned by the Company and those owned by free burghers does need to be stressed; while all slaves initially arrived as the property of the VOC, many were sold to burghers in auctions directly off the slave ships (Shell 1994: 91). Company slaves were used for labour on projects such as the fort construction and other building works at Table Bay, and then also at various outposts such as the woodcutters station at Paradise or even private ventures such as the silver mine on the Simonsberg (see Chapter 2). Throughout the later 17th century, their numbers gradually grew until it stabilized at around 450–500 on average for the 18th century. Although there were both male and female slaves and many births, the mortality rate was so high it kept the population from expanding; indeed it was largely new imports that maintained the figures given (Armstrong and Worden 1989: 126–7). For the most part, Company slaves were kept in a special building, the Slave Lodge, situated outside the Castle in Table Bay. The Lodge was built in 1679, a windowless, rectangular building arranged around a courtyard; it served multiple functions—as a prison for criminals and an asylum for the insane as well a lodge for the slaves. Its architecture encapsulated the classic panopticon principles of surveillance (Markus 1993) and it was run with equal discipline along military lines with an internal hierarchy, which included the slaves themselves (Figure 4.4). While it was VOC servants who basically ensured the building was locked up every night and opened again in the morning, most of the internal discipline was run by its inmates—overseers (*mandoors*), mostly of Creole origin who enjoyed special privileges of their position which included separate rooms and extra rations and supervised the labour required of Company slaves. Another privileged class were a quasi-police force and executioners, known as *caffers*, although they were lower than the mandoors, they were still higher than ordinary labourers. The internal hierarchy of the Lodge reflected the wider evaluation system of slaves at the Cape— *mandoors* tended to be Creoles, while *caffers* tended to be Indian or Indonesian, and the worst manual labour jobs were given to Africans and Madagascans (Shell 1994: 188–9).

Until the establishment of new settlements beyond the Cape flats, in the Stellenbosch and Drakenstein district (see Chapter 3), most slaves were owned by the Company, but with this expanding settlement of free burghers, the numbers of privately owned slaves rapidly increased. Purchase of slaves was a major investment and it required a large initial outlay of capital even if thereafter, their maintenance was relatively cheap. By the mid 18th century, slaves owned by burghers were ten times more numerous than the Company slaves. (Armstrong

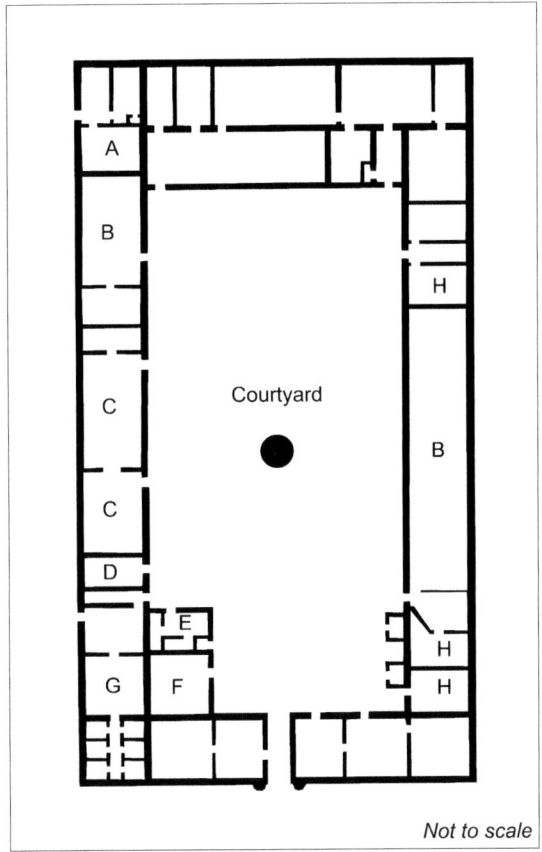

Not to scale

Figure 4.4. Plan of slave lodge (Key: A=Bandits, B=Slaves, C=Hospital, D=Prison, E=Latrine, F=Kitchen, G=Lunatics, H=Overseer). (*Source*: Adapted from De Wildt plan of 1798)

and Worden 1989: 123–4). The main rise in the slave population occurred after 1717 when the VOC decided to stop promoting further settlement and instead, encourage the development of the slave labour force. Throughout the 18th century, the number of privately owned slaves increased, unlike the Company slave population; from 350 privately owned slaves in 1690, the number had risen to 25,754 in 1798 (ibid.: 131–2). This slave population was distributed fairly thinly among the burgher population—large slave plantations typical of the Americas did not exist in the Cape; instead, most slaves lived in small groups of less than 10 on individual farms. Only 1% of slave owners had more

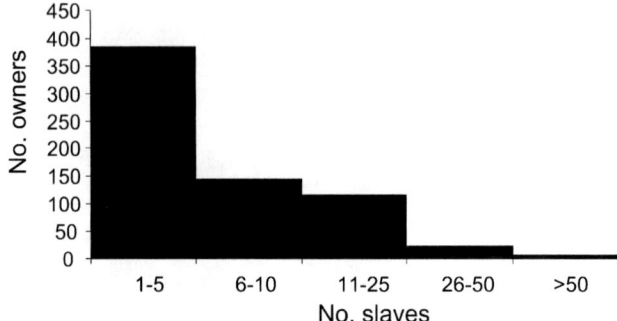

Figure 4.5. Chart of slaves per owner. (*Source*: Adapted from Armstrong & Worden 1989)

than 50 slaves in the mid 18th century (Figure 4.5). Nevertheless, with the increase in some estates during the 18th century, especially the wine and wheat farms of Stellenbosch and Drakenstein, slave populations did grow and these areas had proportionately higher numbers of slaves per farm, a situation even more accentuated with the wine boom of the early 19th century (see Chapter 3).

The slaves owned by burghers were used in farming, at least those in the countryside, while urban slaves were generally employed as domestic servants, but also sometimes in industry. Both urban and rural slaves were sometimes hired out, either to the Company or other burghers. Unlike the Company slave lodge, there was generally no explicit hierarchy of slaves owned by burghers given the small numbers, and they had no separate accommodation provided; they slept in the kitchen, attic or outbuildings. For those larger estates however, separate slave lodges were built and these farms also often appointed an overseer from among the slave group, or occasionally, hired a European (*knecht*)—usually sub-contracted from the Company. Slaves were provided with food and clothing from their owner, and rations of tobacco and wine, and some slaves given plots to grow their own vegetables. No doubt other goods were acquired too. A key element argued for Cape slavery is that they were much more a part of the farm or household unit than an independent, slave community with their own family structures; it has been suggested that because of this, they could not establish a 'slave culture' comparable to that on the large plantations of the Americas (Ross 1983b; Worden 1985). Moreover, the ethnic and linguistic diversity of the slaves would have added to this problem, indeed was often a source of conflict between slaves. This view however needs to be questioned, especially in the more densely populated areas of Cape Town and its hinterland rural areas, including Stellenbosch and

Drakenstein, where neighbouring farms are often less than quarter of an hours walk away. The evidence for a distinct 'slave culture' is most clear in Cape Town, where domestic slaves had much more freedom to move around and the growth of Islam provided a major context in which common identities could be forged and social networks of support established (McKenzie 1993: 93–5; Shell 1994: 357–62).

The issue of whether there was a 'slave culture' at the Cape is perhaps a red herring, insofar as there was not necessarily any tight social cohesion among different groups of the population—settler or slave. Identities were, especially in the 18th and early 19th century, in a process of formation and articulation and it is perhaps only the VOC who can be said to have had any specific sense of self-identity or group-belonging on a colony-wide scale. There were of course the legal identities—free burgher, slave and Khoikhoi and undoubtedly more localized identities, which developed both among slaves and settlers such as the Huguenots. But identity is exactly what is at stake here—identities being formed rather than presumed; identity in flux rather than a stable attribute, and as I have already said, power is the key variable in this formation of identity. In the case of slaves, their identity was defined through grossly unequal power relations. The question is—how was this politics of identity articulated? Robert Shell who has provided perhaps the most detailed study of Cape slavery yet, in his book *Children of Bondage*, argues that it was affected largely through an ideology of the family (Shell 1994). He is critical of previous historians of Cape slavery who over-emphasized the role of overt control and coercion through violence—the threat and exercise of punishment or execution (e.g. Ross 1983b: 29–37; Worden 1985: 119–137). While not denying that violence was used, he suggests that the main form of coercion was in fact more subtle and psychological; slaves were assimilated into the settler family (or even the 'family' of the VOC), as subordinate members—essentially as 'children', and were thus kept under control through paternalism.

Shell's thesis has been criticized on a number of grounds (e.g. see Bank 1995; Ross 1995). There is little doubt that in language and treatment, slaves were frequently regarded in a similar manner to children—like children, they went barefoot and they were addressed as 'boy' or 'girl' regardless of age, or simply by their first name. Moreover, slaves largely lived under the same roof as other members of the family and were provided for from the household resources. All this lends strong support to the idea that slaves were integrated into the family or household unit, and that paternalism rather than overt violence kept them in their place. There is thus, a lot of truth in the ideological role of the 'family' in controlling slaves; but I think it needs to be qualified in several ways. In the first place, just because a slave is seen as a member of the family, does not preclude regular use or threat of violence. A paternalistic ideology can be just as violent towards its 'real' children as any 'ascribed' children, such as slaves; the use of beatings or whippings of children were a common form of discipline in European schools or households in this period and its application on slaves would have been no less common, if not more so given the fact that these 'children' were, actually, mostly adults. Ross has pointed out that moreover that paternalism towards slaves does not necessarily entail a patriarchal relation—i.e. recognized kinship, *even* if many of the slaves were biologically descendant from the male slave owner (Ross 1995). Indeed, the juvenile names used for slaves were *not* the same as those used for the actual (and legitimate) children of the slave owner.

This leads me to the next point; no matter how much slaves were 'infantilized' by their owners, they were clearly still adults, nor were they the same as the slave-owners own children. They may have been 'loved' and treated kindly, but they were also feared and mistrusted; this 'infantilization' needs to be seen primarily as a mechanism for the slave-owner to cope with the inherent dilemma of their ownership of slaves. Paternalism and infantilization as metaphors of the owner-slave relationship is much more the strategy of the owner rather than the slave. While it is perhaps incontestable that slave-owners saw their slaves as children, did the slaves see themselves in the same way?

Kirsten McKenzie has examined the dilemma of a slave-owner at the Cape during the late 18th and early 19th century, through his diaries and other writings (McKenzie 1993). It is a fascinating study of an English immigrant, Samuel Hudson, who himself was once a servant at a stately home in Cambridgeshire, England (Wimpole Hall); he came to the Cape as an employee of Lady Anne Barnard's husband, but eventually worked his way up in Cape society and became a slave-owner. Hudson's dilemma's over first purchasing and then owning slaves are clearly expressed in his writings, and it is undeniable that he reconciled slavery through the ideology of paternalism. While recognizing their humanity, he also believed they were like children and needed a father to look after them, and this included occasional discipline through violence. A slave only really became an adult, in the eyes of the colonial free population, when they were released from the slave status, i.e. manumitted. Needles to say, manumission rates were low—for most of the 18th century and after, about 0.1% of slaves were given their freedom, the lowest of all Dutch colonies (Shell 1994: 383). The example of Samuel Hudson shows, more than anything, that paternalism and infantilization were techniques of the slave-owner, but there is nothing to suggest that slaves themselves shared this ideology. Their behaviour may have helped to sustain it, but this could have been unintentional; indeed it may be the very nature of paternalism that enables it to accommodate a wide variety of behaviours without suffering contradiction. The resistance of slaves to their situation—most blatantly by running away, but also in smaller, overt acts such as disobediance or more subtle forms such as laziness—could all be ascribed as the behaviour of recalcitrant children. And slaves did resist their situation, in any number of ways, but under the ultimate threat of violence or death, the slaves' choices for resistance were limited. The point is, for paternalism to work as a means of controlling slaves, it did not need to have the complicity of the slaves; some may well have adopted the role of a 'child' to their owner, but whether you played the master's game or not, you were always likely to confirm their beliefs about you.

For the slaves, being treated as 'children' of the slave-owner household meant they could never publicly create families of their own; in the first instance, enslavement shattered any families that may have already existed, as fewer than 1% of all slaves imported arrived in family groups and there were no recorded couples (Shell 1994: 125). In the second instance, the male to female ratios were so imbalanced, that it made it impossible for most male slaves to create a family once at the Cape. But even those who could form bonds with female slaves, their chances of maintaining a family unit were always under threat, as they or their kin were sold on. Legally recognized marriages (i.e. Christian) between slaves were extremely rare, and the paternity of children born of slave women was never officially recognized. This meant, that while the bonds of a slave mother and her children may have been recognized by the slave-owner, the woman's partner or children's father hardly ever was. For those slaves who did form relationships and create their own family, it was a difficult unit to hold together as everything was set against them. The men worked and slept in different places to the women, their paternity was not recognized, nor were relationships between men and women, and the ever-present fear of being separated through re-sale all conspired to make family life for slaves almost impossible. Yet still, some did, and even after being separated, there are records of slaves making journeys between farms to visit their kin, and after emancipation, many more making great efforts to try and re-unite with their families (Scully 1997: 64–8).

However, we should also recognize that slaves did not necessarily perceive the concept of family in the same way as their masters; it may be that because of these very conditions of slavery at the Cape, the concept of family became regarded as primarily a matrifocal unit of mother and child(ren), not the nuclear, patrifocal family with the male head (van der Spuy 1992). If nothing else, all this reveals is that slaves did not see themselves in the same way as their owners—they tried to form their own relationships and families, they created a social network and kinship outside the sphere of the paternalistic slave-owner 'family' of which they ostensibly were children, and against great odds. The paternalistic ideology of slavery worked only too well for its owners, as it also made it hard for the slaves to constitute any separate identity for themselves. Yet there were cracks in this ideology, spaces where it did not completely enclose the slave in totality. And it is precisely in these gaps that we find attempts by the slaves to carve out some individuality for themselves. In the rest of this chapter, I want to explore the lives of slaves and their descendants in the study area, addressing some of the general themes already raised but also attempting to give a more close-textured analysis of the situation in one area of the Cape. Of critical importance in this story is what happens after slavery: the post-emancipation era, and thus I will be taking a longer temporal perspective, which at the same time, will need to introduce something of the broader background of developments in Cape society, for the mid-late 19th century and even into the twentieth century.

FROM MADAGASCAR TO THE DWARS VALLEY: THE WORLD OF SLAVES

Tracing the histories of slaves, unlike the European settlers, is much more difficult. Slaves appear as the property of their owners and occur in census and inventories, and then after 1816, slave registers exist which give slightly more detailed information. Nevertheless, some attempt will be made to try and uncover the nature of slave life between the late 17th and early 19th century, through both these documents and material culture. As discussed in the last chapter, most of the farms in the Dwars valley were settled by Huguenot immigrants and within half a century, one family dominated the valley—the de Villiers. There were also a few free black households, at least to begin with, and both these and the Huguenots soon acquired slaves. For example, Jacob van As, the son of a free black who owned Nieuwendorp and was the largest landowner in the valley in the early 18th century, left eleven slaves on his death in 1713—nine males and two females. We even have their names in the inventory: Claas, Anthonij, Jacob, Mars, Moses, Cupido, Samboe, another Anthonij, Flora, Marie and a male child. The number of slaves reflect the general wealth of the estate; on the neighbouring farm of Goede Hoop in 1708, there were no slaves. We do not know what happened to the van As slaves, but in general, free blacks who purchased and owned slaves were more likely than any other sector of the population to manumit; they comprised the smallest group of slave-owners (usually between 2–5% of the free population) yet accounted for about a quarter of all private manumissions (Elphick and Shell 1989: 209; Shell 1994: 92–3; 389). While it is arguable how much Jacob van As identified himself with free blacks, nevertheless, free blacks did own and keep slaves—even if they had a higher manumission rate. It is clear from this that slaves and ex-slaves did not then, necessarily identify with each other just because of their shared status. Indeed, given the ethnic diversity of the slave population, this is perhaps unsurprising; Jacob's mother was from India, and while the origin of most of his slaves is unstated, at least one (Anthonij) is designated as from Madagascar. Indeed, most free blacks were Asians or Creoles, and correspondingly, most manumissions were of the same groups.

Although the ratio of African to Asian slaves imported changed over the 18th century, in general, African and Madagascan slaves were preferred for agricultural labour—and they were cheaper. It is thus likely they formed the majority of imported slaves in the Dwars valley, though Creole slaves of course would have formed an increasingly large number too, especially in the later 18th and early 19th century. The inventory of Nieuwendorp in 1790, after it had been bought up by a de Villiers also lists the names of the 34 slaves but in this case, also their origins: fifteen were Creoles (44%), eleven from Madagascar (32%), three from Mozambique (9%), three from Bengal (9%), and two from Malabar (6%). Aside from the number of slaves, which reflects the continued wealth of the farm as well as the de Villiers, the diversity of ethnic origins gives a fairly typical picture of the slave population in the valley in the later 18th century. At the neighbouring farm of Goede Hoop, the few inventories which exist do not give names or origins of the slaves, but such information does occur in the slave registers for the early 19th century, just prior to emancipation. Between 1816 and 1834, the chief owners of Goede Hoop—Pieter Hendrik de Villiers and his mother, registered 44 slaves, and the pattern clearly shows the decline of imported slaves after the abolition of the slave trade in 1808. 34 of the 44 were Creoles (77%), 14 from Mozambique (14%), one from Bengal (2%), one from Malabar (2%) and two from Bougies (5%). Some of the Creoles registered at Goede Hoop died as infants, and many, if not most, were born on the farm itself; their perspective as slaves must have been rather different to those freshly imported into the Cape. Before discussing what life was like as a slave on the farms in the valley, I want to try and understand the life of those imported slaves, before they were slaves, and specifically, focus on the processes of enslavement.

This is actually a difficult task, as most research has been focused on the slave destination and the slave trade from the perspective of the European slave trade, especially in North America; much less work has been done on enslavement itself and slavery at the source, although there is a significant literature on African slavery (e.g. Alpers 1975; Lovejoy 1983; Meillasoux 1991; Miers & Kopytoff 1977). Moreover, there have been even fewer attempts to integrate the two sides. The American slavery historian Frederick Cooper long ago raised the need to consider the relationship between the two fields and avoid over-dichotomizing European and African slavery; crudely, this portrays European slavery as capitalist with slaves viewed as commodities, while African slavery is seen as absorptionist with slaves assimilated into their owner's household and culture (Cooper 1979). Indeed, there is some debate on the extent to which the European slave trade affected African society—some see its impact as minimal, other have argued for a radical transformation. Lovejoy in particular has argued that it altered several aspects of African society, including the process of enslavement, the African slave trade and the domestic use of slaves in Africa (Lovejoy 1989). The high numbers of people exported as slaves from Africa—estimated at nearly 12 million for the Americas—must have affected social structures, although this must be set against the fact that the *total* export to *all* destinations outside Africa more or less equals estimates for the number of slaves who remained in Africa. Nevertheless, this high figure for Africa may have been stimulated by the European trade. Also the demographic structures would have been affected, for it was generally males who were preferred as slaves, especially from the 18th century, and this would have impacted the nature of gender relations among slave-source communities.

If the situation with respect to African slavery is thus still under-developed, our understanding of slavery in Asia is even worse. At the Cape, about half of all slaves originated from India and Indonesia, yet research on slavery in these countries is extremely hard to find. One major work was published in 1950, but this was largely focused on contemporary issues of serfdom although it did address the historical background of enslavement, and suggested that this increased with the expansion of trade in the Indian Ocean (Lasker 1950: 22). However there is almost a silence on the issue of slavery in Indian historiography, which prompts many questions; part of this may relate to a focus on the economic aspect of slaves as exploited labour, rather than the cultural context of their enslavement (e.g. see the recent study by Chatterjee 1999, which redresses this imbalance). Certainly in the context of exported slaves, they are rarely mentioned except as an aside to other commodities in the Indian Ocean trade, and their significance is often downplayed. Most of the slaves from India appear to have originated along the Coromandel Coast, the major trading area for the Dutch East India Company; during the 17th century, they were exported to the Spice Islands to work on the plantations, but also many went to the Cape (Prakash 1994b: 196–7). The processes of their enslavement however remain obscure; Lasker highlighted five main causes of enslavement in the Asian context: prisoners of war, criminal punishment, kidnapping, sale and debt bondage (Lasker 1950). Very similar if not identical processes have been claimed for African slavery (see below) and while it is tempting to say that Indian slavery was similar to African slavery—i.e. small scale and domestic with slaves integrated into the owner's household—there must have been more specific cultural and historical differences.

Because most of the research has focused on the African context—and because most of the slaves working on the farms in the Dwars valley appear to have originated from East Africa and Madagascar—in the rest of this section I will discuss the context of enslavement in these places. In East Africa, the main focus of the slave trade was in Mozambique, with the port of Quelimane being the funnel through which slaves and traders operated (see Figure 4.1; Campbell 1989). The main region inland from where slaves were acquired was the highlands to the north of the Zambezi, which included the Nsenga, Nyanja and southern Chewa tribes. According to 19th century accounts, these groups subsisted on cultivation of a variety of plant foods (chiefly sorghum, but also maize, sweet potatoes and manioc), with both men and women planting but women mostly harvesting, while the men made and traded textiles (Alpers 1975: 22–27). The social structure was matrilocal and matrilineal, several lineages living together in villages which were organized in a loose hierarchy with territorial chiefs. The people who were enslaved in this region were done so chiefly by purchase or capture. These slaves would rarely have been enslaved by the European traders, but rather through pre-existing systems of enslavement among the groups themselves. An anthropological study among the Sena, a group further to the south, illustrates how this might have happened (Isaacman & Isaacman 1977). *Akporo* (i.e. slaves) were acquired through trade, voluntary enslavement (because of poverty) or kidnapping in exchange for textiles and agricultural produce. Generally only the wealthier households owned slaves who were incorporated into the owner's kinship network through fictitious familial links, and many even married. In general, the *kaporo* system was a means for certain lineages to increase their size and thus their importance.

Slavery in the 17th and 18th centuries was probably similar in terms of its political significance, slavery being used mainly by chiefs and other elites to increase their power. With the demand for slaves by Europeans, such lineages may have seen new opportunities of increasing their status. At Quelimane, the slaves would have been traded for beads, iron, alcohol but most of all, for guns and textiles. However, while the highland tribes such as the Njanja and Chewa were a dominant political force in the region during the 16th and 17th centuries, by the 18th century, their power had waned to new polities in the north. It is possible that the increase in the European trade may have affected their political dominance, indeed towards the end of the 18th century there was a massive increase in slave demands, mainly by the French for their plantations on the Mascarenes. Most of the slaves shipped out of Quelimane by the 19th century were bound either for these islands or Brazil and Cuba (Campbell 1989). This demand for slaves may have affected the indigenous systems of slavery to such an extent that it disrupted part of the power base of local elites. The process is little understood, but in Madagascar, a recent and pioneering study has explored these transformations in a highly illuminating manner (Larson 2000).

Madagascar was a major source of slaves for the Cape in the 18th century, especially after the 1770s when, like Mozambique, there was an increase in the Indian Ocean Trade for the colonial plantations. In his book *History and Memory in the Age of Enslavement*, Piers Larson draws on both historical documents and oral history to provide a new and fresh perspective on the slave trade. In examining the impact of the European slave trade on Madagascan society, he also suggests expanding the concept of the African diaspora to include the enormous numbers of Africans who were displaced *within* Africa through slavery, not just those exported (Larson 2000). Conventionally, enslavement has been seen chiefly as a process of capture through warfare among indigenous tribes, although there are many other recognized causes too, including kidnapping, sale, debt bondage or judicial punishment. Whatever the causes—and I will return to these—enslavement must have had an impact on social and kinship structures as it increased under European demands.

The central point in Larson's study is, I believe, his concept of the 'ethics of enslavement'; what he means by this is the local morality around when it was legitimate or not to enslave someone (Larson

2000: 88). Because we think of slavery as simply wrong under any conditions, we forget that in different times and among different societies, there was a code of conduct, an ethics about enslavement. Larson shows how this ethics was radically changed in Madagascar by the insertion of European traders in the pre-existing slave trade. During the 17th and 18th centuries, Madagascar was an island politically fragmented, and where warfare was common, between mini-kingdoms. There was a loose social hierarchy within any kingdom, which included nobility, commoners and servants of various types, but social mobility was possible as the categories were not that rigid. Before the 1770s, prisoners caught in warfare between these kingdoms were generally ransomed back to their homelands, and those not bought back, would have remained as slaves. Some may have even been sold on to European or Arab traders. After the 1770s with the increased demand by Europeans for slaves, such ransoms were often not offered or put at prices impossibly high, so that prisoners of war were increasingly sold as slaves rather than ransomed back to their homeland. In return for slaves, the Malagasy elite acquired silver, an important prestige item used as both jewelry and a medium of internal exchange; they also acquired textiles, alcohol and guns, the latter being obviously significant to inter-Kingdom warfare (Berg 1985; Larson 2000: 74).

The demand from Europeans however was so great that soon prisoners-of-war could not satisfy it, and the Malagasy elites started to look within their own kingdom for slaves. Once again, there was a pre-existing system which they could exploit, in this case debt bondage or pawnship; people who became indebted to social superiors normally paid off that debt through labour or service for a period of time. There was a strong distinction between such bondsmen and slaves, yet it was a distinction which the elite started to blur, thus potentially turning a bondsman into a slave who could be sold on. Ultimately this lead to major resentment among the commoners and fed a cycle of kidnapping where one lineage might kidnap a member of another to use as a ransom to recover their own bonded kinsman. In short, victims of enslavement started to enslave others themselves, resulting in a complete disintegration of the social fabric. Larson suggested that this fragmentation happened within a space of a decade or two of 1770, and by 1800, enslavement had become endemic across all levels of Malagasy society (Larson 2000: 100). Moreover, it also severely affected gender systems, as most of those enslaved were men; since men were traditionally the ones engaged in agricultural labour, while women in textile production, as communities started to lose their menfolk, women by necessity had to start being involved in agriculture too.

The breakdown in the ethics of enslavement also meant a break-down in trust between social groups, and while there was resistance to this, it was not directed at slavery *per se* but the new forms of enslavement being practiced. The dynamics of slavery in the late 18th century then had a twofold effect: it both increased political fragmentation while at the same time, strengthened the kinship ties within lineages. It was in this highly volatile and unstable social environment that the Merina Kingdom emerged in the early 19th century. This is another story, for in the context of those slaves shipped to the Cape in the later 18th century, they came from a context which was by no means secure. Their landscape, once safe and familiar, had become a dangerous and insecure place where kidnapping was rife. This is not to say that the landscape they we going to was any more pleasant; however bad things were back home, at least there was family, at least it *was home*. For those unfortunate Malagasy who were enslaved and transported to the Cape, among other destinations, they would be entering a completely new world, a new landscape, equally inscribed by fear, but in a very different way.

LANDSCAPES OF SLAVERY

To try and understand how the slaves working and living on the farms in the Dwars valley perceived themselves, and their owners, involves some difficulty, to say the least. I want to explore this perception through the materiality of the world they inhabited, using two main scales of analysis on one farm, Goede Hoop: the close architecture of the *werf* in which they slept and for some, served, and the wider landscape of the farmland in which they laboured. Exploring these landscapes, hopefully will shed some light on how the slaves articulated their lives and their identities. The *werf* was the immediate context of the slaves life, as it was for their owners, but they will have experienced it in very different ways, certainly from the later 18th century when the new Cape Dutch style of architecture was emerging. For those farmers with small, two- or three-bay rectangular house, their slaves, if they owned any, would have probably slept on the floor in the same room as their owners (Shell 1994: 252–3). But for the wealthier farmers with larger homesteads and more than two or three slaves—and that really includes all the farms in the Dwars valley from the later 18th century—there was much greater differentiation and often the provision of separate slave quarters. On the whole, male and female slaves were treated quite differently in this respect; while women would have remained in the main homestead, the male slaves are more likely to have bunked in outbuildings or, if in large numbers, housed in a special building. This difference largely reflected their labour—in the one case domestic, in the other, agricultural.

Within the main home, there was a clear demarcation of the kitchen as the space of female slaves; they spent most of their time there it seems, whether cooking for the household or sleeping at night. It is no accident that, because slaves were cooking for the household, that Cape cuisine rapidly developed a unique Creole style, which owed as much if not more to Asian cooking than it did to European food (Abrahams 1997; 1998). The kitchen was so much so a female and slave space, that the male slave-owner may have hardly ever ventured there, if Samuel Hudson's writings can be generalised (Shell 1994: 256). The kitchen usually lay at the back of the house of the larger homesteads, and Goede Hoop is no exception; here it lies on the back left hand side, with a separate access out to the back and facing the presumed, separate male slave quarters (see Chapter 3, Figure 3.9). For male slaves not sleeping in the main house, their access to it would have been much more restricted; they probably would have come into the kitchen through this back door, but maybe no further. Their main space lay outside, in the outbuildings or the special slave lodge. Slave lodges were not common on rural farms until the later 18th century, and indeed their use is probably closely linked to changes in vernacular architecture and the rise of the Cape Dutch House (Figure 4.6). As discussed in the last chapter, it was suggested that there was an increasing demand for domestic servants associated with this new architecture, as part of broader shifts in consumption, and in this context, the distinction between domestic and agricultural slaves on rural farms would have become more important. It was perhaps this, as much as growing numbers, which created the need for a separate slave lodge on the larger farms in the late 18th century.

Given the proximity of the lodgings of slaves to the main house, it is very difficult to try and separate out any differentiation in material culture, such as ceramics and other objects. Given that the slaves had little or no access to goods other than what was provided for them or handed down from the main house, such differentiation is made even harder. At the site of Vergelegen where there was some distance between the slave lodge and other buildings, such an analysis is made easier, yet in many ways the recovered material culture assemblage was similar to that from any other 18th century site—Chinese porcelain dominated the ceramics (57%), followed by coarse earthenwares (25%) and stonewares, both European and oriental (14%) (Markell 1993).

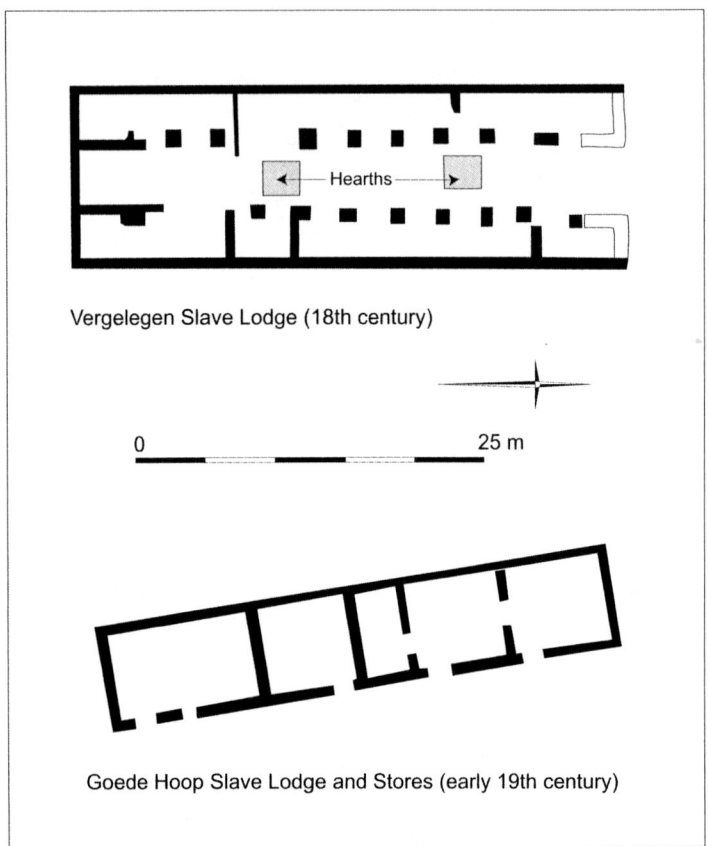

Figure 4.6. Slave lodge at Vergelegen and Goede Hoop. (*Source*: Adapted from Markell 1993 and author's data)

At Goede Hoop, a surface collection of finds was made around the *werf*, and the greatest concentration of material lay in the area between the back of the homestead and the slave lodge. This was clearly an area of primary rubbish disposal, but it was also the first external space that slaves encountered outside their residence—whether female slaves coming out of the kitchen of the main house, or male slaves from their separate lodge. Indeed, it is quite clear that at least by the early 19th century, the *werf* was divided into a front and back space, its main axis defined by the line of the three main buildings. The fronts of one of these buildings, the wine cellar, has a gable fronting its impressive facades, and there is a large open space before it, intended as a vista for both visitors and its owners. In contrast, the slave space is squeezed out of sight, behind the homestead along with the garbage. This is quite intentional and reflects a clear division of the *werf*. This is not to suggest slaves did not walk freely around the *werf* in the day time—their work in the cellars, millhouse and stables would have all necessitated this, but this space was controlled and its very openness, which accentuated the vista of the homestead and cellars, simultaneously rendered it highly suitable for surveillance.

At the center of this space is the bell tower, used for organizing the labour of the slaves, calling them out to and in from the fields. Although the present tower is commemorative and was built in 1934, it is likely a similar one existed in the *werf*, serving this function. The bell would have been an integral part of the slave's life, its ringing tone, a symbol of their life as labour, governing their temporal experience on a daily basis. The work of the male slave on a farm such as Goede Hoop involved a number of different tasks, which varied according to the season. Given that this farm was largely based on viticulture, the annual cycle would have meant cutting and pruning the vines in July and August, weeding in October and November, and harvesting in late February and March (Armstrong & Worden 1989: 144). After picking the grapes, they then had to be processed into wine; this they did by trampling the grapes to extract the juice, which was then poured into vats for fermenting. The work, at peak times such as the harvest, involved long, hard days, and even in the quieter periods, the slaves were probably set for other tasks such transporting produce or acquiring supplies such as wood.

The vineyards around the *werf* was thus a landscape in which male slaves spent much of their life; it would also have been one of the few opportunities for communication with other slaves on neighbouring farms. Their perception of the wider landscape would have been rather different to that of the closely ordered *werf*, but also different to the slaveowners perception of the landscape, a perception which we can try and understand by following some of Upton's cues in his analysis of the Virginian landscape in the 18th century (Upton 1990). For the owners of these Cape Dutch houses and vineyards, the valley would have been seen as an inter-connected network of farms, indeed the landscape would have been perceived as a material inscription of family relations and alliances. The layout of vineyards and who owned them, and what relationship each farmer had to the others would have been clearly understood; the valley would have been conceived as a whole, divisible into individual properties, linked by a network of tracks or roads. For the landed gentry, the valley was a landscape of property and status, articulated through kinship. For the slaves on the other hand, the landscape may have been much more fragmented, especially outside the space of their owners farm; not that slaves would not have traveled to other farms, but this would have been highly controlled and restricted, and for them, each farm in the valley was probably perceived as essentially the same as the one they were on. The valley was a fragmented collection of multiple worlds, each like the other even if varying in detail. In this landscape, the slaves would have been acutely aware—much more so than their owners—of the spaces between farms, the land outside the constituted system of property and ownership. Between and behind the vineyards and *werfs*, lay either common grazing land, or uncultivated wild bush, especially on the slopes of the Simonsberg. The latter especially would have been perceived as a space outside the net of power which ordinarily controlled their lives, outside the landscape of labour which defined their lives (Figure 4.7).

For a while, part of this wild landscape became tamed; during the mid-18th century, the silver mine settlement on the slopes of the Simonsberg would have drastically altered this landscape, but after its abandonment, the empty houses and mine shafts would have offered new potential for exploring behaviour outside the constituted world of the *werf* and slave lodge. No longer just open ground but also houses and rooms now existed in which the slaves could explore an alternative sense of identity for themselves. And there is no doubt these houses were used long after the silver mine was closed; it is quite clear that people were at least using if not fully inhabiting these buildings into the early 19th century, and although it is impossible to know who, this land did not become privately owned until 1822. The latest dating evidence on the site suggests that any squatters left about this time, and it is thus unlikely to have been any free burgher. Of course how easy access slaves would have had to this land is hard to know; certainly they would have been sent up the Simonsberg to collect wood or other natural resources, but illicit trips would also have been very likely. In more recent times, the mine shafts were used as hideaways by people escaping the police and the mines remain a place of huge importance for the local community of the slaves descendants.

The landscape of the slaves was thus a landscape of labour, most of their lives defined between the werf and vineyards; for them, it was a fragmented series of similar spaces, but the holes in this landscape, the space outside the area which constituted their existence, would have taken on special value. This contrasts quite dramatically with the landscape of their owners, for whom it was an ordered and connected world of property and kin, where what mattered most was the connections between places and how these were articulated. Even within their own

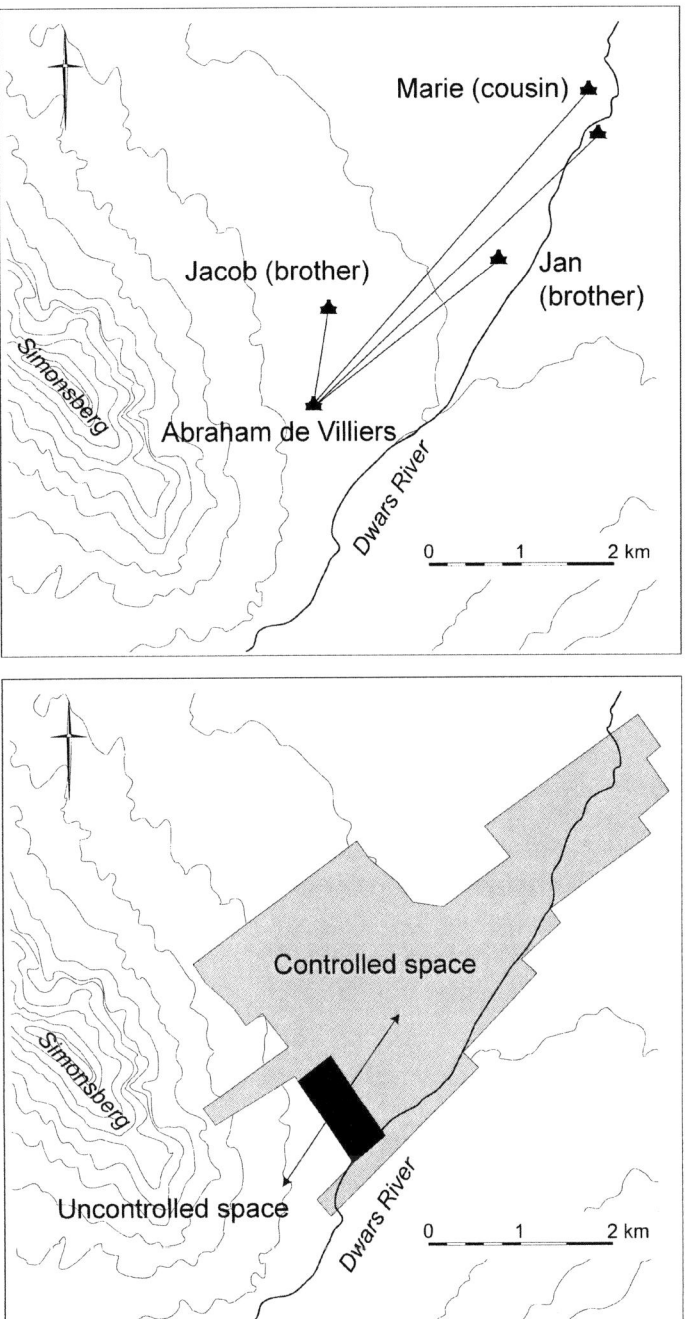

Figure 4.7. Alternate perceptions of the landscape: (top) how Abraham de Villiers might have perceived the Dwars valley in 1740 from his farm Goede Hoop and (bottom) how one of his slaves may have seen it.

werf, the same order applied, with its division of space, both within the main house and within the *werf* as a whole; for the slaves, this order was much harder to articulate differently, their lives were much more tightly regulated. It was only in the larger landscape, where the gaps and holes in this system of power were larger and more open to exploration, that the slaves could perhaps fashion a sense of identity different to that proscribed by their owner. An identity not defined by labour or servitude. Ironically, at the very same time as emancipation happened, this landscape started to close up, as the unclaimed spaces were bought up under new property laws of perpetual quitrent (see Chapter 3).

EMANCIPATION AND THE PNIEL MISSION STATION

On December 1st 1834, slavery was abolished in the Cape colony, following the policy in the rest of the British Empire (Worden and Crais 1994). For the slaves, the transformation was radical—first with the abolition of the slave trade in 1808, and then the abolition of slavery itself in 1834. However, one should not gain from this a rosy picture of a new benevolent and liberal period under the British; in many ways, the British Empire brought an even more segregationist and racist ideology, where identity and difference was far more sharply defined than it had been under the Dutch. Technically, upon emancipation slaves became 'free blacks', but within two years of freedom, the British administration used a new, dual classification at the Cape: 'white' and 'coloured'. The term 'coloureds' lumped together free blacks, ex-slaves and Khoisan, while 'whites' referred to Europeans. For the first time, a distinct classification based on race, rather than legal status was used, though subsequently, the racial duality was overlain with a class one, of Master and Servant (see below). Moreover, despite 1834 being the year of abolition, the slaves were not automatically freed—in fact there was a four year period in which all slaves were obliged to continue working for their former owners under 'apprenticeship', thus it was not until 1838 that slaves finally had the power to leave their former owners farm. Moreover, under the abolition law, many ex-slave children could be indentured if they were considered to be without proper guardians, and this definition was exploited at the Cape in its widest sense to keep children effectively 'enslaved' (Scully 1997: 47–59). After 1838, the indenture clause was repealed along with the end of apprenticeship.

This freedom however, even after 1838, was ultimately little more than a legal technicality for many of the ex-slaves; whilst not downplaying the symbolic importance of freedom and what it meant, for many ex-slaves there were few opportunities or means to articulate this freedom (Ross 1994). They had little or no money or even possessions to speak of, and whatever social network they had, existed in the area and on the farms on which they had been enslaved. After 1838, most ex-slaves continued working for the same people and on the same farms as they had before. While they were now contracted and paid labour, their conditions of contractual labour as set out in the Master and Servants Ordinance of 1841 were heavily stacked in favour of their employers. This new legislation effectively linked conditions of work with class; for example it permitted employers to use certain disciplinary measures (from fines to imprisonment) to regulate the behaviour of this new 'working class', criminalizing acts such as insolence, immorality, drunkenness and negligence (Ross 1994; Scully 1997: 84). Moreover, there was quite tacit recognition that this new class of 'servant' did not include Europeans, but ex-slaves. The original drafting of the law made much more explicit links between race and class, as Scully has shown, but despite dropping the explicit links, it was widely perceived that Masters were 'whites' and Servants were 'coloureds' (Scully 1997: 86). Moreover, when a new legislative assembly was created at the Cape in 1853 based on electoral principles and a property franchise, the vote was restricted to adult males who owned property valued at a substantial price (£25), thus automatically excluding most ex-slaves, except perhaps those on mission stations (Ross 1999b: 170).

Some slaves of course moved on from their previous owners, and a large number of these ended up in the growing number of mission stations being established. Missionary societies were rare at the Cape until after 1795—indeed the only society under VOC rule was the Moravians, which had little impact; after British occupation, missionary societies increased, so that by the time of emancipation, several missionary groups had already established or were prepared to establish stations in rural areas for ex-slaves. One such society was the Apostolic Union, a non-denominational protestant group, based at St. Stephen's Church in Cape Town (formerly a theatre) and established by the Reverend G. W. Stegman and Dr. Adamson for ex-slaves in the town. In 1843, they decided to open a mission station in the Dwars Valley called Pniel, referring to a biblical town meaning the 'face of God'; it was to be run by a (presumed) relative of the reverend, called John Frederick Stegman, who was only about 20 years old and ordained by the Apostolic Union (Silberbauer 1943).

The establishment of a mission obviously needed land, and while the relationship between the Apostolic Union and two landowners in the Dwars valley remains obscure, these land owners—Pieter Izak de Villiers and Johannes Jacobus Haupt—clearly joined to purchase and donate land to the mission, while acting as Directors of the new missionary Institution. De Villiers and Haupt were neighbours, the former on Goede Hoop and the latter in Rhone/Languedoc, and Pniel more or less developed from/in land between these properties. In July 1843, one of these directors, Pieter Izaak de Villiers transferred with Paul Retief (another director) a small area (less than half a hectare) of his farm Goede Hoop to the Institution (plot 1195) for the purposes of building a school and church for the mission station. In December of the same year, the directors purchased a large farm of c. 42 hectares on the southern boundary of Goede Hoop, called Papier Molen, as land and house plots for the mission's new inhabitants (Figure 4.8). This farm was relatively new—it consisted of an amalgamation of a part of Goede Hoop which had been divided off in 1787 (c.16 ha), with a new freehold quitrent of 1822 (c. 25 ha), the land being consolidated under Abraham Johannes Marais. Marais sold some of the land to Carel Albrecht Haupt in 1826 (Johannes Jacobus' father), but most of it went to Abraham Coenraad de Villiers, who owned the adjacent farm of Nieuwendorp and was Pieter Izaak's brother. The Haupt's were fairly new to the valley; they came in 1804, buying the adjacent farms of Languedoc and Rhone but were tied to the de Villiers through multiple marriages. In 1842, the farm was transferred again, but briefly as the new owner became insolvent and in 1843 Papier Molen was bought by the directors of the Institute. Thus by the end of 1843, a substantial parcel of land had been acquired for the

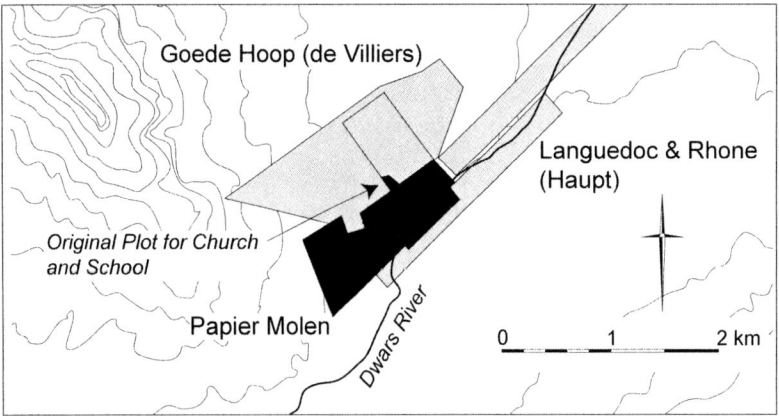

Figure 4.8. Area of farms subdivided off to make Pniel in 1843.

new mission station, and although smaller plots were added over the 19th century, the main core of the mission station was in place within a year of its foundation.

The land set aside for the mission inhabitants was divided into 99 plots, and separated into two zones: an area of housing lots (*erven*) and an area of gardens for them to grow vegetables and keep livestock. According to an addendum to the Master and Servants Ordinance of 1841 on mission stations published in 1849, each building lot or *erf* measured 18.4 by 9.2 m and garden allotment, 22.9 by 19.9 m, for which the holder paid an annual rent of £1, 16s. Thus far, 20 houses had been built with a further eight in construction, while on the allotments, maize, pumpkins, melons and beans were grown while 37 pigs and 11 goats were recorded among the total livestock. At this time, it appears the mission station was only at a little more than half capacity with 49 households registered and a total population of 258 (49 men, 53 women and 156 children); Stegman contested these figures in a rejoinder to the official report, claiming over 200 men and women were living at the station, though this discrepancy seems due to a conflict over the definition of 'adult', with the official inspectors possibly defining many as children whom Stegman considered adult. This report moreover needs to be read in its wider context, for it is very much a document caught up in labour politics in the valley, a point I will discuss further below; but however one reads the figures, it is clear than within five years of its establishment, the mission station was a major attraction to ex-slaves who did not want to live on the farms of their former owners.

The mission's primary objective was of course religious instruction in the Apostolic faith. Throughout the institution of slavery at the Cape, almost no slaves of burghers were baptized, and the reason was simple: Christians under the Dutch Reformed Church were, according to orthodox interpretation, also free citizens and baptism of slaves would thus have effectively been synonymous with emancipation. While the church law was ambiguous and there were slave baptisms—primarily by the VOC of their own slaves in the Lodge, most private slaves remained unbaptised because of the common belief that this would contradict their slave status (Shell 1994: 336–46). Similarly with instruction into the Christian doctrine; while a slave owner could still provide a Christian education for their slaves without baptism, this was rarely done. In such a context, especially in Cape Town and the wealthier rural areas with large numbers of slaves, the growth of Islam became a major attraction, as already mentioned. To what extent Islam had converts in the Dwars valley is very hard to assess, since the impact of the evangelical mission of Pniel would have all but erased any incipient Muslim

community. In general however, Islam seems to have had little impact
in this region. The one, highly equivocal piece of evidence for Muslims
from this project was the recovery of a star and crescent badge on the
site of Silver mine settlement on the Simonsberg. Although it is widely
recognized today as an Islamic symbol, in the 18th century the star and
crescent symbol had wider currency, and its attribution must remain
ambiguous; yet in the context of the above discussion on illicit re-use
of these houses by slaves in the later 18th and early 19th century, it is
nonetheless a provocative artefact.

The establishment of the mission station at Pniel was thus clearly
linked to the fact that most slaves were still 'heathens' and the primary
goal of the Apostolic Union was the absorption and instruction of ex-
slaves into the Christian faith. How the first generation of ex-slaves
regarded this is hard to tell; within the community today, Christian-
ity is a major part of their lives and Stegman is still highly revered,
but this is over a century and half later. The adoption of Chistianity
by ex-slaves may have had great symbolic importance in relation to
their freedom and equality with their former owners, but equally the
presence of a mission station which provided a means of setting up
an independent life must have been extremely attractive. The 1849
report already mentioned, was highly critical of the religious instruction given to the ex-slaves: "It appears to us that this Institution is
not managed upon the principles on which it was actually intended,
namely, to instruct the ignorant and the poor in the word of God, *and
not to draw any profit from them*" (Legislative Council 1849: 51, emphasis in original). Ironically, in Stegman's reply to this unfavourable
report, he attacks the last comment, arguing the station is non-profit
making, but does not really address the issue of religious instruction
except to affirm that it is given to all. Moreover, most of his reply focuses
on the issue of labour, which was the chief cause of concern driving the
report.

The inspectors who produced the report on Pniel were local officials,
the Magistrate and Justice of the Peace of the district of Paarl, and they
were clearly biased for the local farmers. Their report was generally
very unfavourable and critical, its main focus of attack being what the
inspectors saw as the detrimental effect of the Mission station on labour
in the valley—it claimed that those who settled at the station were not
working on the farms, causing a shortage of labour supply and thus
potential ruin of agricultural production. Out of the total population
of 258, the report found only 49 working for farms in the locality. In
Stegman's response appended to their report, were specific responses
contesting some of the inspectors points, followed by detailed and long
lists of the farms and type of labour in which the Pniel residents were

Table 4.1. Ex-slaves at Pniel working on farms in the Dwars Valley in 1849. (*Source*: Legislative Council 1849)

Number of slaves	Farm
9	Boschendal
8	Languedoc/Rhone
5	Meerust/Eenzamheid
5	Bellingham
4	Lekkerwijn
1	Goede Hoop
7	Bellingham
2	Werda
1	L'Ormarins
1	Johannesdal
1	Zandvliet

working, clearly contradicting the official report's findings. At stake here was a larger issue being played out all around the Cape in the wake of emancipation—the farmer's fears of losing labour. In the event, this was not to happen, for as Stegman's reply and history shows, most of those living in the mission station continued to do the same work for the same people on the same land as they had when they were enslaved. In 1849, 43 of the 49 males were listed as working full time on farms, and of these 43, 35 were working on farms in the Dwars valley (Table 4.1). The main advantage they had over those who remained living on these farms was the freedom of their own house and their own community, an advantage by no means to be downplayed Moreover, even though working for the same farmers, they usually worked on a day-to-day basis, which meant they had the freedom to leave their employment any time—another factor which the farmers did not like as it weakened their hold on the labour supply. Despite the farmer's antagonism to mission stations, it did not steal labour—indeed, in many ways missions stations prevented the migration of labour for it offered a context in which ex-slaves could remain in the valley. Indeed, as Ross has pointed out, emancipation only stabilized the rural economy through its tight labour regulations and the mission stations which supported a seasonal labour force for the farmers who only had to keep as many labourers on their farm as they needed for year-round work (Ross 1994). That opinion had so changed by the end of the 19th century is clear from a statement in a 1910 court case (see below), in which, among the religious and educational objectives of the mission, was agricultural training "... with a view to making them useful labourers easily available for the owners of the neighbouring estates." (Silberbauer 1943: 8).

The history of Pniel during the later 19th century is one of growth as more ex-slaves came to settle; the missionary pastor, Stegman remained there until his death in 1909, and appears to have been widely respected. However, a few years before his death, but by which time he had become infirm, a group of *erf*-holders challenged the authority of the Board of Directors and campaigned to run the Mission Station themselves. The primary cause of complaints regarded the property rights of the *erf*-holders. Under the original agreement, *erf*-holders paid rent until the value of the *erf* was paid off—being assessed at £18, and an annual rent of £1, 16s, this meant they became freeholders within 10 years, assuming regular payment. However, it was not until 1905 that trouble started, when several *erf*-holders claimed that since they had long paid off their *erven*, they were now owners of the land and had no need of the Directors. In response, the Directors stated they were the owners and holders of the title deeds, and while the *erf*-holders could sell their property, they were not its owners and were subject to the same conditions of tenancy. After Stegman's death, the Directors took a vote among the community, which backed their position; in response, the detractors filed a court action against them, headed by Garnaat Cyster and Stephanus de Wet. The result was an attempted compromise, which tried to recognize the claims of both sides, yet it is also very clear that the court did not think the residents of Pniel should have self-governorship. In 1911 the court ordered that authority over the Mission station be passed over to a body of eight trustees, "... all such Trustees being men of European race or descent ... "; four of these were the former Directors, while three were to be elected by the *erf*-holders and one by the Church (Silberbauer 1943: 20).

The judicial hearing as reported at the time is interesting because it re-affirms that paternalism was still very much alive as an ideology among the white population, nearly a century after emancipation. The liberal tradition that had swept Britain and its colonies in the 1820s and 1830s leading to emancipation, was already on the wane by the 1840s, ultimately giving way to the harsher imperial ideology and strident racism of the late 19th century (Bank 1999). Nevertheless, paternalism in the form of infantilization of the ex-slave community was still employed as a rhetoric for keeping these people in their place. The report on the court case describes the *erf*-holders who brought the complaint as "... no doubt worthy men in their own station in life, and are possibly well able to manage some of the affairs of such a community ... but I feel certain that it would not be safe to leave them the entire direction of the spiritual ministrations or of the educational requirements of the place. Though some of them are fairly educated, they have not reached a high standard of public life." (Silberbauer 1943: 16). Such sentiments are not that far removed from those expressed by Samuel Hudson a century earlier. Moreover, the reporting of this case suggests the *erf*-holders were dissidents among an otherwise contented population, but this is unlikely. The trusteeship established by the court order did not last long; by the centenary of 1943, administration had passed to the community itself who elected members of its own to manage its affairs (Oberholster 1987: 45). Moreover, in 1917, Pniel Church became part of the Congregational Union of South Africa.

ARCHITECTURE AND THE ARTICULATION OF POST-EMANCIPATION IDENTITIES

I want to now explore the mission station at Pniel in more detail, looking at its layout and architecture, to see how an ex-slave community formed a material world separate from the life of labour it had known under slavery and indeed still knew, as it continued to work on the farms in the valley. I will also draw on oral histories of some of its residents and an archaeological investigation of one house plot in the town. The layout of the town today is clearly divided into two halves (Figure 4.9); to the northeast, lie the regularly laid out plots of the original *erven* and gardens, aligned to the boundaries of the Goede Hoop freehold and occupying the 16 hectares sold off in 1787. The modern road now runs along the boundary between these *erven* and Goede Hoop land, and therefore probably dates to no earlier than the late 18th century in this section. At the northwestern edge of these lots lie the Church and the parsonage. Southwest of this ordered, regular layout, is a much more organic development of plots and twisting roads, which was clearly meant to accommodate any expansion. Although there were less than 50 households in 1849, this is only five years after its founding, and the settlement undoubtedly grew rapidly as the influx of ex-slaves continued and children grew up needing plots of their own. Based on the current population and assuming stable growth rates, Pniel's population may have expanded at an average annual rate of 10%. Certainly this south western half was being occupied by households in the later 19th century. Its more random nature is clearly due to a lack of any centralised planning, which may reflect the speed with which new members of the community arrived and/or the lack of interest on the part of the Directors. Tracing its physical development from records is not as easy as it might appear, because the Directors who held the deeds to the settlement, kept the

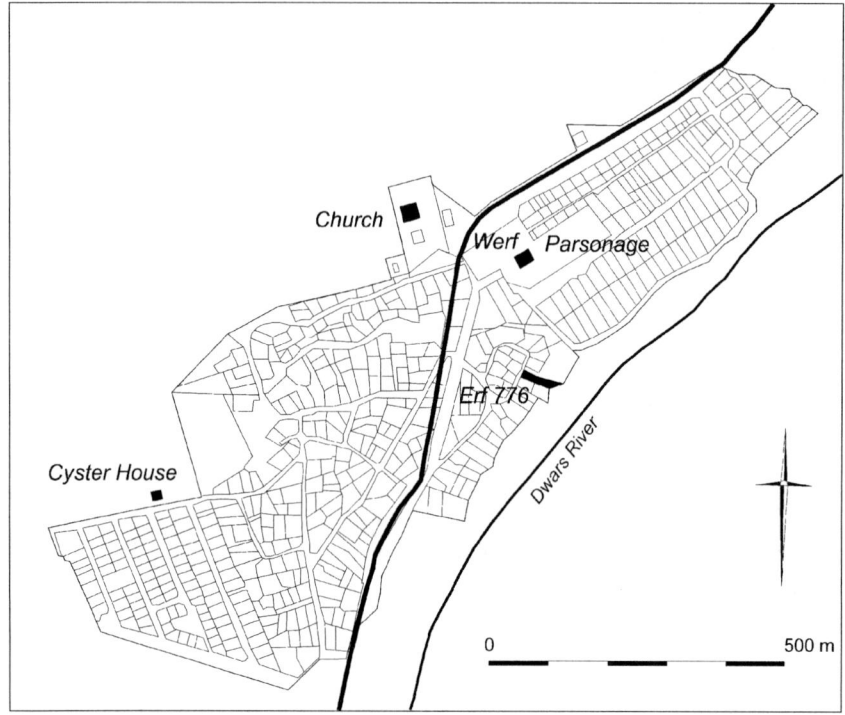

Figure 4.9. Plan of Pniel. (*Source*: Adapted from municipal plan)

land *in toto* (see above); individual *erven* were not registered, and even
after the community took possession, the whole settlement remained
listed as one *erven* belonging to '*Gemmenskap van Pniel*' until 1995/6.
Nevertheless, local memory combined with an architectural study and
archaeology suggest that occupation of the southwest side of Pniel was
established by the later 19th century.

An additional element seems to have been incorporated into the
planned layout of Pniel, that of racial segregation. According to a number of sources among the community today, Stegman and the Directors
separated the lighter-skinned Creole ex-slaves from the darker-skinned
Mozambique ex-slaves, which has left its legacy still today. The area
on the northeastern edge of town, off the main road, is known locally
as Masambiekvlei, Masambiek being a corruption of Mozambique. This
was not just a distinction made by the white Europeans, but also among
the ex-slave community itself, who distinguished themselves as Creole,
Khoisan or Mozambiquan, and was quite widespread (Scully 1997: 156).

Figure 4.10. Photo of old house in Pniel. (*Source*: Photograph by Sarah Winter, taken in 1999)

Such distinctions started to blur and had disappeared in many places by the 1880s as the ex-slaves and authorities adopted the label of 'coloured', which was often used in distinction to the blacks of the Eastern Cape and beyond (Adhikari 1992; Bickford-Smith 1994; 1995). Nevertheless, the distinction certainly between Creole and Mozambiquan descendents is still actively, if quietly used today in Pniel by its inhabitants, while there is no recognition of any Khoisan ancestry whatsoever.

If the planned nature of the north-eastern half contrasts with the randomness of the south west, the architecture of the houses on both sides is fairly similar. Although there is some modern building and repairs or modifications to old buildings, the basic later 19th century house form is square with a central entrance and usually a *stoep* or veranda (Figure 4.10). Sometimes there is back room creating a T- or L-shaped house, usually the kitchen. Nevertheless, there are internal variations—a survey of house plans randomly distributed through Pniel revealed three main types, which occur on both the western and eastern sides of the town (Figure 4.11). Type A has a front entrance leading into a wide central room, which runs the whole depth of the house; either side of it are two, three or four rooms. This form is most reminiscent of the Cape Dutch style—a version in miniature, as the central room is used as a sitting or dining room, while the side rooms are bedrooms

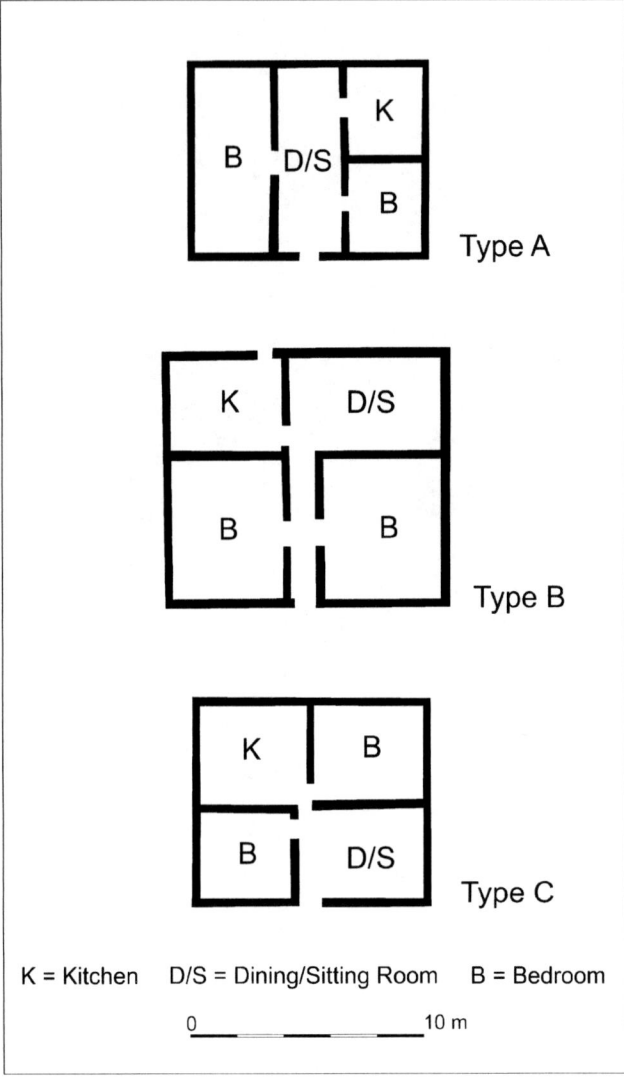

Figure 4.11. Plans of the three main types of houses in Pniel.

and a kitchen, usually a back room. The second house plan, Type B has a front entrance leading to a narrow hall or corridor which only runs half the depth of the house, into a back sitting and dining room. To the other side is the kitchen while the bedrooms occupy the two front rooms flanking the hallway. This form reflects a more English version of vernacular housing with its narrow corridor and hall off which rooms hang. Type C, the third house plan, has no central room, rather the entrance leads directly into the front sitting/dining room on one side, off which are three other rooms—a bedroom on the front and another bedrooms and the kitchen at the back. This type most resembles the original vernacular at the Cape, but modified into a double pile house.

Although the lots were laid out on the eastern side, the ex-slaves built their own houses, and we can be fairly sure that these plans reflect the individual choices of the ex-slaves. There is nothing to suggest any chronological pattern to these types in the context of Pniel, rather all are contemporary but drawing on traditions which were variously older or younger. Thus Type C reflects the oldest tradition, Type A, a mid 18th century tradition, while Type B an early 19th century development. The differences may reflect the architecture that individual householders were familiar with or aspired to on the farms from where they came; yet none of the houses are similar to the single pile, linear slave lodges, which existed on some farms, such as Goede Hoop. Type C is the only one to bear any resemblance to these lodges, but its modification into a double pile house makes it sufficiently different. This is not surprising; the slave lodge architecture was a conversion of an old vernacular, and one that for the ex-slaves, would have carried heavy symbolism of their former status. The adoption of plans that were closer to their owner's residence, the architecture of free burghers, shows quite clearly the importance of the house plan for the slave's new domestic life. This is not to suggest that the houses in Pniel were trying to imitate or copy their former masters; the scale and original variations of these house plans are still distinct, despite the spatial symmetries. The issue really is about what an 'ideal home' should look like for people who for generations, had never had a home of their own; setting up house was of major significance for ex-slaves, for it provided the primary space in which they could articulate their new identities. For slaves who had no other model but their former owners houses, it is inevitable that a similar spatial logic would be employed, but the differences are really how these ex-slaves articulated this space in creating a new identity for themselves.

Oral histories of Pniel provide a wealth of material on life in the community; in particular, genealogies and family history form a key part of their heritage, as many claim descent to the earliest inhabitants of the town. Indeed, genealogical connections to the founding of Pniel provide a degree of status for many in the community, and one family in particular, holds a position of high status—the Cysters. Research is

Figure 4.12. Photo of Cyster house. (*Source*: Photograph by Sarah Winter, taken in 1999)

currently underway into the genealogy of this family in relation to the history of Pniel by a group of its descendants, but I will just sketch out some details as they relate to broader themes. In the 1849 report, a Zyster Bahus or Cyster Bahouss is recorded as having moved to Pniel in the middle of 1848; he was aged about 50 and presumably married to Regina who was about 30 years old; they had five children, three of whom were working. Cyster worked mostly on a de Villiers wheat farm at Kuilenberg, which may be where he originated as a slave. It was a descendant of this family which was at the head of the court action against the Directors in the early 20th century, Garnaat Cyster, and this alone suggests the Cysters were by now, a prominent family in the station. Family history traces descent back to a Carl Cyster, who was probably one of the sons of Cyster Bahouss; a great grand-daughter of Carl, Lillian Idas, now lives on the original plot granted to Carl, which lies on the very western edge of the settlement. The house is unusual in Pniel—a variant of Type A, but conforming closest in style to Cape Dutch architecture, with a T-plan and traces of what used to be an impressive façade (Figure 4.12). The house, both in position and style, clearly reflects the owners articulation of status and identity, vis-à-vis the rest of the community. Nearby is a special graveyard for the Cyster family.

The Cyster's story reflects how, even from the later 19th century, status differentiation may have started within the community, using similar strategies as the burghers had in the mid 18th century. However, I would not push the similarities any further; both the people involved and context are quite different. On the whole, most of the older properties in Pniel are of fairly similar size and elaboration. As a counter example to the Cysters, take the Lackay family; an Abraham Lakey is registered in the 1848 report, aged 26 and married to or living with Delia Arends, aged 45 and 10 children; they had settled in Pniel at the beginning of 1847, and were almost certainly from the locality—a male slave called Lakey was registered in 1816 under the ownership of Carel Albrecht Haupt, who owned the nearby farms of Languedoc and Rhone as well as a portion of Goede Hoop (see above). Lakey was about 30 at the time and came from Mozambique, so the Abraham Lakey who settled in Pniel, if related, was probably his son. The Lakey's owned a plot on the western side of the mission, but which may date to the second generation, as there is also a house still in the family in the eastern half. A great-grandson of the Lakey who owned the western plot, Absolom Lackay, has drawn up the original internal layouts of all of these houses, as they have been substantially altered since his childhood in the 1930s. These houses are of Type C, except one which is a Type B.

Many other family names in Pniel today also appear in the 1849 register, and other such histories could be told. However, these two examples suffice to give some depth to the more general history discussed previously. Tracing the families in Pniel back to slaves on farms in the valley is not an easy task because of the way only single names were given to slaves. Family history often has to provide the main clue, but another comes from surnames. Many family surnames are reputed to derive from the ex-slaves former owners—Williams, a common name in Pniel, is traditionally regarded as an Anglicization of de Villiers, while other surnames are first names of many de Villiers such as David(s) and Hendrick(s). On official Dutch documents, the patronym was often used to identify a burgher in addition to their family name—thus 'Jacob de Villiers Abrahamsz' meant 'Jacob de Villiers, son of Abraham', the 'sz' after Abraham meaning 'son of'. The same form was clearly used by the ex-slaves, hence Davids from David and Hendricks from Hendrick. However, these Christian names were also commonly given to slaves, and its use as a patronym does not especially signify that a de Villiers or any slave-owner was necessarily the father. Indeed, the use of former owners names is in itself ambiguous—it may refer to a social paternity (i.e. ownership) as much as biological paternity. Nonetheless, it is a fact that many slave-owners had children by their female slaves. Such children remained as slaves and in the slave registers, only maternity is recognized, not paternity. This is due to the ideology which denied a family status to slaves in which paternity was considered the key factor, since a family was only such by virtue of its male head. In denying male slaves any legal recognition as fathers, it denied the possibility of a slave family. Correspondingly, in denying owner paternity, it prevented any claims being made by slave children on their father (Scully 1997: 25–33). There is some evidence from oral history that the pastor of Pniel, Stegman, did not want to recognize such 'white' paternity for his flock; family history today ascribes the anglicization of de Villiers to Williams as an explicit effort to erase any association between ex-slaves and former slave-holders, and other examples exist for other family names.

Paternity unsurprisingly became an issue of major importance to emancipated slaves, and in this, the surname obviously played a key role. Paternity and the use of a surname was adopted by almost all of the first generation of male ex-slaves at Pniel, although as we have seen, this was probably regulated by their minister Stegman. In the 1848 report, only seven out of 49 male heads of households gave one name to the inspector, the rest using a surname which in most cases, appears to be a patronym. Wives generally took the husband's surname as did children, thus converting the patronym into a fixed surname within one generation. However, paternity was equally an ideology the missionaries and colonial administration were keen to promote. For the Directors of Pniel Institution, the mission station was regarded as the setting in which to inculcate ideals of the family among the ex-slaves, and at the head of any model family was the father. As Pamela Scully has discussed, the mission stations at the Cape in the mid 19th century were places where the ideology of the patriarchal family was strongly asserted, for emancipation was closely bound up with articulations of gender identity (Scully 1994; 1997). For the missionaries, the family provided the key context for shaping the behaviour of ex-slaves, for 'civilizing' and 'humanizing' them (Philip 1828). It not only provided a curb on the potential hypersexuality perceived to be the hall-mark of former slave women (and men), it also encouraged the familiar European model of the 'separation of spheres': the man working, the woman staying at home and the children at school. In broad terms, it was about inculcating 're-spectability' in a new working class population, whose counterpart was a 'gentility' among the middle and upper classes of Cape society during the same period (see Chapter 3); both shared similar features, especially surrounding gender roles, but with the working class it also included the element of improvement and political representation (Ross 1999b).

As Ross succinctly describes it, the £25 electoral franchise was the cost of respectability (ibid.: 173).

However, what the missionaries hoped to achieve is not quite what happened. Certainly families were constructed and marriages increased dramatically in the wake of emancipation (Scully 1997: 118–119). In many cases, however, this may be a case of the ex-slaves attempting to consolidate previous relationships that went unrecognized under slavery (see above). But where practice differed most from the ideal, was the role of labour in relation to the family, and on two counts. First, while many women did stay at home and children did attend school on missions, it is also clear they engaged in casual or seasonal labour. Part of this was simply economic necessity; the typical wage of a male farm hand in the Dwars valley in the mid 19th century was 9d, which was not even enough to cover the monthy rent of £1 16s at Pniel; though wages went up during harvest season, since this was not a regular income it could not cover this shortfall. Women and children therefore had to work, and both did, especially during the busy harvest seasons, but also in domestic service on the farms, or casual work such as laundry (Figure 4.13). Second, while many men worked on neighbouring farms, in some cases and at certain seasons, many would have been shifted to more distant farms, meaning that they may have lived there during the week or even longer in harvest time. In Pniel, this seems to have been mostly a seasonal issue for the men, who were away on wheat farms principally in Koeberg and Kuilenberg for up to two months of the year. During this time, their role as male head of house was reduced to an economic role, since they may have been absent as much if not more than they were present. The role of work was thus in tension with the ideals of the family, creating a dynamic of actual family life which was very different to the ideal, and one where women soon took on the primary responsibility for maintaining the cultural values and ethics of the mission community (Scully 1997: 139; also see Gaitskell 1983).

Family was and is important in Pniel, as on the farms in the valley, and the significance of the household for the ex-slave community cannot be over-emphasized. The houses which they built came to be the primary arena in which family life was constructed and new identities articulated. However, the family life which they developed was not quite what its founders—or even themselves—necessarily intended, inflected as it was by the conditions of labour to which they were bound. The articulation of post-emancipation identities was enmeshed within a network of conflicting interests—of the missionaries, the farmers, the colonial administration as well as their own, and even though they

Figure 4.13. Laundry washing in Pniel in the early 20th century. (*Source*: Cape Archives AG7560)

were now free, it was a freedom which brought its own burdens as it was a life which was also still largely defined by what it had been under slavery—work. However, it did not remain this way—Pniel today is a very prosperous community and a large part of its population now work in service industries or other trades and business in the region. The wine farms still exist, but much of the work is done by new immigrant labourers, many even from outside South Africa, living in cottages on the estates. In the next section, I want to examine the developments of labour and life in the valley in the 20th century, and how Pniel became what it is today.

FROM EMANCIPATION TO APARTHEID: PNIEL AND THE DWARS VALLEY IN THE 20TH CENTURY

The Twentieth century ushered in radical changes for the Dwars Valley. By 1900, South Africa was a much larger place than the original Cape colony; since the later 18th century, settlers had continued to inch forward both eastward and northward, a frontier which expanded rapidly in the 19th century. By the mid 19th century, the new colony of Natal was formed on the east coast, and by the late 19th century, a new self-proclaimed South African Republic had been formed by the *trek-boers*, in the Transvaal and Orange Free State. The Republic went to war with Britain to assert their independence, but lost, becoming incorporated colonies themselves in 1902. A major cause of the war was control over a new resource, which had been discovered in the Transvaal—gold. Diamonds and then gold had been discovered in the north during the later 19th century and several mining companies were established; the man who made his fortune in these fields was Cecil John Rhodes, who bought out and expanded the De Beers Mining Company, turning the mines into a large-scale industrial operation. Rhodes' imperialistic megalomania is legendary, and his British South Africa Company, set up on a similar model to the 17th century East India Companies, annexed large areas of eastern Africa, including Zimbabwe and Zambia. However, in 1897, Rhodes actions as politician and business manager were severely impugned by the British and in the last years of his life, he directed his attentions to a less controversial sphere. In that year, he started to buy up agricultural land in Drakenstein through his agent, Lewis Lloyd Michell, including the best farms in the Dwars valley (Figure 4.14).

Rhodes knew little of agriculture, but he had already sponsored an English fruit farmer Harry Pickstone, who had cut his teeth in California. Seeing Pickstone's success, he decided to invest in fruit farming on an industrial scale in the Drakenstein, and wanted Pickstone to run them for him; Pickstone helped Rhodes in purchasing the farms and directed them for the first six years (until 1903), establishing the infrastructure and importing managers from California to handle their daily running (Baker 1934: 61–3; Gertenbach, pers. comm.). Rhodes died soon after acquiring these properties, but just before his death in 1902, Mitchell transferred the land to a newly formed subsidiary of De Beers, Rhodes Fruit Farms (RFF). Given that precious minerals formed the major concern of de Beers, it is interesting to note an unusual purchase RFF made in 1914. Property 1199 lies up on the slopes of the Simonsberg—this is not cultivable land and is a strange acquisition for a fruit farm to make, but in 1914, they bought the quitrent for a little over £29. Prior to this, it had been common or government land. Plot 1199 does however encompass the mine shafts dug in the mid 18th century for silver (see Chapter 2). But if RFF was aware of the history of the mines, then so was the government, for there were statements not usually seen on a title deed, reserving the rights to all precious minerals to the government, not the deed holder. Not that this would

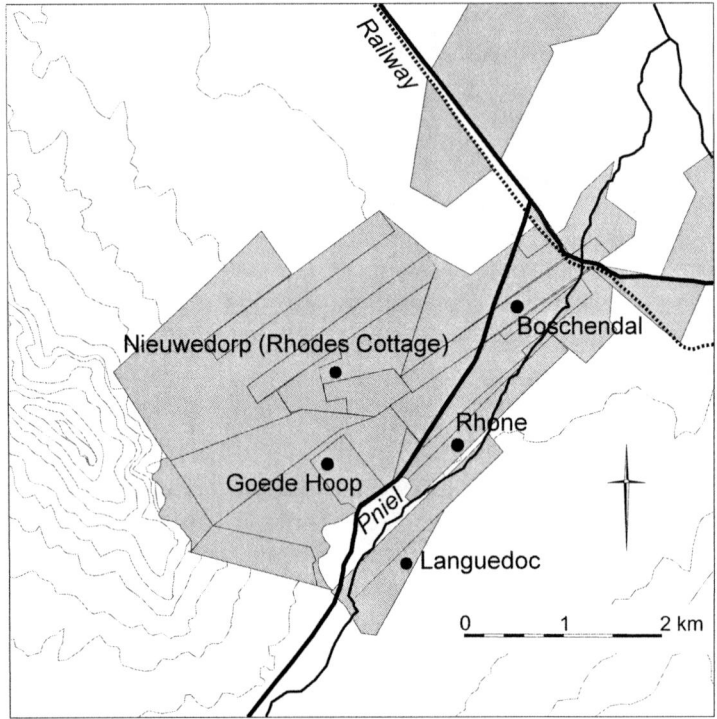

Figure 4.14. Plan of Rhodes Fruit Farms properties. (*Source*: Adapted from map in possession of Anglo-American)

have excluded RFF from mining or profiting, but it shows, even in the early 20th century, that the legacy of the silver mines on the Simons-berg was still strong enough for people to be cautious about dismissing its potential altogether. Goede Hoop, which bordered the mines and on whose land the ruins of the mining settlement now lay, was also com-monly known as 'Silvermine' (Zilvermyn) among the local population. In 1937, RFF was sold to an old friend of Rhodes, Abe Bailey who re-tained the property until his death when it was bought by a syndicate of businessmen who sold it in 1969 to Anglo-American Farms (AAF or Amfarms), with whom most of the land still belongs. Amfarms is a sub-sidiary of the multi-national corporation Anglo-American, founded in 1917 by Ernest Oppenheimer, who in 1926 gained a majority share in De Beers and was later chairman, thus incorporating the company into Anglo-American.

In the early 20th century, RFF began fruit farming on a mass-scale and completely altered the landscape of the valley; although fields, boundaries and houses were largely left intact, the land was now within

Figure 4.15. Pay Day at the workers cottages at Languedoc in the early 20th century. (*Source*: Cape Archives AG7532)

the hands of a single owner, and right at the beginning of the twentieth century, corporate capitalism started to change the nature of life in the valley (Figure 4.14). In 1904 a railway line was brought into the mouth of the valley and then a cannery and jam factory (all instigated by Pickstone), while much of the labour working for RFF continued to come from Pniel (Gertenbach 2000). Nevertheless, the scale of the operations and the fact that many of the former labourers for previous farmers still lived on the farms and not in Pniel, meant that new workers accommodation was needed. Herbert Baker, the famous colonial architect of the British Empire who worked in India designing the urban plan for New Dehli (Irving 1981), was a close associate of Rhodes, and designed a new labourers village on the farm of Languedoc, now part of RFF (Figure 4.15; Baker 1934: 66–7). Rhodes' attitude to these labourers however was less than respectful, if Rhodes' views on the coloured population can be generalized (ibid.: 66).

Baker also built a house for Rhodes on the farm of Nieuwedorp, Rhodes Cottage (which Rhodes however never occupied), in the revivalist style of Cape Dutch architecture. Baker had already built two houses for Rhodes near Cape Town (the Woolsack and Welgelegen) as well as re-building an old homestead (Groote Schuur; Baker 1944). Both Baker and Rhodes admired the Cape Dutch style and Baker recalled Rhodes' admiration of this architecture in his biography (Baker 1934; 1944); indeed when buying up properties in the Drakenstein, Rhodes specifically requested preference be given to farms with "the more beautiful and stately of the old homesteads" (Baker 1934: 64). However, this was more than pure aesthetic admiration here; Rhodes motives must have also been driven by the need to maintain an appearance of continuity; his wish to preserve and maintain what he saw as a disappearing landscape would have also served an important ideological role for the local community, of both farmers and labourers. By renovating and up-keeping old farmsteads, an illusion of individual farms was sustained, masking the fact that this was now a landscape of corporate ownership.

However, while many of the farm labourers lived in the new village, the administrative and management staff lived in these former homesteads, particularly Goede Hoop. For most of the 20th century, Goede Hoop was the official residence of the managing director of RFF/AAF, and today, it remains as a guest house for visiting management which now works primarily from Vergelegen, Willem Adriaan van der Stel's former estate (see Chapter 3). Interviews with the wife of a former manager of the farm have revealed something of the use of the buildings and life in the valley from one perspective in the mid 20th century (Dressler, pers.comm.). The homestead was occupied by the General Manager, while the former millhouse by a factory manager; the farm manager and their family lived in a house outside the main werf, close to the graveyard. This house had been built in the latter half of the 19th century, and was probably the residence of Paul Retief, who seems to have been a co-occupant of Goede Hoop and partner of the official deed holder, Pieter Izak de Villiers. Retief died in 1873 and was buried in the family graveyard. In the main werf, the wine cellars and stables continued to function as before, while the long house behind the homestead served as domestic servants quarters and a store room although a stable boy had living quarters in the stables where there was also offices.

The managing director and his family living at the homestead, had three domestic servants—a cook, housemaid and a laundress, but for the other management, domestic servants were less common. The farm manager only employed a casual worker occasionally to help around the house, and then later, a part time maid whose husband worked on the farms. By the 1940s, many of the labourers on the farm were migrant workers from the Eastern Cape, housed at the factory, although the majority of the workers still came from Pniel or the new village of Languedoc. Later on, new housing for these migrants were built on Goede Hoop, but at some distance away from the *werf*. Migrant workers still live there. The fruit industry was and is, very labour intensive, especially during harvest. In the 1940s, wagons and horses were still used in the orchards and manual labour was used to tend the trees and vines, the soil was tilled with shovels and forks. During harvest time, the fruit was placed into wicker baskets carried by the fruit pickers, which were then emptied into "packing cases" on the back of horse-drawn wagons (and later tractors) and the fruit was then transported to the packing store or canning factory. Mostly men were employed, although today women are a far more common part of the labour force, while children would sometimes work during the holidays to earn pocket money.

Reading the landscape of the Dwars valley under the corporate ownership of RFF/AAF reveals some interesting developments. On the one hand, there is a new vision of the landscape, where everything is on a larger scale than before; the new industrial scale of production even brings in new migrants to the valley, working for the company. But in other ways, there is a great deal of continuity—the integration of many of the workers into the company as 'family'; people who worked for the company, also live in houses built by them, on land owned by them, while the management occupy the former homesteads. In many ways the class divisions and organization of labour has changed little, in the shift from multiple, private farmers to a single corporation. But there have also been many changes, in particular, among the community of Pniel which has become much more independent than it was in the 19th century. The community is able to exert a much stronger sense of autonomous existence and identity than it had previously, a characteristic that has undoubtedly flourished in the post-apartheid years.

Expansion on the southern and western sides of Pniel has been taking place since the 19th century and is continuing still today, as Pniel is a thriving and increasingly wealthy community. Nevertheless, many of the amenities are very recent—while the first house in Pniel had electricity in the 1920s, most did not get this until much later. Similarly piped water was only introduced in the early 20th century, and then in communal taps—piping direct to homes occurred much later. Refuse was thrown at the back of the lot or taken to a communal dump by the river, but municipal collection only started in the 1980s. Until the mid 20th century, most residents relied on food produced by themselves on their allotments; here they grew sweet potatoes, potatoes, green beans, peas, carrots, tomatoes and onions among others, and kept chickens and pigs. While fish hawkers regularly visited Pniel (and still do), the first butchery only opened in the 1940s giving the community access to a wider selection of meat, including beef and mutton. Over the latter part of the 20th century, food bought from shops increasingly replaced home produce and there are a number of small groceries in the town today. While all these changes are significant, it is the social context of life in Pniel in the 20th century that is most revealing, particularly about how the family is articulated and how this relates to the early days of the settlement in the mid 19th century.

Throughout the 20th century, family remained a key mode of articulating identity in Pniel, as evident in interviews conducted with several elderly residents of Pniel. Households ideally consisted of the nuclear family of the married couple and children, although some relatives may have also lived with this unit, depending on the size of the house. Generally, a married couple would always strive to set up a new home, thus accounting in large part, for the rapid growth of Pniel. Gender seems to have been clearly demarcated in the household, as boys and girls slept in separate rooms, and even if there was insufficient room, this separation would be maintained. For example, in one case where an uncle lived with the family, he shared with the boys, while in another where there was no spare room, the boys slept in the dining room. Sundays became an important regular occasion for bringing the family together for a special meal at midday where roasted meats were eaten in contrast to the usual weekday evening meal of vegetable stews, fish, and pies. These meals were eaten in the dining room, instead of, as on other days, the kitchen. Other religious days such as Easter and Christmas also served the same function, as did weddings and twenty-first birthdays. Weddings in particular used to be very significant events incorporating a wide extended family, although today usually only close family are invited. The family then, remained a key social ideal in Pniel, and one which still adhered to the patriarchal model. Men were considered the main breadwinners, while the role of women was to raise the family and care for the household, with the assistance of children. Most of the men still worked for RFF/AAF, working Monday through to Saturday morning, but during harvest time also on Sundays, when women also often worked too. They would usually walk to work and the day would start at 5 am in the summer and 7 am in the winter. Some managed to maintain a living as builders and carpenters, but this was seasonal and dependent on available work.

Such are the contours of life reflected in local memory. I want to now study one house lot in some detail, using chiefly archaeology to try and understand the micro-history of life in Pniel in the 20th century.

ERF 776: THE ANATOMY OF A HOUSE LOT

The lot excavated in 2001 lies in the south western part of Pniel (see Figure 4.9); a house stood on the plot until the mid 1980s when it was razed but local memory recalled it as an old structure, made of mudbrick on stone foundations (Fortuin, pers. comm.). Removal of a demolition layer exposed the base of all internal walls which were built of mudbrick on cobble base and the floor—layers of linoleum over a stamped brick fragment and mortar (i.e. grock) floor. The external walls had been demolished quite extensively and only the stone foundations remained, but probably consisted of mud brick as local memory suggests (Figure 4.16). The excavation of the house revealed a surprisingly complex history; in short, it was found that originally a small, two cell structure stood on this plot, oriented east-west and dating to sometime in the mid-19th century (Figure 4.17). Toward the end of the century, this was expanded into a four room house, now oriented north-south and onto the street, which may have been laid out around the same time. This later house underwent some internal modification, probably quite early on, mostly affecting the northern end, and thereafter, seems to have remained unchanged until its demolition (though additional elements may have been added to its back). The house as recalled by the owner's daughter, consisted of a large central living room

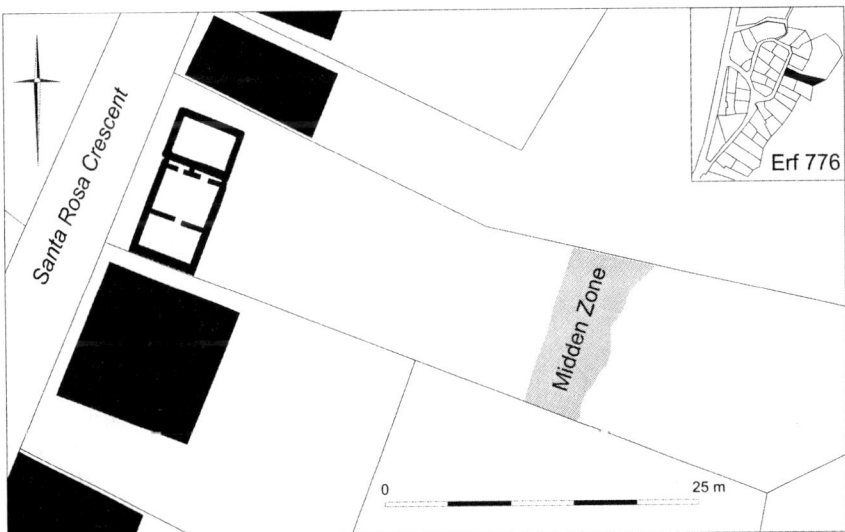

Figure 4.16. Erf 776.

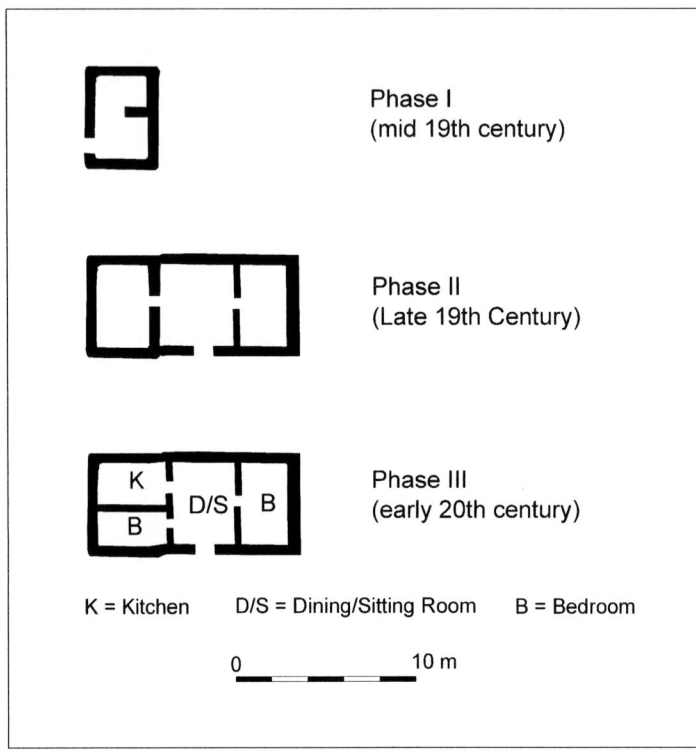

Figure 4.17. The development of erf 776.

through which access to and from the street was made and off this a
bedroom to the south, and a kitchen and other bedroom to the north
(Louisa Adams, pers. comm.). The layout of this house clearly conforms
to the Type A discussed above.

There were no services to the house, so water must have been acquired from one of the communal taps, while lighting came from paraffin
lamps, two of which were recovered from the demolition layer over the
house. Cooking would have been done on a wood burning or gas stove.
Behind the house, the ground sloped steeply down toward the river, but
is had been terraced on several levels; the immediate level behind the
house probably had a lean-to shelter or shed, and there was probably
an outdoor privy or use of chamber pots. Test pits were dug at intervals
in a transect down the back of the property, and while the upper test
pits recovered little material and showed a shallow soil profile, the lowest test pit at the base of the slope had a much thicker accumulation

of soil. Here also lay the main midden, which was evident both from local memory and surface inspection. A large assemblage of ceramics, glass, tin and some bone among other finds were retrieved in the long sondage cut at the base of the slope, the majority of the material dating to the 20th century. At the base of the sequence, only a small amount of 19th century material was recovered.

Comparing the Pniel house to other archaeological examples of working class housing in the Cape is difficult given the limited research. There has been some recent investigations on another mission station, Genadendal (Malan pers. comm.), but the best examples come from Cape Town—in District Six and Bo-Kaap. There have been a few excavations in District Six, mostly uncovering the foundations of buildings, which had been leveled in the wake of forced removals in the late 1979s and early 1980s (see below). The archaeological evidence, combined with archive research and oral history has provided a rich history of the area, which challenges many myths while at the same time yielding a detailed picture of life of working class people in the 20th century (Malan and Van Heyningen 2001). The excavations on one erven in Horstley Street, show terrace rows of cottages—small, two-roomed houses with a corridor or passageway to one side, and with stone foundations and poorly fired brick walls, bonded and rendered with mud mortar and plaster (Figure 4.18). At the back was an open yard, which was soon after modified by the extension of another room used as a kitchen and the installation of drains and an outdoor privy. The house was originally built in 1897, but may have suffered from overcrowding fairly soon—archaeological evidence suggested the extensions occurred at the same time as the corridor started to be used as a living space rather than just a corridor. Moreover, there seem to have been intense use of the back space of the lots in District Six, from unauthorized additions to workshops (Hall et al. 1994; Halkett and Hart 1996; Malan and Van Heyningen 2001: 51).

District Six housed a diverse ethnic community during the late 19th and 20th century, and it was only towards the mid 20th century that it became predominantly coloured, including a strong muslim element. Bo-Kaap lies on the other side of Cape Town to District Six, and is commonly known as the 'Malay' quarter of Cape Town, a term used to designate 'coloureds' who were muslims (Townsend and Townsend 1977). However this area too probably includes a complex and heterogeneous population history, indeed the very term 'Cape Malay' is largely a creation of the 1940s and 1950s and is closely linked to attempts by certain members of the elite Muslim community living in Bo-Kaap to carve out an identity which downplayed their slave origins in favour

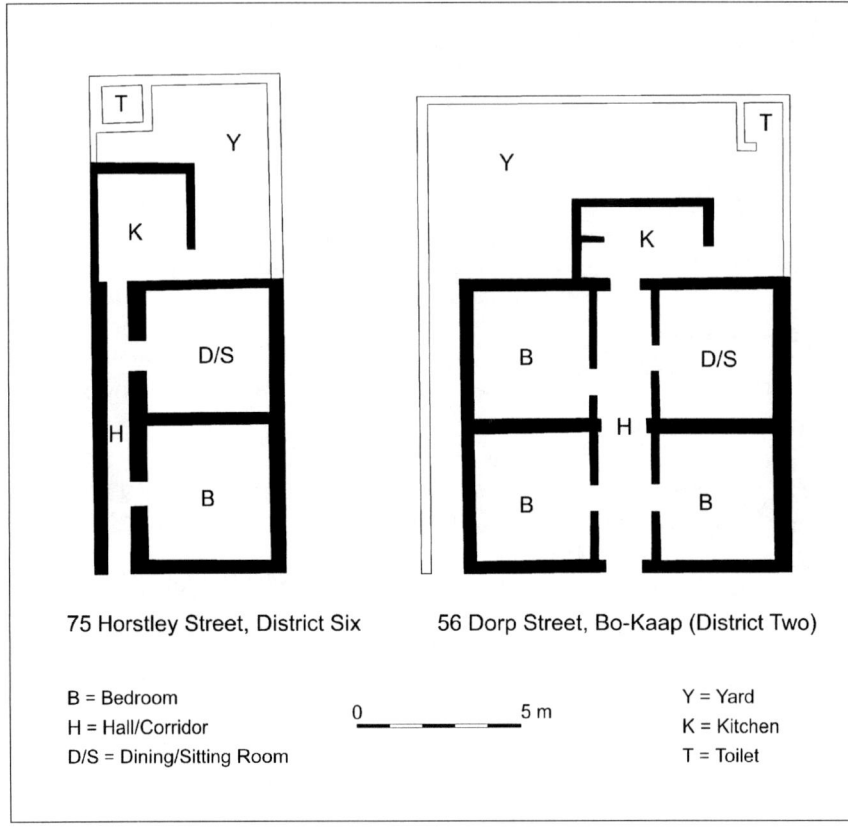

Figure 4.18. Plans of working class housing in Cape Town. (Adapted from Malan & van Heyningen 2001 and Irvine 1990)

of ethnic affiliation (Ward and Warden 1998: 208). The housing in Bo-Kaap is both similar and different to District Six—certainly it is a much older part of the urban fabric as many of the houses were built in the later 18th century. Unlike District Six, it did not suffer forced removal as it was designated a coloured area, and many of the old houses still stand today as part of the quarter was declared a national monument. James Walton identified two main types of original house in this area—one is very similar to the type in District Six in form, a narrow corridor down one side and rooms off it to the right, while the other is more symmetrical, with a central hall or passageway, with rooms off each side. Both types had a stoep and a backyard, which was a focus of much activity, as in District Six (Walton 1995: 112–115). Excavations in the back yard of one house of the second type, on Dorp Street, produced a small assemblage of material, but on the whole, the back area was fairly clean (Irvine 1990; Figure 4.18). Similarly, little artefactual material was recovered from the excavations in District Six, generally finds were small and what had accumulated under floorboards. Moreover, the back yard of Horstley Street was concreted while that of Dorp Street cobbled, suggesting an attempt was made to provide a cleanable outdoor surface. The picture of squalor which was often painted of working class areas such as District Six and Bo-Kaap—both of which were regarded as slums by the municipal authorities—is not necessarily borne out by the archaeology. However, the Dorp street house, like that in Horstley Street, did show a number of additions to the back part of the property including a kitchen and outdoor privy, which are suggestive of overcrowding, but this in itself does not so much indicate squalor as an active attempt by inhabitants to deal with problems of large households. Indeed, archaeology is increasingly providing a contested narrative of the 'slum' nature of poorer or working class areas of cities, an image which developed in the 19th century among middle classes and is imbued with a particular ideology (Mayne and Murray 2001; Yamin 2001).

Cleanliness and lack of clutter was considered key attributes of respectability, and it is clear this ideology was something that was strived for, even in the worst urban conditions, and even if it fell short of white, middle class ideals (Ross 1999b). In the mission stations, such as Pniel however, the opportunities to maintain these ideals were much better, given the space available. Erf 776 in Pniel contrasts with the tight space of Horstley Street for example, with its spacious back yard and larger rooms. Overcrowding does not seem to have been an issue in Pniel either, even if some households may have had large or extended families living there. However in other ways, Pniel lacked many of the things one sees in urban working class households; services, though initially not installed at Horstley street for example, soon were, while in Pniel they came much later, and on erf 776, not at all. Furthermore, household goods, such as ceramic tablewares and bottled commodities too are very rare in the Pniel site until the mid 20th century. In contrast, assemblages from working class housing in Cape Town from the later 19th century are comparable to those of contemporary middle class households (Table 4.2)—although quantities may be less and there may also be more subtle differences in the quality and types of vessels. This last has not really been explored but is certainly worthy of further research; an exploratory comparison by decoration suggests that poorer households may have had more sponge and slipwares, unsurprisingly perhaps as they were cheaper (Table 4.3). Such household goods would

Table 4.2. 19th Century Ceramic Assemblages from Cape Town. (*Source*: adapted from data in Klose & Malan 2000, Irvine 1990, Sealy 1998 and ACO 1991)

	Working Class Households				Middle Class Households			
	Tenant Street (c.1840–1880)		Dorp Street (c. 1790–1850)		Riverstone Road (c.1840–1900)		Harrington Street (c.1860–1890)	
	MNV	%	MNV	%	MNV	%	MNV	%
Oriental porcelain	31	4.68	31	22.79	2	0.86	24	2.87
European porcelain	5	0.75	7	5.15	42	18.03	50	5.97
Oriental stoneware	4	0.60	0	0.00	0	0.00	0	0.00
European stoneware	49	7.39	13	9.56	26	11.16	78	9.32
Coarse lead-glazed earthenware	21	3.17	4	2.94	7	3.00	2	0.24
Refined Industrial earthenwares & stonewares	553	83.41	81	59.56	156	66.95	683	81.60
Total	*663*	*100*	*136*	*100*	*233*	*100*	*837*	*100*

have also been an important way of articulating respectability, especially given the importance attached to family meals, and while their absence in Pniel may relate to issue of access which do not apply for an urban working class household, still this lack would have carried some implications. Whatever advantages a Pniel household had with regard

Table 4.3. Comparison of types of decoration at different Cape Town sites. (*Source*: Adapted from data in Klose & Malan 2000, Irvine 1990, Sealy 1998 and ACO 1991)

	Working Class Households				Middle Class Households			
Main Decorative types	Tenant Street (c. 1840–1880)		Dorp Street (c. 1790–1850)		Riverstone Road (c. 1840–1900)		Harrington Street (c. 1860–1890)	
	MNV	%	MNV	%	MNV	%	MNV	%
Banded	0.00	0.00	3.00	4.05	7	5.43	11.00	2.18
Sponge	9.00	1.91	10.00	13.51	2	1.55	56.00	11.11
Slip	78.00	16.53	10.00	13.51	5	3.88	90.00	17.86
Transfer	285.00	60.38	26.00	35.14	92	71.32	305.00	60.52
Shell-edge	6.00	1.27	4.00	5.41	0	0.00	9.00	1.79
Plain	94.00	19.92	21.00	28.38	23	17.83	33.00	6.55
Total	*472*	*100*	*74.00*	*100*	*129*	*100*	*504*	*100*

to space, it was not until the 1940s that it had comparable access to the range of such commodities available to its urban counterpart.

APARTHEID AND IDENTITY

In 1910 all the four colonies of southern Africa—Cape, Natal, Transvaal and Orange Free State—had been brought together under the Union of South Africa, with its own parliament and prime minister. The country remained part of the British Empire or Commonwealth until 1961 when it was expelled and formally declared itself a Republic, but by this time it had already implemented its apartheid policies. Dominating the politics of the country during most of the 20th century was the Nationalist Party, who after the elections of 1948, introduced their programme of apartheid which aimed to carve out separate regions with their own governing bodies for different ethnic groups. Four groups were classified in the Population Registration Act of 1950: Whites, Coloureds, Asians and Blacks. Basically, apartheid was a policy of fragmentation by segregation, splitting the country into incipient African nations off from a white South Africa. They key practical applications of this programme were effected through the concepts of 'homeland' and 'group area'; homelands (or Bantustans as they became known) were those regions designated for separate political and economic development, and chiefly applied to blacks; group areas on the other hand were enclaves of mainly coloured and asian populations within white South Africa. These policies led to forced removals under the Group Areas Act of 1950, where a large proportion of the population (10%—3.5 million people), were suddenly designated as living in the wrong area.

However violent the policies of apartheid were, it is now recognized that they were an extension and adaptation of pre-existing structures written into the 1910 constitution of the Union of South Africa (Beinart and Dubow 1995). Under the term 'segregation', a number of policies were established which aimed to regulate the relationship between the minority of whites (c. 20%) and majority non-whites, including residential segregation in towns and the countryside (e.g. Native Lands Act 1913, Natives Urban Area Act 1923). There have been various perspectives on where and how segregation was first articulated, and they have been variously tied to British imperial ideologies of race as well as the economic conditions of the new industrial settlements in the north, linked to the diamond and gold mines. Certainly the mineral revolution and increasing industrialization did have an impact on urban populations which resulted in greater concern by whites for segregation—which may have stimulated as well as been stimulated by an increasing sense of white ethnicity (Bickford-Smith 1995). In so doing, the racialization of the rest of the population may have just followed on. During the early 20th century, many of the material policies of segregation anticipated those of apartheid, especially in terms of architecture and town planning (Lemon 1991; Le Grange 1985; Smith 1992). One can even see such processes occurring in Pniel with separation of coloureds from blacks in Stegman's vision of the townscape, as discussed above. However, such policies were much more prevalent in urban areas such as Cape Town.

By the 1920s, housing had become a critical problem in Cape Town, especially in the working class areas such as District Six, the area to the west of the Castle and old town. Health concerns were the pretext for the forced removal of many black Africans in the city in 1897 to a camp on the Cape Flats, later named Ndabeni, as racial ideologies entwined with ideologies of sanitation and hygiene (Swanson 1977). Such ideologies continued to play a role well into the 20th century as the housing shortage became critical, for the municipal population had quadrupled between 1890 and 1920 from over 50,000 to over 200,000 people. In 1920 the Housing Act was passed which recommended state intervention in the provision of housing, and the solution in Cape Town was to adopt the model of the Garden City, developed in Britain (Le Grange 1985). The Garden City model offered town planners two key principles: low density housing which decreased health problems and 'green belts', which segregated the urban landscape as well as providing a buffer zone between residential areas. The same model had been used in Britain to maintain class distinctions and consciously or not, its segregationist potential was exploited in South Africa for the new non-white, working class suburbs and townships. Thus to replace the 'temporary' camp of Ndabeni, by now severely overcrowded, the new township of Langa was conceived on these principles, as were other municipal housing schemes such as Maitland Garden Village, developed for the coloureds,. From the 1920s to the 1940s, housing shortages only got worse and similar projects were initiated, so that by the time of the 1950 Group Areas Act, the forced removal of large numbers of black and coloured Capetonians to the Cape Flats in new townships such as Mitchells Plain had established precedents. Such removals continued late into the apartheid era—the infamous removals from District Six, a key working class part of the city, took place over several years between 1976 and 1982, and the area today mostly remains as it was after it was bulldozed: an urban wasteland, a testament to the cruelty and vanity of apartheid (De Kok 1998; Malan and Van Heyningen 2001).

The ideology of segregation and later, apartheid was always in tension however, with the economic need for labour in towns and cities, and consequently all manner of strategies were needed to accommodate this such as the pass laws. However, at the same time such segregation also worked in favour of a certain type of labour: the migrant worker. Migrant workers formed a major part of the labour force in the diamond and gold mines of the Transvaal, since the 19th century—for the industrialists, they were cheap to accommodate, as their families, if they had them, lived elsewhere. Indeed, these families, whom the mining companies did not have to feed or accommodate, provided a ready source of new workers (Wolpe 1972). When the homelands were created under apartheid, this reinforced the migrant system by confining the labourers' families to reserves, who maintained the burden of reproducing the workforce for the mines. It has been pointed out that the migrant labour system was as much a product of the African communities as the industrialists, and in particular was linked to the gendered nature of migrant labour and the patriarchal organization of these societies (Beinart 1985; Bozzoli 1983). Certainly this gives the labouring groups a more active role in this history, even it was unintentionally to the benefit of the government's segregationist ideology.

Against this background, in 1968, Pniel was designated as a rural 'Coloured Area'. Pniel of course, lay in the heart of rich agricultural land owned by individual farmers and companies, and most of this land was designated as 'white'. Yet being agricultural, it depended heavily on the labour of the 'coloured' population; places like Pniel—former mission stations—effectively provided ready made 'townships', and reserves of labour, which farmers and companies like AAF did not have to maintain—they were self-reproducing and provided most of the necessary labour for agriculture in the valley. The interests of Amfarms in the valley and its need for labour was ultimately served by towns like Pniel, as it had done for the farmers before in the years after emancipation. But equally, the presence of a community such as Pniel, a 'coloured' enclave in the heart of a 'white' Cape, with its own sense of identity and traditions, contradicted the very premise of segregation. Its people worked on the white land for white farmers and companies, their presence, indeed their ancestry, an ever-constant reminder of the fantasy of apartheid.

Wider community networks in Pniel have always been maintained through the Church, which has helped to sustain a sense of communal identity. Regular church services and functions, either on Sundays or special days, such as Easter, the church's birthday or the church bazaar, served to maintain its sense of identity and distinction within the valley.

The importance of the church as a focus, and the *werf* in the center of the settlement provided a communal space for such activities, although today the community hall and sports hall, have become the key venues. This has probably taken on increasing significance as new settlements emerged in the 20th century, namely Johannesdal and Kylemore, many of whose inhabitants nevertheless have family connections to Pniel. But equally, the communal identity has emerged in distinction to the corporate identity of RFF/AAF, for whom many still work. The relationship of Pniel to Amfarms today is not unaffected by the era of apartheid, and many in the community see the company as having unscrupulously profited from this system. Many large companies enjoyed economic success under apartheid and its labour laws, particularly Anglo-American who bought out many smaller companies, including foreign firms who quit under the call for sanctions so that by 1987, it owned 60% of all shares on the Johannesburg stock exchange (Innes 1984; Ross 1999a: 132). More generally however, the relationship between Amfarms and Pniel in the later 20th century encapsulates the key relation, even contradiction, at the heart of apartheid: between the ideology of segregation and the economy of labour.

Ultimately of course, apartheid failed—the persistent resistance to it by the majority of the population and the increasing isolation of South Africa in the international community, caused it to crumble and in 1994, the first universal franchise elections were held, leading to the inauguration of the ANC as the new government. Under the new constitution, new policies about urban and rural landscapes were produced, and in particular, the promotion of Integrated Development Plans (IDP) aimed to manage development in a fair and progressive manner. In 2001, Pniel became incorporated into the Stellenbosch Municipal Council, which produced their own IDP with a vision of an "...integrated and reconciled community, free from all forms of discrimination" (Stellenbosch Municipality 2002: 110). As part of the production of the IDP, a full review of the state of municipality was conducted, and an interim document gives some detailed data on the current state of Pniel as of 2001. The population was 2556, with a total of 623 *erven* or lots, 600 of which were developed with housing. All of these had electricity, piped water and sewage pipes. Pniel remains very much a residential settlement—only three business' are registered, two shops and a garage. There is still a local council in Pniel, and the Church is as strong as ever, but its heritage is becoming a major focus for many members of the community, and a Museum Committee has now been established.

Heritage and tourism are closely linked in the new IDP, and Pniel is keen to explore this aspect, part of which is occurring under the

umbrella of the UNESCO slave route project. There are also more local initiatives in the community, such as genealogical research linked
to the history of Pniel, or conservation oriented strategies, focused on
material remains such as the silver mines (Winter 1999). Moreover,
there is a committed effort on the part of Anglo-American to facilitate
new heritage initiatives in tandem with Pniel. Amfarms own many
examples of Cape Dutch farms, which they have restored and opened
to the public, including Boschendal, which is a major tourist attraction; but they are also keen to integrate their programmes with local
heritage initiatives, such as those discussed above (Gertenbach 2000).
There are however conflicts over the heritage of Pniel and the Dwars
valley—not only between Amfarms and some of the people in Pniel, but
also within Pniel itself. However, so much is still at the preparation
and proposal stage that it is hard to say how the heritage of the valley will ultimately be presented; nevertheless, consensus may be less
interesting and provocative than difference of opinion. The valley remains a place which is heterogeneous, where politics and identity are
still in flux, especially so since the end of apartheid. People are trying
to make sense of their past, now more than ever—and in many ways,
perhaps ironically, it is the distant past of slavery and slave origins,
not apartheid that is forming the key focus among all parties. Many of
the elderly informants interviewed in Pniel spoke of how their parents
and grandparents would not talk about their slave origins—it was still
too close. A similar amnesia was found with the residents of another
mission station, Mamre (Ward 1994: 333), indeed in many ways the
heritage of slavery in South Africa has been largely suppressed, not
only by the 'white' government, but also by its 'coloured' population,
despite some active attempts to the contrary (Ward and Worden 1998).
It is only recently, since the mid 1990s, that the slaves descendants
are more actively seeking to remember their past. Now, people in Pniel
talk openly about it, indeed crave to know more about their past, and
who they are; it is perhaps only with the ending of apartheid and years
of oppression, that such questions of identity, can for the first time be
really addressed—indeed demand to be addressed.

Forging Identities | 5

In each of the preceding chapters I have examined the ways in which identity has been created and sustained for a number of different sections of the population at the Cape from the late 17th to the early 20th centuries. In Chapter 2, I discussed the nature of VOC power and identity, and the ambiguity involved between official and private enterprise through the example of the silver mine. More specifically, these ambiguities were expressed through the foreman of the mine works who, as an ex-serviceman, aspired to a certain status as a free citizen in the colony and who saw the mine as the means for achieving this. His failure, indeed the whole context of his attempt, contrasts with the first Huguenot settlers who came to the same valley over half a century earlier. As Chapter 3 discusses, the fortunes of these settlers varied too, but the really successful farmers, such as the de Villiers family, were eventually able to develop a distinct identity for themselves. They helped to forge a class of landed gentry whose wealth and status was independent of the VOC, creating a landscape which was their own and in which their identity was deeply inscribed. However, this landscape was only made possible by the labour of their slaves, people whose own power of expression was severely curtailed. In Chapter 4, I explored the lives of the slave and slave-descendant population and their incorporation into an ideology of the family, both before and after emancipation, though expressed in quite different ways. I have tried to show how they both used and contested this ideology, and to affirm their agency even under conditions which tried hard to negate such autonomy.

The study has by no means been exhaustive, indeed it explicitly focused on one small area, the Dwars Valley, in order to try and present something of the 'micro-physics' of these processes. My concern has been to show how real people, individuals were caught up in larger social and cultural processes and how they articulated their sense of who they were in this context. In so doing, they not only responded to the situation but helped to shape it. Moreover, the identity of each 'community' was bound up with that of the others, and the manner in which one group articulated this affected the behaviour of the others. Indeed, it was perhaps precisely the tensions which emerged through drawn lines within one group which fuelled the drive for self-circumscription by another. The issue I want to address in this concluding chapter is how these processes can be tied in to larger themes, specifically questions of identity, colonialism and capitalism, and how this contributes to a global historical archaeology. In other words, my concern is to explore the historical intersection of a local politics of identity, as illustrated in the main part of this book, and a global politics of capitalism.

RACE, CLASS AND GENDER

The current theoretical focus on identity politics is very much defined by a trinity of concepts which seem to be the primary means of articulating questions of identity. Race, class and gender—once addressed by scholars from separate angles, are increasingly being viewed as interrelated and mutually constitutive categories of society (see, for example, the excellent study by McClintock 1995). Race and class were perhaps the first pair to be associated, especially in the context of South African historiography. Marxist inspired studies of colonial and imperial histories have seen the development of the slave trade as establishing the grounds upon which later class divisions formed, with racial divisions underlining class divisions so that the two become mutually reinforcing. In a seminal volume of South African working class formation, Shula Marks and Richard Rathbone stressed the links between race and class, showing how industrial capitalism in the wake of the mineral revolution of the 1870s, exploited racism in the creation of a labouring class (Marks & Rathbone 1982: 4). Their emphasis is very much on the diamond and gold mines of the north and the emergence of a new urban proletariat from the late 19th century. This undoubtedly had a wider impact though, for its repercussions were felt all the way down to Cape Town, where the slave-descendant population appropriated the term 'Coloured' in order to differentiate themselves from the influx of Blacks from the eastern Cape and elsewhere after the 1870s (Bickford-Smith 1994; 1995). Previously an umbrella designation applied by the British colonial authorities and the white population in general to ex-slaves, free blacks and Khoisan, it became a means of unifying a population who previously were highly fragmented and differentiated and certainly did not share a common consciousness. In appropriating a label given by others, it became a means of creating a new community, defined by a common slave past and a creolized ancestry (Adhikari 1992).

In many ways, although perhaps not explicitly articulated until the last decades of the nineteenth century, the basis for this development of a 'coloured consciousness' was laid in the wake of emancipation in the 1830s. Indeed, Robert Ross argues that already by this time, the Cape economy was fully commercialised and its labour proletarianized (Ross 1986; 1993: 13–49). Certainly rural communities such as Pniel would have developed a sense of discrete identity fairly soon after establishment, an identity only hardened by the continuation of the same labour structures as before. Even in the towns, sections of the population such as the Muslims would have forged some sense of community too. However, it is perhaps fair to say the notion of a wider class consciousness is something which only comes with industrialization and the connection between labour and political representation. Indeed, for a long time it was imperial notions of respectability which seemed to be at stake in political enfranchisement (Ross 1999b: 175), not class consciousness and in fact such ideologies may have helped to retard the formation of a class consciousness in relation to labour structures.

Respectability in fact is very much entangled in the second relation—between gender and class. As early as 1983, Belinda Bozzoli argued for a consideration of the relation between these two terms, and the vital importance of integrating gender within economic critique (Bozzoli 1983). Crucially, she argued for the need to relate class struggle and class identity to the domestic context, not just the working context, and to examine the politics within the home as well as between the home and the capitalist sphere. A classic paper examining just such themes was Deborah Gaitskill's study of the conflicts of gender and labour among working class women in Johannesburg, published in the same year (Gaitskill 1983). Similar studies of Cape communities came much later, but it is now a fully entrenched part of scholarship, particularly influenced by the ideology of separate spheres which is argued to have emerged in England by the 1830s (Davidoff & Hall 2002). The notion that women are associated with the home and men with work was a middle class ideology that developed in the wake of the industrial revolution in England, and conjoined the notion of respectability with that of class. Essentially, it articulated the power structures of class difference based on labour by representing class as a cultural or social achievement—respectability. Class was about behaviour, about manners, about gender relations.

The legacy of this remains strong today, certainly in Britain, but as an ideology it was also exported to the British colonies, including South Africa. We have already seen how it operated both among the urban middle classes of Cape Town as well as the working classes of mission stations (Scully 1997). In many ways, there was a powerful link between the imperial project and this ideology of social improvement, and this came together precisely in locations such as mission stations (McClintock 1995: 35–6). The English missionary John Philip was quite explicit about the civilising role of missionary work and how it complemented Britain's imperial goals:

> While our missionaries, beyond the borders of the colony of the Cape of Good Hope, are everywhere scattering the seeds of civilization, social order, and happiness, they are by the most unexceptionable means, extending British interests, British influence, and the British Empire. (Philip 1828: ix–x).

By this means, the Empire became a cultural project, not simply an economic one. The effects of such imperial missionary work rebounded back home of course, and indeed there were soon parallels drawn between the missionary work among 'savages' and that in English towns among the working classes, who were likened to such 'savages' (McClintock 1995: 52–6, also esp. ch.2; Young 1995: 56–9). This link between empire and class through the notion of 'culture' brings us to the third pair, gender and race. Once again, it is in colonial and post-colonial studies that these terms have taken on their most dynamic force, especially through the notions of hybridity and creolisation (Young 1995). In the more specific context of the VOC and Dutch colonialism, Ann Stoler has addressed the tensions between gender and race in several papers (e.g. Stoler 1991; 2000). She argues that the racial distinctions between colonizer and colonized were secured through gender and the sexual control of domestic arrangements. On the one hand, there were no real prohibitions against inter-racial mixing, indeed the VOC condoned the practices of concubinage between its servants and local women. It not only generated a population who were bound to the colony, it also removed the burden of costs for maintaining families away from the VOC and onto the local population (Stoler 1991: 58).

However there were consequences of this policy that were perhaps unforeseen. In the first place, a colonial population emerged who were neither European nor local; the process of creolisation was highly problematic in the context of nationalism, for it challenged the question of national identity (Stoler 2000; also see Bhabha 1994). Who were such people and where did they belong? Moreover, the very question of creolisation, of hybridization connected the concept of identity with that of sexuality (Young 1995). Secondly, as the number of European women in the colonies increased during the later 19th century, so the question of sexual relations between races became more of an issue; it has long been remarked that an increase of racism and segregation occurred as the numbers of European women rose, and this was often ascribed to women being more racist than men. However, this has been shown to reflect not female attitudes to race, but male ones towards race and gender. It was men who feared sexual relations between European women and local men, and who encouraged the ideology of the 'black peril' to prevent such relations. Indeed, it was only with the entry of European women in the equation, that the whole connection of race and gender became contentious. Both of these consequences—the influx of European females and the growth of a creole population—seriously threatened the colonial order, because of the conceptual contradictions they highlighted. It was only in this context, toward the end of the nineteenth and especially the early twentieth century, that racial segregation became such a major issue. It reflected a real crisis in colonial power, which was only exacerbated by the developments of a working class consciousness and ultimately, the emergence of a national consciousness within the colony itself. In the case of South Africa, this was incredibly complicated since the divisions of race did not neatly align with those of colonizer and colonized. Moreover, given the multi-racial composition of South Africa, it did not even always align with class divisions either. National, racial and class consciousness thus remained loosely entwined.

The interplay of race, class and gender is undoubtedly more complex than I have portrayed here, but I have tried to give some idea of their intersection. Indeed, the previous chapters in this book have, I hope, provided a better sense of this complexity. Such themes are also now very much in the forefront of historical archaeologies in general (e.g. Delle et al. 2000; Orser 2001; Seifert 1991; Wall 1994; Wurst & Fitts 1999) However, it needs to be emphasized that this trinity of concepts are not so much categories of analysis for colonial (or any other) identity as historical formations specific to the period being discussed in this book; archaeology and other social disciplines, often use these concepts as if they were universal dimensions of analysis, yet I think we need to remember that race, class and even gender, are all constructions of European culture of the last few centuries, especially of the last two hundred years. Archaeologists generally do not extend the concepts of race or even class into the medieval period or even prehistory, rather they use broader terms such as ethnicity or social stratification, although gender has always seemed to retain a more general meaning. However, even ethnicity and social stratification remain ambiguous terms and it is questionable how separable they are from ideologies of race and class, or more generally from the specific social conditions of the modern world.

Race is not a universal of human society—few if any anthropologists today would argue that there are separate races of humanity and most agree that racial difference—as a biologically significant difference—is socially constructed. This construction of race emerged exactly as Europeans started to settle around the globe and where cultural differences between Europeans and others were articulated around perceived physical differences, especially skin colour. In particular, slavery and the slave trade played a major role in *constituting* ideologies of race—as much as they were justified by such ideologies. Indeed, the heyday of race ideology occurred after slavery and the slave trade had been abolished. Given this, what is especially interesting therefore is that the articulation of race ideology was not necessarily the same everywhere. It is very easy to subsume all European discourse on race under an essentially similar racial ideology—and in terms of scientific discourse, this may be partially correct. However, concepts of racial difference and racism were not exclusively scientific but used in everyday life; in fact, a systematic scientific discourse on race is undoubtedly much later, emerging in the late 18th and 19th century. During the 17th and earlier 18th centuries, racial ideologies were probably much more fluid and varied, and consequently one would expect them to have very different histories in South Africa as to North America or elsewhere. Because the social and cultural conditions in these different places varied—including the practices of slavery, these must have affected the way racial attitudes were articulated, even if in most cases, there was a broader politics that placed Europeans above others. In the context of the Cape, one sees this homogenisation of racial difference occurring only in the late 19th century, as both official British categorization and a newly emerging class consciousness drew up lines between White, Coloured and Black. Trying to understand race ideology prior to this classification is difficult; a common theme in this book and other studies is the notion of hybridity and creolisation, as a way of expressing the more fluid nature of social relations (e.g. see papers in Dawdy 2000). However, one needs to be wary of the way in which concepts such as creolization and hybridity presuppose the very thing they contest—i.e. 'pure' races; indeed, as Robert Young has argued, such concepts, which seem peculiarly post-colonial, always existed, even in the heart of Victorian racial theory (Young 1995). Nevertheless, the fact that they do unsettle the essentialism of race, guarantees their usefulness as concepts.

The concept of class is equally problematic; although it gained wide currency as part of Marxist analysis of the modern state from the late 19th century, anthropologists in the mid 20th century started to use the concept of class in a broad sense to define groups within a society with unequal status, whatever the basis for group differentiation (i.e. work, kinship, age or gender). While providing the means to extend Marxist approaches to pre-capitalist societies, there was always the danger of overplaying the analogy to class formations in modern society (McGuire 2002: 181; also see Saitta 1994). Moreover, while the general principle of looking at internal conflict within any society is undeniably a valuable asset, the extent to which this anthropological broadening of the concept of class may have weakened the original Marixst concept cannot be overlooked. This is particularly the case in historical archaeology.

For example, a weak definition of class would simply equate it with socio-economic status, which can then be measured in terms of simple indices such as income or surrogates for income, such as the purchasing ability of households for items such as ceramics (e.g. Miller 1991; Spencer-Wood 1987). Although it is recognized that the relation between consumer choice and income is not that straightforward, the relationship between income and class is less theorized in archaeology (Wurst & Fitts 1999: 2). Indeed, class in the above sense is simply a generalised status model, which ignores the specific historical and cultural context of class difference, and is similar to archaeological studies of status from prehistory. However, it is questionable how useful such general models are—in any period. Social differentiation is surely always related to the historical and culturally specific social conditions of the time and place; in the case of class, to the very particular changes affecting conditions of production and consumption in society associated with capitalism. The development of wage labour, factory production and new property rights among other changes, all affected social differentiation. Clearly based on Marxist (and also Weberian) analysis, archaeological approaches to class in this sense, focus on conflict, power and ideology rather than simple issues of status (e.g. Paynter & McGuire 1991; Wurst & Fitts 1999).

However, because class is historically specific, it will also vary between places and times within the modern era; class cannot be reduced to simplistic dualities such as worker and capitalist or even hierarchies such as lower, middle and upper, for they should not be seen as fixed or stable categories. Class is relational and constructed through specific practices, from factory labour to home furnishing, and while these practices may coalesce within communities or sections of the population, this is never fixed, but always open to change. Indeed, in many ways the concept of class is a fiction if we assume it to mean stable, internal social divisions within society; class is always situated, positional and cannot be separated from a consciousness of that position. Thus at certain periods and places, a community will have a strong sense of coherence, a 'class consciousness', but this should never be treated as a given, but rather something to be explored in relation to the specific practices of the community concerned. Nor does this deny social inequality or differentiation—the issue is not about whether there are social relations particular to capitalism, but whether it is useful to solidify these in terms of a concept such as class. Indeed as we have seen, issues of race and gender are also bound up here, serving to fragment and decentre any single relational term such as class, as primary (Laclau & Mouffe 1985).

Gender has been a major concept in recent scholarship, including archaeology, and arguably one of the most important dimensions of identity. The study of gender has been brought to all periods in archaeology, from the Palaeolithic to the present day, its universality presumed—while specific constructions of gender (i.e. man, women or third/fourth genders) are historically and culturally specific, gender as a category of analysis is deemed universal. This universality is largely based, explicitly or implicitly, on the distinction of sex from gender, and the fact that biological sex is also assumed to be a universal. However, with third wave feminism, the distinction between sex and gender, indeed the universality of sex as a natural division, has been contested, with sex and sexuality increasingly viewed as a social construct (e.g. see Laqueur 1990; Meskell 1999). The implications of this have destabilised the category of 'woman' as a universal (and by implication, 'man', though with little explicit discussion)—and also, less clearly, destabilised the category of gender. Gender may still be a useful category of analysis for all archaeological periods, but it is much more context-dependent, and transected by any number of other axes of identity.

For archaeologists working in the post 1500 era however, gender is undoubtedly of key interest—our very concepts of gender and sex which we operate with and which feminism has contested, were created at this time through specific practices which archaeologists can explore. The separation of two spheres—household and work or private/public have been closely connected to the sharp differentiation between 'men' and 'women', and ideologies associated with their construction as categories of subjectivity (Davidoff & Hall 2002). Historical archaeologists have been increasingly exploring such practices, particularly in relation to the mutual constitution of domesticity and women in the 19th century (e.g. Wall 1994). However, as with the construction of race in the same period, the ideals of gender construction and the dichotomy of the sexes was never that simple, but always countered by other practices—especially when gender is transected by race or class—studies of prostitution or female prisons being prime examples (e.g. Casella 2000; Seifert et al. 2000). What it was to be a man or a woman in a middle class home in New York differed quite sharply from a convict prison in

Australia at the same time; yet perhaps the question historical archaeologists should be asking is not simply how the construction of 'woman' differed in such contexts, but how a discourse emerged which could categorise them in the same terms at all. How did a universalising discourse of gender emerge at this time, in the face of a reality where experiences were so diverse?

It is important to reiterate therefore that race, class and gender are not so much categories of analysis, but subjects of analysis; they are not the universal concepts we often take them to be, but rather specific products of the modern world and moreover, ones which even then vary between period and place within this historical context. Indeed, it is even debatable how useful they are as concepts to understand identity prior to the 19th century, since people may not have perceived identity in these terms—certainly not in the late 17th or early 18th century. Certainly one might argue that to understand how these concepts crystallized in the 19th century, they need to be seen as the product of an earlier period, but equally one needs to beware of the danger of reducing issues of identity of this earlier period to a teleology of the 19th century. Indeed, while race, class and gender are incontestably key terms in understanding identity in the modern world, they are not the only ones, and although it may seem obvious to state it, others may be equally if not more significant depending on the context (e.g. religion, kinship).

QUESTIONS OF IDENTITY AND CULTURE

Identity is not a given or imposed set of attributes, but something that is produced and in constant articulation. Identity should be viewed as an interpellation or chaining of multiple discourses about subjectivity to form a position which constitutes—and is constituted by—the individual (S. Hall 1996; also see Butler 1993). These discourses are constructed through specific contexts and practices surrounding people's relationships to each other, from the general (e.g. enslavement, marriage or wage labour) to the particular (e.g. dining, sleeping, shopping). And as has been pointed out, all such identifications, always involve a politics of exclusion, of separation; the moment a Cape farmer acquired—or even encountered—their first slave, they had to reconfigure their own identity as a *non*-slave, and what this meant was continually refined and articulated in their daily relationship to that slave and all slaves. Similarly with all identifications, such as man/woman, master/servant, relative/stranger, French/Dutch—though one needs to remember that such pairs are not only strategic and context-dependent, they are also not simply structural oppositions so much as structural exclusions, with one term often remaining *discursively* blank, constituted only by its opposite. An archaeology of colonial identity is largely a study of how such subjectivities are constituted in the context of colonialism in terms of quotidian practice and the role material culture plays—through landscapes, buildings and everyday domestic objects.

Identity is clearly multi-faceted, and highly dependent on context; the use of broad terms such as race, gender and class therefore often subsume a lot of complexity, even if entwined with each other. Nevertheless, if a broad context is taken—such as European expansion in the post 1500 era, broad concepts are needed. The reason race, class and gender are so prevalent, is because they have been defined as critical arenas in the development of European capitalism (Mrozowski et al. 2000). Slavery, wage labour and domestication (of the home) were all key practices through which these discourses were created, practices which can be seen as emerging through the broader process of capitalism. Within historical archaeology, especially as it is practised in North America, there is a dominant (but by no means exclusive) focus on capitalism as a thematic lens through which to analyse the archaeological record of the modern world (Leone 1995; Leone and Potter 1999; Orser 1996). This has, recently, started to be questioned, especially by archaeologists working outside North America (e.g. Funari et al. 1999), but while it is important to recognize that other historical archaeologies need to carve out distinct research approaches according to their local context, the globalization of the modern world through European capitalism cannot be so easily dismissed as a North American perspective. However, the issue is not simply one of North American perspective, but more critically, that of a eurocentric perspective and master narrative (Johnson 1999). For some—inspired by post-colonial theory—a Marxist based approach to historical archaeology incorporates the same totalising and eurocentric vision as colonialism and imperialism, which it seeks to critique, insofar as it attempts to see the development of the modern world through the lens of a single system, capitalism, which emanates from Europe. Moreover, it has been argued that this ultimately also risks privileging class above race and gender, and subsuming feminist and post-colonial critiques under a critique of capitalist economic formations.

While such criticisms may be pertinent, they do not necessarily mean we should abandon such a generalizing perspective. Indeed, without some kind of platform, there is the greater danger that no critique is possible at all, and therefore one simply serves the status quo. Specific strategies within Marxist scholarship to decentre class yet still retain grounded critique have been proposed (e.g. Laclau & Mouffe 1985), while more generally, the notion of strategic essentialism has been argued to counter the problems raised within postmodernist discourse (Moore Gilbert 1997:198). I think it is legitimate to try and understand how the articulations of race, class and gender, or rather of identity in general as discussed in this book, are bound up in larger scale processes, especially the development of capitalism. Fragmentation of master narratives is no doubt a positive move—we need to be wary of accounts which erase or flatten out too much cultural variability or historical detail, but too much fragmentation also means we lose any position from which to critique larger scale processes and connections; granted that an archaeology of capitalism is a partial and situated perspective, it remains a powerful tool of understanding and critique.

How do we begin to explore the relationship between the construction of colonial discourses of subjectivity against larger scale processes such as capitalism and imperialism? Is it even possible? As just mentioned, one of the persistent problems in postcolonial theory is the danger—ironically—of eliding the political force of critique because of the lack of any grounded position. If all identity and subjectivity is purely discursive, constituted by and within discourse, then inequality is relativized, and there are no grounds from which to critique social inequality (e.g. see Ahmad 1992). Conversely however, affirming such a position—such as inequality through control or access to resources or the means of survival—means privileging an economic base over ideology. This return to a vulgar materialism is no more acceptable, but then perhaps this was always a caricature of all the but the most simplistic of Marxist positions. The problem is not with materialism but with a discourse that reduces or associates the material world (and the related concept of 'economy') to a naturalism born from late 18th century philosophy. But the material world is as much a cultural construct as discourse—yet at the same time, one which still exceeds the power of discourse to capture it totally. Rather than cling to outdated terms such as: culture=discourse and nature=materiality, it is preferable to view culture as both discourse/materiality.

Rather than a fault, one of the strengths of Marxist theory is to embrace this tension through the domains of ideology and economy. It only becomes a weakness if these terms are ossified and kept separate—such as through base-superstructure models. Ideology is economic, and the economy is ideological. In this sense however, even to privilege the terms of ideology and economy is perhaps too risky; rather, we should seek to disperse social structure into more specific historical and cultural practices, yet ones that retain a tension between discourse/materiality. To return to the question of identity—the construction of subjectivities is both discursive and material, where identity is as much materialized as it is discursively constructed—from the homes we live in, the clothes we wear, to—and especially—the bodies we perform (e.g. see Butler 1993). However, if we explode totalising visions of society (such as the economy-ideology structure) into multiple, specific practices, can we say anything about historical processes which exceed the local? I believe so, only the point now, is rather than seeking grand historical narratives, we explore the connections between local practices, which constitute global processes. An archaeology of colonial identity needs to consider how the specific practices at any place and time, are articulated with others. In doing this, we may counter the tendency to produce both grand and eurocentric narratives of the past. In the next section, I want to look at the development of connections between Europe, South Africa and Asia in terms of movement of objects and people, and explore the development of capitalism as something that emanated not from Europe, but rather from an ambiguous, in-between space created through European and Asian interaction.

THE NATURE OF COLONIAL SPACE AND THE DEVELOPMENT OF CAPITALISM IN THE INDIAN OCEAN

When the VOC first established their post at Table Bay, they relied for much of their provisions—especially meat—on trade with local Khoikhoi pastoralists. These transactions were conducted purely on barter basis: copper and tobacco for sheep and cattle. This was subsistence trade and nothing more, even if the goods exchanged or the conditions under which they were traded, were variously unequal—although even this depends on one's perspective. It is ironic though that it was a very different kind of exchange which brought the Dutch there in the first place: long-distance trade of exotics (spices, tea, silks, porcelain etc.) with urban communities in India, Japan, China and Indonesia, for which they had to pay in gold and silver. This was mercantile capitalism at its most developed, but it depended on the almost industrial nature of production of these goods in Asian countries. From one perspective, South Africa resides in a very marginal place in this trade: it was simply a refreshment station for ships and while it developed into a colony, it was neither a major producer nor consumer of this trade. It was merely an 'in-between' place, neither Asia nor Europe. In what way can its archaeology contribute to our understanding of global processes of capitalism?

I think in many ways, it is precisely because it was an 'in-between' place that its role is significant. To explore this, it is first necessary to broaden the scope to consider the nature of all European colonies as they developed under mercantile capitalism and assess their relationship to both the development of European industrial capitalism and the Asian economies. Perhaps the first thing to stress is the effect the Asian trade had on Europe. In a now classic study, Chaudhuri has charted the development and nature of trade in the Indian Ocean before and during the rise in European sea trade (Chaudhuri 1985; also see Das Gupta & Pearson 1987). He points out how the demand in Europe for Asian goods such as textiles actually stimulated the development of industrial production in Europe (ibid.: 82). Indeed, it is interesting to consider how almost all of the Asian commodities transported back to northern Europe in massive quantities, were at various times, soon copied or produced in Europe too. Tobacco was grown in the Netherlands since the 1630s—and to some success (Schama 1991: 193–4), while cotton and silk industries thrived in the late 17th and early 18th century (Israel 1995: 998–9). Similarly, there were various attempts to copy porcelain—both decoratively in tin-glazed earthenware, and substantively in European soft-paste porcelains. Many of these goods—especially the objects such as textiles and pottery rather than the foodstuffs, were at the forefront of industrial, factory-based production in northern Europe, which really expanded in the 18th century. Mercantile capitalism—if this is not an oxymoron (see Wolf 1982: 79)—led to industrial capitalism when the locus of production shifted away from Asia to Europe.

However, this transformation was by no means simple, despite the ease with which I make this claim. Nor was it wholesale—indeed, the development of colonial plantations in both Asia and the Americas remained key locations for the production of many raw materials as well as foodstuffs. In fact, it is precisely in the colonies that this transformation was articulated before it could be applied back in Europe. The industrial revolution in Europe was only made possible because of the experience gained in colonial contexts, both commercial and agricultural. One of the major features of the East India Companies, especially the VOC, was their integrated organization in local production and trade. They did not simply come and leave according to trade cycles, but established a network of permanent bases with resident personnel and in the case of the VOC, a major settlement in Batavia which acted as a node through which most of the Dutch-Asiatic trade passed. It was largely this that resulted in the accumulation of reserve stocks and capital (see Chapter 2). Moreover, even though the Company's warehouses and posts were often set apart from the local community in any one port, their relationship to Asian merchants was not simply one of buyers—they affected both the nature of what was produced and often the nature of trade in these ports (Brennig 1977; Das Gupta 1994).

The connection between pure mercantilism and the production of commodities was one feature of this integration which changed in a major way when the first colonial plantations were established. As early as the 1620s, the Dutch had spice plantations set up in the Moluccas, but the major period of European plantation development was the 18th century, and while there were several major plantations operating in the Indian Ocean, the greatest plantation colonies were in the Caribbean and the Americas. It is possible to see these plantations as the forerunners of industrial agriculture in Europe, places where the transition from mercantile to industrial capitalism was first rehearsed, was first articulated. Moreover, the establishment of colonies as sites of production radically altered the attitude of colonizing nations to their colonies, as colonies came to be viewed as part of the colonizing nation—another region within it, constitutive of its identity as well as shaping the identity of the colony. This is not simply colonialism, but imperialism—when the colony changes status from being a port of trade to an integral part of the nation and in the process, changing the perception of the nation.

From this perspective, the colonies move from out of the shadows into centre stage, playing the key, vital role in the transition from mercantile to industrial capitalism. But how does the Cape colony fit into this story? It did not have the large plantations, nor did it have any key commercial position, for as I mentioned earlier, it was not a key producer or source of any of the commodities going back to Europe. The answer emerges when we move away from the narrow focus on economy to consider the social aspect of colonial society. Regardless of the quantitative value of the Cape colony to the European capitalist system, it still acted as a theatre in the transition to industrial capitalism through two chief characteristics: the alienation of labour from production and the role of alienated commodities in articulating social identity. The use of a slave labour force on farms throughout the Cape produced a system whereby those who worked, did so not to reap the produce of their work but for subsistence provided by the owner. They may not have been paid, their labour may have been coerced, but like any industrial proletariat, they were alienated from the object of production. Their labour was a commodity, bought and sold, even if not by them but by their masters. In this sense, the use of slaves on farms, in urban service industries or as domestic servants all prefigured the emergence of a European working class. In this respect, they differed substantially from slaves owned by the VOC, who were effectively servants of the Company like the soldiers and sailors, even if their status and autonomy was radically less.

Although the Cape was not a major consumer of many of the products bound for Europe, it still nevertheless had access to most if not all of these goods, as the ships would stop off via the Cape on their way back to Europe. Moreover, while the amount of legal trade and off-loading of such cargo may have been small, illicit private trading was of sufficient scale to provide commodities sufficient to meet demand. This meant its free population could acquire most of the same exotic and luxury items as their counterparts in the Netherlands, items that played a major role in articulating status and identity. Moreover, it often acquired them at much cheaper cost, owing to the shorter shipping distance and the availability of cheaper versions such as Provincial porcelain, which were not normally exported back home. In this context, the availability of such commodities to a comparatively wide spectrum of the free population created a consumer who grew largely dependant on such goods, especially in the domestic context. The critical thing about such goods was of course their exotic nature; they did not form part of the Cape production system, let alone part of household domestic production. While such goods have almost always formed a part of any household consumption, their quantity and significance has usually been small. The reliance of colonies on imported goods, and colonial households especially, was perhaps more than in Europe, a situation which in many ways prefigured the modern consumer culture.

These two features—an alienated labour force and an alienated consumer—were related in many complex ways at the Cape, but the use of slave labour was almost certainly proportionate to the wealth of the slave owner and their acquisition of alienated commodities. Each fuelled each other in the development of a landed gentry and urban elite in the mid 18th century. Once again, the nature of consumption was rather different among the VOC servants, and yet the allure of personal consumption was a constant temptation which, if developed to extremes as with Willem Adriaan van der Stel at Vergelegen, could be their downfall (see Chapter 3). Thus the Cape colony—like many others—occupies a very significant space in the development of European capitalism, articulating the transition from mercantile to industrial forms through its organisation of social relations, specifically in terms of labour and consumption. Moreover, just as it anticipated many of the themes of later industrial society in Europe, so also it has played a key role in late capitalism. It is ironic that gold, one of the major currencies in the Asian trade of the 17th and 18th centuries, was found to the north of the Cape in the later 19th century.

Along with the diamond mines, the gold fields ushered in the industrialisation of South Africa, nearly a century after northern Europe. Yet unlike European industrialism, this was, from early on, advanced monopoly capitalism—yet one exploiting an unskilled, migrant labour force dependant on pre-capitalist social structures (Marks & Rathbone 1982: 9–10). A key player in this new capital has of course, been Anglo-American who are currently one of the wealthiest multi-national companies thriving on the capitalist periphery (Innes 1984). Their success questions the notions of core-periphery in capitalist world systems, as the development of capitalism is something generally seen to have emerged from Europe. Yet the whole perspective which I have taken in the preceding discussion, has reinforced the crucial importance of the 'colonial space' in this process. The significance of a corporation such as Anglo-American to this perspective is of special interest insofar as it seems to have anticipated major shifts in global capitalism of the late 20th century. As companies relocate their primary production centres outside of Europe back into the space of former colonies because of cheapness of labour and raw materials, it seems as if we have come full circle. Indeed, as distribution networks have increasingly improved— through air freight to the internet, the whole notion of core-periphery is elided, and even if many of the largest company 'homes' lie in Europe or the States, the dispersed nature of multi-nationals means that such companies are no longer defined by national boundaries. Late, multi-national capitalism, like the colonies of mercantile and industrial capitalism, resides in a space 'in-between'; the only real terms we have for articulating it, and its material culture, are those of the global and local.

It is perhaps an irony that just as the old European colonies were being transformed into new nations in the earlier 20th century, so the whole nature of nationalism and nation states was soon to be undermined by this new form of capitalism. In many ways, the seeds of this was sown at the moment such colonies were established; colonial spaces were a conceptual problem under European nationalism, and the only solution ultimately was to turn a colony into nation. This of course only transferred the problem onto the colonized people, albeit in a new form, who could only define themselves—and their bid for independence— in the same terms as their former masters (Fanon 1961). For capitalism to continue to expand in the face a globally nationalized world— i.e. in the absence of colonies—it had to change its basis and its mode of operation. In a compelling and radical perspective of the expansion of capitalism in the late 20th century, Antonio Negri and Michael Hardt have argued that capitalism always needs an outside—an 'other', i.e. the non-capitalist world (Negri & Hardt 2000). They see imperialism as the last stage of a capitalism which still has such an 'outside'— i.e. its colonies. Today, in a post-imperialist world where capitalism is inserted everywhere—where it has no outside, where there is no colonial space anymore, where colonies are nation states—a completely new form of globalization exists, which they call 'Empire'. This empire has no centre—it is dispersed, mobile, yet highly unstable, riven by inequalities and tensions which cannot be easily aligned along traditional divisions of the nation state. Indeed, if there is no longer a colonial space, then nations can no longer serve as centres of capitalism; power needs to be reconfigured in ways which transect national boundaries.

Negri and Hart's views are in many ways closely aligned with ideas in post-colonial theory as well as adding a new twist on Marxist theories of late capitalism (e.g. cf. Jameson 1991; Mandel 1978). Such texts are a crucial part of trying to understand larger processes in the modern world. Yet the idea that there is no outside for capitalism today—no colonized versus the colonizer—was in many ways prefigured in the heyday of imperialism. In traditional Hegelian dialectic, the distinction between colonizer and colonized was ambiguous the moment the relationship was established. Insofar as former colonies adopted nationalism over the 20th century, so colonialism played a key role in defining nationalism in the metropoles. Nationalism was always closely entwined with colonialism. Perhaps then, it is not so much there is no longer a colonial space, as *everywhere* has become a colonial space *as well as a national one*. The mutually constituting nature of colony and metropole is increasingly a subject of study (Hall 2002; McKenzie 1986), and for historical archaeologists working in both Europe and its former colonies, there is a growing need for such recognition (Lawrence 2003b). In many ways therefore, an archaeology of colonial identity is as much an archaeology of national identity, increasingly so over the 19th and 20th century. If most of my story in this book has been about the construction of identity in a colony, it is perhaps only fitting to end with a short story about the role of the Cape colony in the construction of identity in the metropole—England.

COLONIAL IDENTITY AND MATERIAL CULTURE IN THE METROPOLE

Figure 5.1 shows a two-shilling coin of the South African Republic, dated 1897. On one side is a triptych—a lion, a voortrekker and a wagon, symbols of the Afrikaaner *volk*, and on the reverse, a profile of Paul Kruger, first president of the Republic. The South African Republic (more commonly known as the Transvaal) was named in 1853, one year after it had been recognized as an independent territory by the

Figure 5.1. Souvenir of the South African War. (*Source*: Photograph by the author)

British. Between 1836 and 1846, c. 14,000 people moved out of the Cape colony northward to occupy areas later known as the Orange Free State and Transvaal: away from the restrictions of British colonial rule and toward new farm land. Throughout the 1840s, various small Boer republics were proclaimed, but none recognized by the British, until Transvaal in 1852, followed two years later by the Orange Free State. Such independence however, did not last out the century—from the late 1870s, British policy shifted towards confederation of the various colonies in southern Africa, and in 1877, they annexed the Transvaal— only to eventually withdraw in 1881 after their troops were defeated by the Boers. With the re-establishment of the South African Republic in 1881, Paul Kruger was elected its first president.

The British attitude to the Boer republics however was changing rapidly; when in the 1850s, they were granted independence, this was seen as the most beneficial policy—there was little return in trying to control a few renegade, non-threatening territories, and more sense in consolidating their position in the Cape colony. Initial moves towards confederation in the 1870s were largely precipitated by tensions with African chiefdoms in the northeast, however it was only with the discovery and mining of gold and the fact that by the1880s, the Transvaal was one of the world's largest producers of gold, that British policy made a complete turn around (Ross 1999a: 69). A famous yet failed attempt to bring down the South African Republic—the Jameson Raid—was instigated by Rhodes in 1895 in order to influence gold production to the benefit of Britain. Although not officially sanctioned, the motives behind the Jameson Raid were similar to the pressures brought by Britain against the Republic in the years following, and which ultimately led to war in 1899. The Boer War or South African War lasted until 1902 and saw at its peak, 200,000 British troops fighting in the two Boer republics. After the Boers capitulated, both republics were annexed as colonies, followed in 1910 by unification with Natal and the Cape as a single Union of South Africa.

The coin in figure 5.1, dated 1897, was minted just two years before the war. What I want to explore here is not so much the coin as a symbol of a short-lived Boer republic—but as a symbol of British imperialism. The coin belonged to my great grandmother's brother; he went out to serve as a soldier with the British army in the South African War and brought this coin back, no doubt as a memento. I do not know how he acquired this object, nor when it was inserted into the frame, which turns the coin into a badge. Perhaps it was taken from a Boer; perhaps he just wanted to memorialise this period of his life. Either way, as the object has been passed down into my hands, I cannot help seeing it as a small piece of the materialization of British imperial ideology in the metropole and the effect this has had—and continues to have—on what it means to be British. Nor can I help but see this in personal terms. This coin/badge acts as the matrix or intersection of personal, national and colonial histories and identities, and what strikes me most, is that *in this object*, these strands are inextricable.

It is also important to see this object within its contemporary context, in particular the mass production of imperialist souvenirs and ephemera, which pervaded British life in the late 19th and early 20th century. From the 1870s, there was an increase in mass material culture 'in miniature'—from packaging to postcards—which explicitly presented and promoted the imperial connections of Britain to the domestic market. As John McKenzie has put it:

> New advertising techniques were central to all this activity, and companies creating and supplying the new tastes were concerned not just to sell their own product, but also the world system which produced it. The most aggressive and innovative advertisers of the day were companies dependent on the imperial economic nexus, in tea, chocolate, soaps and oils, tobacco, meat extracts, shipping and later rubber. They set out not only to illustrate a romantic view of imperial origins, a pride in national possession of what Joseph Chamberlain called the 'imperial estates', but also to identify themselves with royal and military events, and to score from the contemporary cult of personality. (McKenzie 1986: 16).

The power of such ephemera—especially when allied with photography and other media of pictorial representation—brought the Empire and its connection to Britain and British identity into the homes of effectively everyone in the country. Imperial subjects from people to places and events were a common feature of such ephemera. Postcards were a major craze between c. 1890 and 1920 and were widely available in any corner shop where they were avidly collected. Similarly with cigarette cards and related items such as tea and confectionary cards. Even I remember tea packets containing such cards in the late 1960s and early 1970s. More than perhaps any time before or since, the period between the late 19th and mid 20th century was a period when British history and British identity was closely bound with its colonies and empire and this relationship was forged in large part through material culture.

Anne McClintock provides a valuable and provocative study of the role of domestic commodities in forging concepts of identity in the English home during this period (McClintock 1995, see especially chapter 5). In particular, she highlights the link between imperial and colonial images on goods associated with domestic order and hygiene—especially soaps and other cleaning products. Notions of domestic respectability (i.e. a clean house) were inextricably linked to notions of racial hierarchy and progress, from the use of general symbols of colonialism or imperialism to specific images on Pears soap of black children becoming white through the use of soaps or related products. The home became a contested site, requiring constant attention and work to maintain its respectability and cleanliness and avoid degeneration to dirt and a 'lower class', just as in the colonies, the English required constant vigilance to avoid 'degenerating' to the level of natives. At stake was the maintenance of identity and borders, and commodities such as cleaning products, became key arenas to articulate this struggle.

But it was not just through packaging of everyday domestic goods, but also through a wide array of media such as popular entertainment in theatres, books and later cinema as well as exhibitions, that connections between colonial and national ideologies were forged. Moreover, through commemorative objects such as table and teacloths as well as ceramics, such media could be brought into the home as a constant reminder of this link. Commemorative plates and mugs have a long history, but it is only in this period that they become mass produced and mass consumed, and included subjects such the South African War of 1899 (McKenzie 1986: 27). Commemorative ceramics in a particular occur not infrequently in archaeological assemblages of the late 19th/early 20th centuries (Figure 5.2). While not mass produced (as a memento), and indeed, highly personal, my great granduncle's coin/badge nevertheless operated within this context, within the circulation of mass produced imperialist ephemera. In a similar way, it helped to articulate images of 'Britishness', especially for my grandmother who inherited it before it came to me via my mother. Yet also,

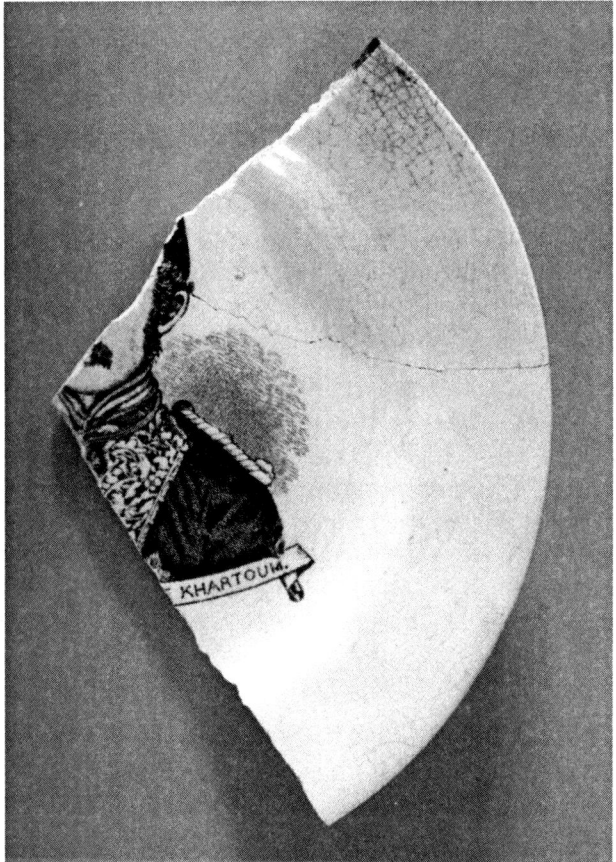

Figure 5.2. Fragment of a commemorative plate of Gordon of Khartoum, from a late 19th century assemblage from Cambridge. (*Source*: Photograph by the author)

because it was personal, it perhaps made the imperial connections more real, more attached; indeed, perhaps the very success of mass produced imperialist ephemera is partly related to the fact that most families may have had a relation, somewhere and sometime, who was involved directly in the imperial nexus in one way or another.

So what is colonial identity? An ambivalent, ambiguous construction which exists in an in-between space—neither colony nor metropole; is it any different to national identity? As long as there were nations and colonies, I think it is justifiable to talk about the distinction, even if the construction of national identity was bound up with colonial space and vice versa. My great grand uncle no doubt thought of himself as British, certainly not a colonial, but similarly the Boers he fought probably thought of themselves as South Africans or Afrikaaners. Part of their struggle was to *not* see themselves as colonials, but nationals too. The height of imperialism was also the beginning of postcolonialism—in the purely political sense of the term. However, perhaps national identity was always a more centrifugal construction than colonial identity; a century before the South African War, c. 1800, how strongly did the Cape colonists see themselves as possessing a distinct, colonial identity? Perhaps unlike national identity, colonial identity was always a more centripetal, dispersed and fragmentary construction. The colonial existed far more as a coherent identity in the mind of nationals in the metropole than among colonists themselves (whether colonizers or colonized). Perhaps the only moment when a colonial identity is felt as belonging to oneself (as opposed to another), is the moment when one wants to shake it off and substitute it with a national identity. This book has attempted to explore an archaeology of colonial identity, but the diversity and variability of what constitutes such identity belies the coherence implied by the term. And what strikes me as I end this book, is that maybe it is a colonial identity—dispersed, centripetal—which dominates in the world today, even in the nationalistic heartlands of the former metropoles. If everyone belongs to a nation today, the nature of national identity may be much more like the colonial identities of 1900 than the nationalist ones of the same period: fluid, unstable and highly ambiguous.

References

Abrahams, G.
  1984a The development of historical archaeology at the Cape, South Africa. *Bulletin of the South African Culture History Museum* 5:20–32.
Abrahams, G.
  1984b Gouda clay pipes from excavated historical sites in Cape Town. *Bulletin of the South African Culture History Museum* 5:
Abrahams, G.
  1987 Seventeenth and Eighteenth Century Glass Bottles excavated from Fort de Goede Hoop, Capetown. *Annals of the South African Cultural History Museum* 1:1–38.
Abrahams, G.
  1993 The Grand Parade, Cape Town: Archaeological Excavations of the Seventeenth Century Fort De Goede Hoop. *South African Archaeological Bulletin* 48:3–15.
Abrahams, G.
  1994 Coarse Earthenwares of the VOC period: 18th century pottery excavated from the Grande Parade at the Cape. *Annals of the South African Cultural History Museum* 6:1–52.
Abrahams, G.
  1997 Mid-eighteenth century foodway traditions at the Cape: archaeological and inventory information. *Quarterly Bulletin of the South African Library* 52:28–37, 60–69.
Abrahams, G.
  1998 Archaeology and Local Cuisine: Signatures of the Cape around 1750. *Annals of the South African Cultural History Museum* 10:1–66.
ACO
  1991 *Archaeological Excavations at 109 Harrington Street. 'The Granite Lodge'.* Archaeology Contracts Office, University of Capetown, Capetown.
Adhikari, M.
  1992 The Sons of Ham: Slavery and the Making of Coloured Identity. *South African Historical Journal* 27:95–112.
Ahmad, A.
  1992 *In Theory: Classes, Nations, Literatures.* Verso, London.
Alpers, E. A.
  1975 *Ivory and Slaves in East Central Africa.* Heinemann, London.
Alston, M.
  1929 *From an Old Cape Homestead.* The Bodley Head, London.
Armstrong, J.
  1983 Madagascar and the slave trade in the seventeenth century. *Omaly sy Anio* 17:
Armstrong, J. and Worden, N.
  1989 The slaves, 1652–1834. In *The Shaping of South African Society 1652–1840,*

edited by Elphick, R. and Giliomee, H., pp. 109–183. Maskew Miller Longman, Capetown.

Aymard, M.
1982 *Dutch Capitalism and World Capitalism*. Cambridge University Press, Cambridge.

Baart, J. M., Krook, W. and Lagerweij, A. C.
1986 Opgravingen aan de Oostenburgermiddenstraat. In *Van VOC tot Werkspoor*, edited by Kist, J. B., pp. 81–142. Matrijs, Utrecht.

Baart, J. M.
1987 Dutch Material Civilization: Daily Life between 165–1776. Evidence from archaeology. In *New World Dutch Studies. Dutch Arts and Culture in Colonial America 1609–1776*, edited by Blackburn, R. and Kelley, N., pp. 1–11. Albany Institute of History and Art, Albany.

Baart, J. M.
1990 Ceramic Consumption and supply in early modern Amsterdam: local production and long-distance trade. In *Work in Towns 850–1850*, edited by Corfield, P. J. and Keene, D., pp. Leicester University Press, Leicester.

Baker, H.
1934 *Cecil Rhodes*. Oxford University Press, London.

Baker, H.
1944 *Architecture and Personality*. Country Life Ltd., London.

Bank, A.
1995 Slavery without slaves: Robert Shell's social history of Cape slave society. *South African Historical Journal* 33:182–193.

Bank, A.
1999 Losing faith in the civilizing mission: the premature decline of humanitarian liberalism at the Cape, 1840–60. In *Empire and others: British encounters with indigenous peoples, 1600–1850*, edited by Daunton, M. and Halpern, R., pp. 364–383. UCL Press, London.

Barrow, J.
1801 *An Account of Travels into the Interior of Southern Africa in the Years 1797 and 1798*. A. Strahan, London.

Bartels, M., Clevis, H. and Zeiler, F. D., (ed.)
1993 *Van huisvuil in Hasselt. Opgravingen aan het Burg Royerplein*. Stichting Archeologie Ijsseæ/Vechtstreek, Kampen.

Bartels, M., (ed.)
1999 *Steden in Scherven / Cities in Sherds. Finds from cesspits in Deventer, Dordrecht, Nijmegen and Tiel (1250–1900)*. Stichting Promotie Archeologie/Rijksdienst voor het Oudheidkindig Bodemonderzoek, Zwolle/Amersfoort.

Beinart, W.
1985 Chieftancy and the concept of articulation: South Africa c. 1919–1950. *Canadian Journal of African Historical Studies* 19:

Beinart, W. and Dubow, S., (ed.)
1995 *Segregation and Apartheid in Twentieth-Century South Africa*. Routledge, London.

Bell, P.
1998 The fabric and structure of Australian mining settlements. In *Social Approaches to an Industrial Past. The Archaeology and Anthropology of Mining*, edited by Knapp, A. B., Pigott, V. C. and Herbert, E. W., pp. 27–38. Routledge, London.

Bensusan, A. D.
1966 *Silver Images. A History of photography in Africa*. Howard Timmins, Capetown.

Berg
1985 Sacred Muskets. *Comarative Studies in Society and History* 27:261–279.

Bhabha, H.
1994 *The Location of Culture*. Routledge, London.

Bickford-Smith, V.
1994 Meanings of Freedom. Social Position and Identity among the ex-slaves and their descendants in Cape Town, 1875–1910. In *Breaking the Chains. Slavery and its Legacy in the Nineteenth Century Cape Colony*, edited by Worden, N. and Crais, C., pp. 289–312. Witwatersrand University Press, Johannesburg.

Bickford-Smith, V.
1995 *Ethnic Pride and Racial Prejudice in Victorian Cape Town*. Cambridge University Press, Cambridge.

Bitter, P., Dijkstra, J., Roedema, R. and van Wilgen, R., (ed.)
1997 *Wonen op niveau. Archeologie, bouwhistorie en historie van twee percelen aan de Langestraat*. Gemeente Alkmaar, Alkmaar.

Boonzaier, E., Berens, P., Malherbe, C. and Smith, A.
1996 *The Cape Herders. A History of the Khoikhoi of Southern Africa*. David Philip Publishers (Pty) Ltd., Capetown.

Botha, C. G.
1919a *The French Refugees at the Cape*. Cape Times, Cape Town.

Botha, C. G.
1919b Early Cape Land Tenure. *South African Law Journal*.

Boucher, M.
1981 *French Speakers at the Cape in the first hundred years of Dutch East India Company Rule: The European Background*. University of South Africa, Pretoria.

Boxer, J. R.
1965 *The Dutch Seaborne Empire, 1600–1800*. London.

Bozzoli, B.
1983 Marxism, Feminism and Southern African Studies. *Journal of Southern African Studies* 9:139–171.

Bradlow, E.
1987 Women at the Cape in the mid-nineteenth century. *South African Historical Journal* 19:51–75.

Brennig, J. J.
1977 Chief Merchants and the European Enclaves of Seventeenth century Coromandel. *Modern Asian Studies* 11:321–340.

Brink, Y.
1990 The Voorhuis as a central element in early Cape houses. *Social Dynamics* 16:38–54.

Brink, Y.
1992 *Places of Discourse and Dialogue. A Study in the Material Culture of the Cape Colony during the Rule of the Dutch East India Company, 1652–1795*. PhD Degree, Department of Archaeology, University of Capetown, Capetown.

Brink, Y.
2001 The meaning of the eighteenth century Cape farmstead. *Vernacular Architecture Society of South Africa (VASSA) Journal* 5:1–23.

Bull, M. and Denfield, J., (ed.)
  1970 *Secure the Shadow: The Story of Cape Photography from its beginning to the end
        of 1870.* Capetown.
Bult, E. J., (ed.)
  1992 *IHE Delft Prospers on a Cesspit. Archaeological Research between Oude Delft
        and Westvest.* IHE, Delft.
Burman, J.
  1969 *The Cape of Good Intent.* Human & Rousseau Publishers, Cape Town.
Butler, J.
  1993 *Bodies that Matter: on the discursive limits of 'sex'.* Routledge, London.
Cairns, M.
  1985 Freeblack landowners in the southern suburbs of the Cape peninsula during the
        eighteenth century. *Kronos* 10:23–31.
Campbell, G.
  1981 Madagascar and the Slave Trade, 1810–1895. *Journal of African History* 22:203–
        227.
Campbell, G.
  1989 Madagascar and Mozambique in the Slave Trade of the Western Indian
        Ocean 1800–1861. In *The Economics of the Indian Ocean Slave Trade in the
        19th century,* edited by Clarence-Smith, W. G., pp. 166–193. Frank Cass,
        London.
Casella, E.
  2000 Bulldaggers and gentle ladies: archaeological approaches to female homosexu-
        ality in convict-era Australia. In *Archaeologies of Sexuality,* edited by Schmidt,
        R. A. and Voss, B. L., pp. 143–159. Routledge, London.
Chatterjee, I.
  1999 *Gender, Slavery and Law in Colonial India.* Oxford University Press, Oxford.
Chaudhuri, K. N.
  1985 *Trade and Civilization in the Indian Ocean. An economic history from the rise
        of Islam to 1750.* Cambridge University Press, Cambridge.
Clevis, H. and Smit, M., (ed.)
  1990 *Verscholen in vuil. Archeologische vondsten uit Kampen 1375–1925.* Stichting
        Archeologie Ijssel/Vechtstreek, Kampen.
Coertzen, P.
  1988 *The Huguenots of South Africa 1688–1988.* Tafelberg Publishers Ltd., Capetown.
Coetzee, J. M.
  1988 *White Writing. On the Culture of Letters in South Africa.* Yale University Press,
        New Haven.
Cohn, B. S.
  1987 The Census, Social Structure and Objectification in South Asia. In *An Anthro-
        pologist Among Historians and Other Essays,* edited by Cohn, B. S., pp. 224–254.
        Oxford University Press, Oxford.
Cooper, F.
  1979 The Problem of Slavery in African Studies. *Journal of African History* 20:103–
        125.
Cowan, R., Cowan, Z. and Marsden, P.
  1975 The Dutch East Indiaman *Hollandia* wrecked on the Isles of Scilly in 1743.
        International Journal of Nautical Archaeology 4:267–300.
Daniell, S.
  1820 *Sketches representing the Native Tribes, Animals and Scenery of South Africa
        from drawings by the late Mr Samuel Daniell.* London.

Das Gupta, A. and Pearson, M. N., (ed.)
1987 *India and the Indian Ocean Trade 1500–1800*. Oxford University Press,Calcutta.
Das Gupta, A.
1994 *Merchants of Maritime India 1500–1800*. Variorum, Aldershot.
Davidoff, L. and Hall, C.
2002 *Family Fortunes. Men and Women of the English Middle Class 1780–1850*. Routledge, London.
Dawdy, S. L., (ed.)
2000 *Creolization*. Historical Archaeology. 34:3
De Bosdari, C.
1953 *Cape Dutch Houses and Farms*. A. A. Balkema, Capetown.
De Kok, I.
1998 Cracked heirlooms: memory on exhibition. In *Negotiating the past*, edited by Nuttall, S. and Coetzee, C., pp. 57–71. Oxford University Press, Capetown.
de Wet, G. C., (ed.)
1984 *Resoluties Van Die Politieke Raad (Resolutions of the Political Council)*. Die Staatsdrukker, Pretoria.
de Wet, G. C.
1987 White settlement in the Drakenstein Valley up to 1700. In *Paarl Valley 1687– 1987*, edited by Oberholster, A. G., pp. 13–22. Human Sciences Research Council, Pretoria.
Deacon, H. J. and Deacon, J.
1999 *Human Beginnings in South Africa: Uncovering the secrets of the Stone Age*. David Philip, Cape Town.
Delle, J. A., Mrozowski, S. and Paynter, R., (ed.)
2000 *Lines that Divide. Historical Archaeologies of Race, Class and Gender*. University of Tennessee Press, Knoxville.
Diener, T.
1993 *The Colonial Archaeology of the Franschoek Valley*. Honours Degree, Archaeology, Stellenbosch, Stellenbosch.
Dubow, J.
2001 Rites of Passage: Travel and the Materiality of vision at the Cape of Good Hope. In *Contested Landscapes. Movement, Exile and Place*, edited by Bender, B. and Winer, M., pp. 241–255. Berg, Oxford.
Duco, D. H.
1981 The Clay Tobacco Pipe in Seventeenth-Century Netherlands. In *The Archaeology of the Clay Tobacco Pipe*, edited by Davey, P., pp. BAR International Series, Oxford.
Duco, D. H.
1982 *Merken van Goudse pijpenmakers: 1660–1940*. Uitgeversmaatschappij De Tijdstroom Lochen, Poperinge.
Eisler, W.
1995 *The Furthest Shore. Images of Terra Australis from the Middle Ages to Captain Cook*. Cambridge University Press, Cambridge.
Elphick, R.
1985 *Khoikhoi and the founding of White South Africa*. Ravan Press, Johannesburg.
Elphick, R. and Giliomee, H., (ed.)
1989 *The Shaping of South African Society 1652–1840*. Maskew Miller Longman, Capetown.
Elphick, R. and Malherbe, V. C.
1989 The Khoisan to 1828. In *The Shaping of South African Society 1652–1840*,

edited by Elphick, R. and Giliomee, H., pp. 3–65. Maskew Miller Longman, Capetown.

Elphick, R. and Shell, R.
  1989 Intergroup relations: Khoikhoi, settlers, slaves and free blacks, 1652–1795. In *The Shaping of South African Society 1652–1840*, edited by Elphick, R. and Giliomee, H., pp. 184–242. Maskew Miller Longman, Capetown.

Elphick, R. and Giliomee, H.
  1989 The origins and entrenchment of European dominanc at the Cape, 1652-c. 1840. In *The Shaping of South African Society 1652–1840*, edited by Elphick, R. and Giliomee, H., pp. 521–566. Maskew Miller Longman, Capetown.

Fagan, G. and Fagan, G.
  n.d. *Boschendal Renascent. A history of Boschendal*.

Fairbridge, D.
  1924 *Lady Anne Barnard at the Cape of Good Hope 1797–1802*. Clarendon Press, Oxford.

Fanon, F.
  1961 *The Wretched of the Earth*. Penguin, Harmondsworth.

Forbes, V. S.
  1965 *Pioneer Travellers of South Africa 1750–1800*. A.A. Balkema, Capetown.

Franken, J. L. M.
  1978 Die Hugenote aan die Kaap. *Archives Year Book for the South African Library* XLI:

Fransen, H. and Cook, M. A.
  1980 *The Old Buildings of the Cape*. Balkema, Capetown.

Fredlund, J.
  1997 *Gammalt Porslin. Svenska Serviser 1790–1990*. ICA Bokforlag, Vasteras.

Freund, W.
  1989 The Cape under the transitional governments, 1795–1814. In *The Shaping of South African Society 1652–1840*, edited by Elphick, R. and Giliomee, H., pp. 324–357. Maskew Miller Longman, Capetown.

Funari, P. P. A., Hall, M. and Jones, S., (ed.)
  1999 *Historical Archaeology. Back from the edge*. Routledge, London.

Gaastra, F. S.
  1983 The exports of precious metal from Europe to Asia by the Dutch East India Company, 1602–1795. In *Precious Metals in the Later Medieval and Early Modern Worlds*, edited by Richards, J. F., pp. 447–475. Carolina Academic Press, Durham.

Gaitskell, D.
  1983 Housewives, Maids or Mothers: some contradictions of domesticity for Christian women in Johannesburg 1903–39. *Journal of African History* 24:241–256.

Gawronski, J.
  1992 *Hollandia Compendium. A contribution to the history, archaeology, classification and lexicography of a 150 foot Dutch East Indiaman*. Elsevier-Rijks Museum, Amsterdam.

Gertenbach, M.
  2000 *Conservation Plan for Goede Hoop*. AmFarms.

Geyl, P.
  1961 *The Netherlands in the 17th century*. Ernest Benn, London.

Gilroy, A., (ed.)
  2000 *Romantic Geographies. Discourse of Travel 1775–1844*. Manchester University Press, Manchester.

Glamann, K.
  1958 *Dutch-Asiatic Trade 1620–1740*. Martinus Nijhoff, The Hague.
Gleeson, J.
  1998 *The Arcanum. The Extraordinary True Story of the Invention of European Porcelain*. Bantam Press, London.
Green, J. N.
  1977 *The loss of the VOC Jacht Vergulde Draeck, wrecked western Australia 1656*. BAR, Oxford.
Guelke, L.
  1976 Frontier Settlement in Early Dutch South Africa. *Annals of the Association of American Geographers* 66:25–42.
Guelke, L. and Shell, R.
  1983 An early colonial landed gentry: land and wealth in the Cape Colony 1682–1731. *Journal of Historical Geography* 9:265–286.
Guelke, L.
  1988 The anatomy of a colonial settler population: Cape Colony 1657–1750. *The International Journal of African Historical Studies* 21:453–473.
Guelke, L.
  1989 Freehold farmers and frontier settlers 1657–1780. In *The Shaping of South African Society 1652–1840*, edited by Elphick, R. and Giliomee, H., pp. 66–108. Maskew Miller Longman, Capetown.
Halkett, D.
  1993 *Archaeological Investigation of the Elsenburg Herehuis*. Archaeology Contracts Office, University of Capetown, Capetown.
Halkett, D. and Hart, T.
  1996 *Excavations in District Six: a residential property at the corner of Stuckeris and Roger Streets*. Contracts Office, University of Capetown, Capetown.
Hall, C.
  2002 *Civilizing Subjects. Metropole and Colony in the English Imagination 1830–1867*. Polity, Cambridge.
Hall, M.
  1988 Historical Archaeology and Colonial Expansion. *Kronos* 14:3–10.
Hall, M.
  1991a High and Low in the Townscapes of Dutch South America and South Africa: the dialectics of material culture. *Social Dynamics* 12:41–75.
Hall, M.
  1991b Fish and the fishermen: archaeology and art. *South African Journal of Art and Architectural History* 2:
Hall, M.
  1992a Small Things and the Mobile, Conflictual Fusion of Power, Fear and Desire. In *The Art and Mystery of Historical Archaeology. Essays in Honour of James Deetz*, edited by Yentsch, A. E. and Beaudry, M. C., pp. 373–399. CRC Press, Boca Raton.
Hall, M.
  1992b *People in a changing urban landscape: excavating Cape Town*. University of Capetown, Capetown.
Hall, M.
  1993 The Archaeology of Colonial Settlement in Southern Africa. *Annual Review of Anthropology* 22:177–200.
Hall, M.
  1995 The Architecture of Patriarchy: Houses, Women and Slaves in the Eighteenth

Century South African Countryside. In *The Written and the Wrought: Complementary Sources in Historical Anthropology. Essays in Honour of James Deetz*, edited by D'Agostino, M. E., Prine, E., Casella, E. and Winer, M., pp. 61–73. Kroeber Anthropological Society Papers No.79,

Hall, M.
  1996a The Proximity of Dr. Bleek's Bushman. In *Miscast. Negotiating the Presence of Bushmen*, edited by Skotnes, P., pp. University of Capetown Press, Capetown.

Hall, M.
  1996b *Archaeology Africa*. James Currey, London.

Hall, M.
  1997 Patriarchal Facades. The ambivalences of gender in the archaeology of colonialism. In *Our Gendered Past. Archaeological Studies of Gender in Southern Africa*, edited by Wadley, L., pp. 221–236. Witwatersrand University Press, Johannesburg.

Hall, M.
  2000 *Archaeology and the Modern World. Colonial Transcripts in South Africa and the Chesapeake*. Routledge, London.

Hall, M. and Markell, A.
  1993 Introduction: Historical Archaeology in the Western Cape. *South African Archaeological Society Goodwin Series* 7:3–7.

Hall, M., Brink, Y. and Malan, A.
  1988 Onrust 87/1: an early colonial farm complex in the Western Cape. *South African Archaeological Bulletin* 43:91–99.

Hall, M., Halkett, D., Huigen van Beek, P. and Klose, J.
  1990a "A stone wall out of the earth that thundering cannon cannot destroy"? Bastion and moat at the Castle, Cape Town. *Social Dynamics* 16:22–37.

Hall, M., Halkett, D., Klose, J. and Ritchie, G.
  1990b The Barrack Street Well: Images of a Cape Town Household in the Nineteenth Century. *South African Archaeological Bulletin* 45:73–92.

Hall, M., Malan, A., Amann, S., Honeyman, L., Kiser, T. and Ritchie, G.
  1993 The Archaeology of Paradise. *South African Archaeological Society Goodwin Series* 7:40–58.

Hall, M., Cox, G., Halkett, D., Hart, T., Rubin, K. and Winter, S.
  1994 *A shadow in stone. Archaeology in Horstley Street, District Six*. University of Capetown, Capetown.

Hall, S.
  1996 Introduction: Who Needs Identity? In *Questions of Cultural Identity*, edited by Hall, S. and du Gay, P., pp. 1–17. Sage, London.

Hardesty, D. L.
  1998 Power and the industrial mining community in the American West. In *Social Approaches to an Industrial Past. The Archaeology and Anthropology of Mining*, edited by Knapp, A. B., Pigott, V. C. and Herbert, E. W., pp. 81–96. Routledge, London.

Harley, J. B.
  1989 Maps, Knowledge and Power. In *The Iconography of Landscape*, edited by Cosgrove, D. and Daniels, S. J., pp. 277–312. Cambridge University Press, Cambridge.

Hart, D. and Winter, S.
  2001 The politics of remembrance in the new South Africa. In *Archaeologies of the*

Contemporary Past, edited by Buchli, V. and Lucas, G., pp. 84–93. Routledge, London.

Heller, D.
1949 *A History of Cape Silver 1700–1870*. David Heller (Pty) Ltd., Capetown.

Henkes, H. E.
1994 *Glass without Gloss: Utility Glass from Five Centuries Excavated from the Low Countries, 1300–1800*. Coordinatie Commissie van Advies inzake Archeologisch Onderzoek binnen het Ressort Rotterdam, Rotterdam.

Huizinga, J. H.
1968 *Dutch Civilization in the Seventeenth Century and other essays*. Fontana, London.

Hurst, J. G., Neal, D. S. and van Beuningen, H. J. E.
1986 *Pottery produced and traded in north-west Europe 1350–1650*. Stichting 'Het Nederlandse Gebruiksvoorwerp', Rotterdam.

Innes, D.
1984 *Anglo American and the Rise of Modern South Africa*. Heinemann, London.

Irvine, M.
1990 *Scratching the Surface: the archaeology of 56 Dorp Street, Bo-Kaap*. Degree, Archaeology, University of Capetown, Capetown.

Irving, R. G.
1981 *Indian Summer. Lutyens, Baker and Imperial Delhi*. Yale University Press, New Haven.

Isaacman, B. and Isaacman, A.
1977 Slavery and Social Stratification among the Sena of Mozambique. A study of the Kaporo system. In *Slavery in Africa. Historical and Anthropological Perspectives*, edited by Miers, S. and Kopytoff, I., pp. 105–120. University of Wisconsin Press, Madison.

Israel, J.
1989 *Dutch Primacy in World Trade, 1585–1740*. Oxford University Press, Oxford.

Israel, J.
1995 *The Dutch Republic. Its Rise, Greatness, and Fall 1477–1806*. Oxford University Press, Oxford.

Jameson, F.
1991 *Postmodernism, or, the Cultural Logic of Late Capitalism*. Verso, London.

Johnson, M.
1999 Rethinking Historical Archaeology. In *Historical Archaeology. Back from the edge*, edited by Funari, P. P. A., Hall, M. and Jones, S., pp. 23–36. Routledge, London.

Jordan, S. C.
2000 Coarse Earthenware at the Dutch Colonial Cape of Good Hope, South Africa: A History of Local Production and Typology of Products. *International Journal of Historical Archaeology* 4:113–143.

Jorg, C. J. A.
1982 *Porcelain and the Dutch China Trade*. Martinus Nijhoff, The Hague.

Jorg, C. J. A.
1986 *The Geldermalsen. History and Porcelain*. Kemper Publishers, Groningen.

Jowett, R., Kain, J. P. and Baigent, E.
1992 *The Cadastral Map in the Service of the State: A History of Property Mapping*. Chicago University Press, Chicago.

Kertzer, D. I. and Ariel, D.
  2002   Census, Identity formation and the struggle for political power. In *Census and Identity. The Politics of Race, Ethnicity and Language in National Census*, edited by Kertzer, D. I. and Ariel, D., pp. 1–42. Cambridge University Press, Cambridge.
Klose, J.
  1993   Excavated Oriental Ceramics from the Cape of Good Hope: 1630–1830. *Transactions of the Oriental Ceramic Society* 57:69–81.
Klose, J. and Malan, A.
  1993   *Ceramics of the southwestern Cape 1650 to 1850.* Historical Archaeology Research Group, Capetown.
Klose, J. and Malan, A.
  2000   The Ceramic Signature of the Cape in the Nineteenth Century, with particular reference to the Tenant Street Site, Cape Town. *South African Archaeological Bulletin* 55:49–59.
Kolb, P.
  1967   *The Present State of the Cape of Good Hope.* Johnson Reprint Corporation, New York.
Laclau, E. and Mouffe, C.
  1985   *Hegemony and Socialist Strategy, Towards a Radical Democratic Politics.* Verso, London.
Lakdusinghe, S.
  2001   *The Katuwana Archaeological Heritage Project. Excavation Report 2000.* Institute of Archaeology, University of Kelaniya, Colombo.
Laqueur, T.
  1990   *Making Sex: Body and Gender from the Greeks to Freud.* Harvard University Press, Cambridge MA.
Larson, P. M.
  2000   *History and Memory in the Age of Enslavement. Becoming Merina in Highland Madagascar, 1770–1822.* James Currey, Oxford.
Lasker, B.
  1950   *Human Bondage in Southeast Asia.* University of Carolina Press, Chapel Hill.
Lawrence, S.
  1998   Gender and community structure on Australian colonial goldfields. In *Social Approaches to an Industrial Past. The Archaeology and Anthropology of Mining*, edited by Knapp, A. B., Pigott, V. C. and Herbert, E. W., pp. 39–58. Routledge, London.
Lawrence, S.
  2003a Exporting Culture: Archaeology and the Nineteenth Century British Empire. *Historical Archaeology* 37:20–33.
Lawrence, S., (ed.)
  2003b *Archaeologies of the British. Explorations of identity in Great Britain and its colonies 1600–1945.* Routledge, London.
Le Grange, L.
  1985   Working Class Housing, Cape Town 1890–1947. Segregation and Township Formation. *South African Review* 13–37.
Legislative Council
  1849   *Master and Servant Addenda to the Documents on the working order in council of the 21st July 1846: including memorials etc. and reports by the resident magistrates on the missionary institutions.* Legislative Council, Cape Town.

Lemon, A., (ed.)
  1991 *Homes Apart. South Africa's Segregated Cities*. Indiana University Press, Bloomington.
Leone, M.
  1988 The Georgian Order as the Order of Merchant Capitalism in Annapolis, Maryland. In *The Recovery of Meaning. Historical Archaeology in the Eastern United States*, edited by Leone, M. and Potter, P. B., pp. 235–262. Smithsonian Institute, Washington.
Leone, M.
  1995 A Historical Archaeology of Capitalism. *American Anthropologist* 97:251–268.
Leone, M. and Potter, P. B., (ed.)
  1999 *Historical Archaeologies of Capitalism*. Kluwer Academic/Plenum Press, New York.
Lewcock, R.
  1963 *Early Nineteenth Century Architecture in South Africa. A Study in the interaction of two cultures 1795–1837*. A. A. Balkema, Cape Town.
Lighton, C.
  1956 *Arthur Elliot. A memoir of the man and the story of his photographic collection*. A. A. Balkema, Cape Town.
Löfgren, O.
  1999 *On Holiday. A History of Vacationing*. University of California Press, Berkeley.
Losman, A.
  1988 Skokloster—Europe and the World in a Swedish Castle. In *The Age of New Sweden*, edited by Losman, A., Lundstrom, A. and Rivera, M., pp. 84–101. Livrustkammaren, Stockholm.
Lovejoy, P. E.
  1983 *Transformations in Slavery. A History of Slavery in Africa*. Cambridge University Press, Cambridge.
Lovejoy, P. E.
  1989 The Impact of the Atlantic Slave Trade on Africa: A Review of the Literature. *Journal of African History* 30:365–394.
Lucas, G. and Regan, R.
  2003 The Changing Vernacular: archaeological excavations at Temple End, High Wycombe, Buckinghamshire. *Post-Medieval Archaeology* 37:165–206.
Malan, A.
  1990 The Archaeology of Probate Inventories. *Social Dynamics* 16:1–10.
Malan, A.
  1997 The Material World of Family and Household. The Van Sitterts in Eighteenth Century Capetown 1748–1796. In *Our Gendered Past. Archaeological Studies of Gender in Southern Africa*, edited by Wadley, L., pp. 273–301. Witwatersrand University Press, Johannesburg.
Malan, A.
  1999 Chattels or Colonists? 'Freeblack' women and their households. *Kronos* 25:50–71.
Malan, A. and Malherbe, J. E.
  1996 *List of Huguenots who came to the Cape*. Huguenot Memorial Museum, Franschoek.
Malan, A. and Harris, S.
  1999 *Archives and Archaeology*. 2, Historical Archaeology Research Group, Capetown.

Malan, A. and Van Heyningen, E.
  2001 Twice Removed: Horstley Street in Capetown's District Six, 1865–1982. In *The Archaeology of Urban Landscapes. Explorations in Slumland*, edited by Mayne, A. and Murray, T., pp. 39–56. Cambridge University Press, Cambridge.
Malan, A. and Klose, J.
  2003 Nineteenth century ceramics in Cape Town, South Africa. In *Archaeologies of the British: Explorations of identity in Great Britain and its colonies 1600–1945*, edited by Lawrence, S., pp. Routledge, London.
Malherbe, J. E.
  1997 *Cape Vernacular Architecture*. Huguenot Memorial Museum, Franschoek.
Mandel, E.
  1978 *Late Capitalism*. Verso, London.
Markell, A.
  1993 Building on the Past: the architecture and archaeology of Vergelegen. *South African Archaeological Society Goodwin Series* 7:71–83.
Marks, S.
  1972 Khoisan resistance to the Dutch in the seventeenth and eighteenth centuries. *Journal of African History* 1:55–80.
Marks, S. and Rathbone, R., (ed.)
  1982 *Industrialization and Social Change in South Africa. African Class formation, culture and consciousness 1870–1930*. Longmann, London.
Marsden, P.
  1972 The wreck of the Dutch East Indiaman *Amsterdam* near Hastings, 1749. *International Journal of Nautical Archaeology* 1:73–96.
Marsden, P.
  1978 A reconstruction of the treasure of the *Amsterdam* and the *Hollandia* and their significance. *International Journal of Nautical Archaeology* 7:133–148.
Maxwell, A.
  1999 *Colonial Photography and Exhibitions. Representations of the 'Native' and the making of European Identities*. Leicester University Press, Leicester.
Mayne, A. and Murray, T., (ed.)
  2001 *The Archaeology of Urban Landscapes. Explorations in Slumland*. Cambridge University Press, Cambridge.
McClintock, A.
  1995 *Imperial Leather. Race, Gender and Sexuality in the Colonial Contest*. Routledge, London.
McCracken, G.
  1990 *Culture and Conumption*. Indiana University Press, Bloomington.
McGuire, R.
  2002 *A Marxist Archaeology*. Percheron Press, New York.
McKendrick, N., Brewer, J. and Plumb, J. H.
  1982 *The Birth of Consumer Society: The Commercialization of Eighteenth Century England*. Indiana University Press, Bloomington.
McKenzie, J.
  1986 *Propaganda and Empire*. Manchester University Press, Manchester.
McKenzie, K.
  1993 *The Making of an English Slave-owner. Samuel Eusebius Hudson at the Cape of Good Hope 1796–1807*. University of Capetown Press, Capetown.
McKenzie, K.
  1997 'My own Mind Dying within Me': Eliza Fairbairn and the Reinvention of

Colonial Middle-Class Domesticity in Capetown. *South African Historical Journal* 36:3–23.

Meillasoux, C.
1991 *The Anthropology of Slavery*. Athlone Press, London.

Mentzel, O.
1925 *A Geographical and Topographical Description of the Cape of Good Hope*. Van Riebeeck Society, Capetown.

Meskell, L.
1999 *Archaeologies of Social Life: Age, Sex, Class etc. in Ancient Egypt*. Blackwell, Oxford.

Meyer, L.
1996 *Contact between indigenous Khoikhoi and European settlers*. Huguenot Memorial Museum, Franschoek.

Miers, S. and Kopytoff, I., (ed.)
1977 *Slavery in Africa. Historical and Anthropological Perspectives*. University of Wisconsin Press, Madison.

Miller, G. L.
1991 A revised set of CC index values for classification and economic scaling of English ceramics from 1787 to 1860. *Historical Archaeology* 25:1–25.

Moore-Gilbert, B.
1997 *Postcolonial Theory. Contexts, Practices, Politics*. Verso, London.

Mrozowski, S., Delle, J. A. and Paynter, R.
2000 Introduction. In *Lines that Divide. Historical Archaeologies of Race, Class and Gender*, edited by Delle, J. A., Mrozowski, S. and Paynter, R., pp. xi–xxxi. University of Tennessee Press, Knoxville.

Naidoo, R.
2000 *The Commanders Slaves*, SABC Channel 3 (South Africa).

Negri, A. and Hardt, M.
2000 *Empire*. Harvard University Press, Cambridge, MA.

Oberholster, A. G.
1987 Local Government. In *Paarl Valley 1687–1987*, edited by Oberholster, A. G., pp. 38–51. Human Sciences Research Council, Pretoria.

Obholzer, A. M., Baraitser, M. and Malherbe, W. D.
1985 *The Cape House and its Interior*. Stellenbosch Museum, Stellenbosch.

Orser, C.
1996 *A Historical Archaeology of the Modern World*. Plenum Press, New York.

Orser, C., (ed.)
2001 *Race and the Archaeology of Identity*. University of Utah Press, Salt Lake City.

Ostkamp, S., Roedema, R. and van Wilgen, R., (ed.)
2001 *Gebruikt en Gebroken. Vijf eeuwen bewoning op drie locaties in het oostelijk stadsdeel*. Gemeente Alkmaar, Alkmaar.

Parker Pearson, M.
1997 Close encounters of the worst kind: Malagasy resistance and colonial disasters in Southern Madagascar. *World Archaeology* 28.393–417.

Parker Pearson, M., Godden, K., Ramilisonina, Retsihisatse, Schwenninger, J.-L. and Smith, H.
1999 Lost Kingdoms: oral histories, traveller's tales and archaeology in southern Madagascar. In *Historical Archaeology. Back from the edge*, edited by Funari, P. P. A., Hall, M. and Jones, S., pp. Routledge, London.

Paynter, R. and McGuire, R., (ed.)
 1991 *The Archaeology of Inequality*. Blackwell, Oxford.
Peires, J. B.
 1989 The British and the Cape, 1814–1834. In *The Shaping of South African Society 1652–1840*, edited by Elphick, R. and Giliomee, H., pp. 472–520. Maskew Miller Longman, Capetown.
Penn, N.
 1999 *Rogues, Rebels and Runaways. Eighteenth Century Cape Characters*. David Philips Publishers (Pty) Ltd., Capetown.
Philip, J.
 1828 *Researches in South Africa*. James Duncan, London.
Prakash, O.
 1994a Precious metal flows in Asia and world economic integration in the seventeenth century. In *Precious Metals and Commerce. The Dutch East India Company in the Indian Ocean Trade*, edited by Prakash, O., pp. 81–96. Variorum, Aldershot.
Prakash, O.
 1994b The Dutch East India Company in the Trade of the Indian Ocean. In *Precious Metals and Commerce. The Dutch East India Company in the Indian Ocean Trade*, edited by Prakash, O., pp. 185–200. Variorum, Aldershot.
Pratt, M. L.
 1992 *Imperial Eyes. Travel Writing and Transculturation*. Routledge, London.
Raven-Hart, R.
 1967 *Before Van Riebeeck. Callers at South Africa from 1488 to 1652*. Struik (Pty) Ltd, Cape Town.
Reid, A., (ed.)
 1983 *Slavery, Bondage and Dependency in Southeast Asia*. St. Lucia.
Robinson, A. M. L., (ed.)
 1994 *Cape Journals of Lady Anne Barnard 1797–8*. Van Riebeeck Society, Capetown.
Ross, R.
 1983a The Rise of the Cape Gentry. *Journal of Southern African Studies* 9:193–217.
Ross, R.
 1983b *Cape of Torments. Slavery and Resistance in South Africa*. Routledge, London.
Ross, R.
 1986 The Origins of Capitalist Agriculture in the Cape Colony: A Survey. In *Putting a Plough to the Ground. Accumulation and Dispossession in Rural South Africa 1850–1930*, edited by Beinart, W., Delius, P. and Trapido, S., pp. 56–100. Ravan Press, Johannesburg.
Ross, R.
 1989 The Cape of Good Hope and the world economy 1652–1835. In *The Shaping of South African Society 1652–1840*, edited by Elphick, R. and Giliomee, H., pp. 243–282. Maskew Miller Longman, Capetown.
Ross, R.
 1993 *Beyond the Pale. Essays on the History of Colonial South Africa*. Wesleyan University Press, Hanover.
Ross, R.
 1994 'Rather Mental than Physical': Emancipation and the Cape Economy. In *Breaking the Chains. Slavery and its Legacy in the Nineteenth Century Cape Colony*, edited by Worden, N. and Crais, C., pp. 145–167. Witwatersrand University Press, Johannesburg.

Ross, R.
  1995 Paternalism, Patriarchy and Afrikaans. *South African Historical Journal* 32:34–47.
Ross, R.
  1999a *A Concise History of South Africa*. Cambridge University Press, Cambridge.
Ross, R.
  1999b *Status and Respectability in the Cape Colony, 1750–1870. A Tragedy of Manners*. Cambridge University Press, Cambridge.
Ryan, S.
  1994 Inscribing the Emptiness. Cartography, exploration and the construction of Australia. In *De-scribing Empire. Anti-colonialism and textuality*, edited by Tiffin, C. and Lawson, A., pp. Routledge, London.
Ryan, S.
  1996 *The Cartographic Eye. How Explorers Saw Australia*. Cambridge University Press, Cambridge.
Ryan, J. R.
  1998 *Picturing Empire. Photography and the visualization of the British Empire*. University of Chicago Press, Chicago.
Saitta, D.
  1994 Agency, Class and Archaeological Interpretation. *Journal of Anthropological Archaeology* 13:201–227.
Schama, S.
  1991 *The Embarrassment of Riches. An Interpretation of Dutch Culture in the Golden Age*. Fontana Press, London.
Schoeman, K.
  1996 *The Face of the Country: a South African family album, 1860–1910. Photographic portraits from the collections of the South African Library*. Human & Rousseau, Capetown.
Schoffer, I. and Gaastra, F. S.
  1982 The import of bullion and coin into Asia by the Dutch East India Company in the 17th and 18th centuries. In *Dutch Capitalism and World Capitalism*, edited by Aymard, M., pp. 215–233. Cambridge University Press, Cambridge.
Schrire, C.
  1987 The historical archaeology of colonial-indigenous interactions of South Africa: proposed research at Oudepost I, Cape. In *Papers in the prehistory of the western Cape, South Africa*, edited by Parkington, J. and Hall, M., pp. BAR, Oxford.
Schrire, C.
  1988 The historical archaeology of the impact of colonialism in 17th-century South Africa. *Antiquity* 62:214–25.
Schrire, C.
  1990 Excavating Archives at Oudepost I, Cape. *Social Dynamics* 16:11–21.
Schrire, C.
  1995 *Digging Through Darkness. Chronicles of an Archaeologist*. Witwatersrand University Press, Johannesburg.
Schrire, C. and Merwick, D.
  1991 Dutch-Indigenous Relations in New Netherland and the Cape in the Seventeenth Century. In *Historical Archaeology in Global Perspective*, edited by Falk, L., pp. 11–20. Smithsonian Institution Press, Washington.

Schrire, C. and Cruz-Uribe, K.
  1993 The Site History of the Historical Site at Oudepost I, Cape. *South African Archaeological Society Goodwin Series* 7:21–32.

Schutte, G.
  1989 Company and colonists at the Cape, 1652–1795. In *The Shaping of South African Society 1652–1840*, edited by Elphick, R. and Giliomee, H., pp. 283–323. Maskew Miller Longman, Capetown.

Scott, P. E. and Deetz, J.
  1990 Building, Furnishings and Social Change in Early Victorian Grahamstown. *Social Dynamics* 16:76–89.

Scully, P.
  1994 Private and Public Worlds of Emancipation in the Western Cape, c. 1830–1842. In *Breaking the Chains. Slavery and its Legacy in the Nineteenth Century Cape Colony*, edited by Worden, N. and Crais, C., pp. 201–223. Witwatersrand University Press, Johannesburg.

Scully, P.
  1997 *Liberating the Family? Gender and British Slave Emancipation in the Rural Western Cape, South Africa, 1823–1853*. David Philip Publishers (Pty) Ltd., Capetown.

Sealy, E.
  1998 *Riverstone Road 1993. A study of the history and material culture from two nineteenth century households in Wynberg, Cape Town*. BA Honours Degree, Department of Archaeology, University of Capetown, Capetown.

Seifert, D. J., (ed.)
  1991 *Gender in Historical Archaeology*. Historical Archaeology. 25,

Seifert, D. J., O'Brien, E. B. and Balicki, J.
  2000 Mary Ann Hall's first-class house: the archaeology of a capital brothel. In *Archaeologies of Sexuality*, edited by Schmidt, R. A. and Voss, B. L., pp. 117–128. Routledge, London.

Shell, R.
  1994 *Children of Bondage. A Social History of the Slave Society at the Cape of Good Hope, 1652–1838*. Witwatersrand University Press, Johannesburg.

Silberbauer, C. C.
  1943 *Pniel and its first missionary superintendent*. Citadel Press, Capetown.

Smith, D. M., (ed.)
  1992 *The Apartheid City and Beyond. Urbanization and Social Change in South Africa*. Routledge, London.

Sparrman, A.
  1975 *A Voyage to the Cape of Good Hope 1772–1776*. Van Riebeeck Society, Capetown.

Spencer-Wood, S., (ed.)
  1987 *Consumer Choice in Historical Archaeology*. Plenum Press, New York.

Stavorinus, J. S.
  1969 *Voyages to the East Indies*. Dawsons, London.

Steensgaard, N.
  1982 The Dutch East India Company as an institutional innovation. In *Dutch Capitalism and World Capitalism*, edited by Aymard, M., pp. 235–257. Cambridge University Press, Cambridge.

Stellenbosch Municipality
  2002 *Greater Stellenbosch 2002–2006 Integrated Development Plan*. Stellenbosch Municipal Council, Stellenbosch.

Stoler, A. L.
   1991   Carnal Knowledge and Imperial Power. Gender, Race, and Morality in Colonial Asia. In *Gender at the Crossroads of Knowledge: Feminist Anthropology in the Post Modern Era*, edited by di Leonardo, M., pp. 51–101. University of California Press, Berkeley.

Stoler, A. L.
   2000   Sexual Affronts and racial frontiers; European identities and the cultural politics of exclusion in colonial Southeast Asia. In *Hybridity and its Discontents*, edited by Brah, A. and Coombes, A., pp. 19–55. Routledge, London.

Swanevelder, C. J.
   1987   The evolution of the Drakenstein Valley Landscape. In *Paarl Valley 1687–1987*, edited by Oberholster, A. G., pp. 1–12. Human Sciences Research Council, Pretoria.

Swanson, M.
   1977   "The Sanitation Syndrome": Bubonic Plague and Urban Native Policy in the Cape Colony 1900–1909. *Journal of African History* 18:

Tagg, J.
   1988   *The Burdern of Representation. Essays on Photographies and Histories.* University of Minnesota Press, Minnesota.

Taylor, J. G.
   1983   *The Social World of Batavia. European and Eurasian in Dutch Asia.* University of Wisconsin Press, Madison.

Thunberg, C. P.
   1986   *Travels at the Cape of Good Hope 1772–1775.* Van Riebeeck Society, Capetown.

Townsend, L. and Townsend, S.
   1977   *Bokaap: faces and facades.* Howard Timmins, Cape Town.

Trotter, A. F.
   1903   *Old Cape Colony. A Chronicle of Her Men and Houses From 1652 to 1806.* Archibald Constable & Co Ltd, London.

Upton, D.
   1990   Imagining the early Virginia Landscape. In *Earth Patterns. Essays in Landscape Archaeology*, edited by Kelson, W. M. and Moss, R., pp. University Press of Virginia,

Valentyn, F.
   1971   *Description of the Cape of Good Hope.* Van Riebeeck Society, Capetown.

van der Meulen, J.
   2003   *Goudse pijpenmakers en hun merken.* CIP-gegevens Koninklijke Bibliotheek, Den Haag.

van der Spuy, P.
   1992   Slave women and the family in 19th century Cape Town. *South African Historical Journal* 27:50–74.

Visagie, J. C.
   1987   Council of Landdrost and Heemraden. In *Paarl Valley 1687–1987*, edited by Oberholster, A. G., pp. 23–32. Human Sciences Research Council, Pretoria.

Volker, T.
   1971   *Porcelain and the Dutch East India Company.* E. J. Brill, Leiden.

Vos, H. N.
   1985   Coarse Provincial Ware at the Cape. *Antiques in South Africa* 16:15–18.

Vos, H. N.
   1992   *Unpublished Letter to Roger Jones.*

Wall, D. d.
  1994 *The Archaeology of Gender: Separating the Spheres in Urban America.* Plenum
        Press, New York.
Wallerstein, I.
  1982 Dutch hegemony in the seventeenth century world economy. In *Dutch Capi-
        talism and World Capitalism*, edited by Aymard, M., pp. 93–145. Cambridge
        University Press, Cambridge.
Walton, J.
  1965 *Homesteads and Villages of South Africa.* van Schaik, Pretoria.
Walton, J.
  1995 *Cape Cottages.* Kagiso Publishers, Capetown.
Ward, K.
  1994 Links in the Chain. Community, Identity and migration in Mamre 1838–1938.
        In *Breaking the Chains. Slavery and its Legacy in the Nineteenth Century Cape
        Colony*, edited by Worden, N. and Crais, C., pp. 313–333. Witwatersrand Uni-
        versity Press, Johannesburg.
Ward, K. and Worden, N.
  1998 Commemorating, suppressing and invoking Cape slavery. In *Negotiating the
        past. The making of memory on South Africa*, edited by Nuttall, S. and Coetzee,
        C., pp. 201–217. Oxford University Press, Capetown.
Wastfelt, B., Gyllensvard, B. and Weibull, J.
  1991 *Porcelain from the East Indiaman Gotheborg.* History Department, University
        of Gothenborg, Gothenborg.
Weibull, J.
  1991 The Swedish East India Company and the final voyage of the East Indiaman
        Gotheborg, 1743–45. In *Porcelain from the East Indiaman Gotheborg*, edited by
        Wastfelt, B., Gyllensvard, B. and Weibull, J., pp. 11–29. History Department,
        University of Gothenborg, Gothenborg.
Werz, B.
  1993 Maritime Archaeological Project Table Bay: Aspects of the first field season.
        South African Archaeological Society Goodwin Series 7:33–39.
Winer, M. and Deetz, J.
  1990 The Transformation of British Culture in the Eastern Cape, 1820–1860. *Social
        Dynamics* 16:55–75.
Winer, M.
  1995 The Painted, Poetic Landscape: Reading Power in Nineteenth Century Textual
        and Visual Representations of the Eastern Cape Frontier. In *The Written and the
        Wrought: Complementary Sources in Historical Anthropology. Essays in Honour
        of James Deetz*, edited by D'Agostino, M. E., Prine, E., Casella, E. and Winer,
        M., pp. 74–109. Kroeber Anthropological Society Papers No.79,
Winer, M.
  2001 Landscapes, Fear and Land Loss on the Nineteenth-Century South African Colo-
        nial Frontier. In *Contested Landscapes. Movement, Exile and Place*, edited by
        Bender, B. and Winer, M., pp. 257–271. Berg, Oxford.
Winter, S.
  1999 *Heritage Conservation Component of the Structure Plan for the Dwars River
        Valley.* Henschilwood, Yates & Winter, Capetown.
Wolf, E.
  1982 *Europe and the People without History.* University of California Press,
        Berkeley.

Wolpe, H.
   1972   Capitalism and Cheap Labour Power in South Africa: from Segregation to Apartheid. *Economy and Society* 1:

Wood, D.
   1992   *The Power of Maps.* Guilford Press, New York.

Woodward, C. S.
   1974   *Oriental Ceramics at the Cape of Good Hope 1652–1795.* A. A. Balkema, Cape Town.

Woodward, C. S.
   1983   From multi-purpose parlour to drawing room: the development of the principal voorkamer in the fashionable Cape house 1670–1820. *Bulletin of the South African Culture History Museum* 4:5–19.

Worden, N.
   1985   *Slavery in Dutch South Africa.* Cambridge University Press, Cambridge.

Worden, N. and Crais, C., (ed.)
   1994   *Breaking the Chains. Slavery and its Legacy in the Nineteenth Century Cape Colony.* Witwatersrand University Press, Johannesburg.

Worden, N., Van Heyningen, E. and Bickford-Smith, V.
   1998   *Cape Town. The Making of a City.* David Philip Publishers, Cape Town.

Wurst, L. and Fitts, R. K., (ed.)
   1999   *Confronting Class.* Historical Archaeology. 33:1,

Yamin, R., (ed.)
   2001   *Becoming New York: The Five Points Neighbourhood.* Historical Archaeology. 35: 3,

Young, R.
   1995   *Colonial Desire. Hybridity in Theory, Culture and Race.* Routledge, London.

Zandvliet, K.
   1998   *Mapping for Money. Maps, plans and topographic paintings and their role in Dutch overseas expansion during the 16th and 17th centuries.* Batavian Lion International, Amsterdam.

Index